The Battle of Quiberon Bay, 1759

The Battle of Quiberon Bay, 1759

*Admiral Hawke and the
Defeat of the French Invasion*

Nicholas Tracy

Pen & Sword
MARITIME

First published in Great Britain in 2010 by
Pen & Sword Maritime
an imprint of
Pen & Sword Books Ltd
47 Church Street
Barnsley
South Yorkshire
S70 2AS

ISBN: 978-1-84884-116-1

A CIP catalogue record for this book is
available from the British Library.

Typeset in 11/13pt Sabon by
Concept, Huddersfield, West Yorkshire

Printed and bound in England by
the MPG Books Group

Pen & Sword Books Ltd incorporates the Imprints of Pen & Sword
Aviation, Pen & Sword Maritime, Pen & Sword Military, Wharncliffe
Local History, Pen & Sword Select, Pen & Sword Military Classics,
Leo Cooper, Remember When, Seaforth Publishing and
Frontline Publishing.

For a complete list of Pen & Sword titles please contact
PEN & SWORD BOOKS LIMITED
47 Church Street, Barnsley, South Yorkshire, S70 2AS, England
E-mail: enquiries@pen-and-sword.co.uk
Website: www.pen-and-sword.co.uk

Contents

On the whole, this battle ... may be considered one of the most perilous and important actions that ever happened in any war between the two nations; for it not only defeated the projected invasion, which had hung menacing so long over the apprehensions of Great Britain; but it gave the finishing blow to the naval power of France.

(Tobias Smollett, *The History of England*, vol. 4, 1800)

Should England attempt to seclude France entirely from the North American fishery, it would not only be inadmissible by them, but would give umbrage to Spain and all other maritime Powers, as it would be a great step towards gaining the monopoly of a trade, which is the great source of all maritime power, and might be as dangerous for us to grasp at, as it was for Lewis the 14th when he aspired to be the Arbiter of Europe, and might be as likely to produce a grand Alliance against us, as his ambitious views did against him.

(Bedford to Newcastle, 9 May 1761)

In his vision of England as sole mistress of the sea, [Pitt] fell into an error as enticing and as fatal as that which brought the Grand Monarque and Napoleon to their ruin. Magnificent as was his strategy, it broke the golden rule.

(Sir Julian Corbett, *England in the Seven Years War*, 1907)

It is the distinctive and distinguished significance of Hawke's career that during so critical a period he not only was the most illustrious and able officer of her navy – the exponent of her sea-power – but that by the force of his personality he chiefly shaped the naval outcome. He carried on the development of naval warfare, revolutionised ideas, raised professional standards, and thereby both affected the result in his own time, and perpetuated an influence, the effect of which was to be felt in the gigantic contests of later days. In this eminent particular, which involves real originality, no sea officer in the eighteenth century stands with him; in this respect only he and Nelson, who belongs rather to the nineteenth, are to be named together.

Forty-odd tall ships, pursuers and pursued, under reefed canvas, in fierce career drove furiously on; now rushing headlong down the forward slope of a great sea, now rising on its crest as it swept beyond them; now seen, now hidden; the helmsmen straining at the wheels, upon which the huge hulls, tossing their prows from side to side, tugged like a maddened horse, as though themselves feeling the wild 'rapture of the strife' that animated their masters, rejoicing in their strength and defying the accustomed rein.

(Alfred Thayer Mahan, *Types of Naval Officers*)

Preface

This year is the 250th anniversary of Hawke's victory over the French fleet, fought in a full gale among the rocks, shoals and tide races of Quiberon Bay on the Breton south coast. The enduring consequence was that an end was brought to French domination of the north and west of America, and that Canada became a part first of the British empire, then of the Commonwealth, and with the final union with Newfoundland in 1949, a bilingual nation stretching from the Atlantic to the Pacific and almost to the north pole. 1759 has been accepted as the year in which Britain began its history as a world empire, one that only came to a conclusion in the 1960s.

Sir Julian Corbett's history of *England in the Seven Years War* was written in 1907. Corbett was the unofficial historian of the Admiralty and his study is a masterpiece of strategic analysis, dealing as much with the diplomatic as the naval and military aspects of the war. In 1960 Geoffrey Marcus published the first account of the battle that made full use of Royal Navy log books and dispatches, and five years later Ruddock Mackay published his monumental biography of Admiral Hawke. This he followed in 1990 with the publication of a selection of Hawke's correspondence, as part of the series of Naval Records Society publications. Unfortunately, neither Marcus's *Quiberon Bay, the Campaign in Home Waters, 1759* nor Mackay's *Admiral Hawke* are currently in print. But even if they were, the perspective of the 1960s is not that of the present generation that have come to look for sustainable relationships rather than simple, and problematic, victories. The conquest of New France sewed angry dragon's teeth in Acadia and along the St Lawrence which still have the potential for political conflict, and at the same time ended the relationship of mutual need between Britain and her American colonies. In the 1980s and early 1990s

I published *Navies, Deterrence and American Independence* and *Attack on Maritime Trade*, both of which considered the triumph of 1759 in a wider perspective, and other scholars, notably Jonathan R Dull with his *The French Navy in the Seven Years War*, have continued to extend the context. In the nineteenth century brief accounts of the action were included in general works of naval warfare by French authors, but they were all limited in their scope, and sometimes rather passionate in their perspective. These limitations have now been addressed by Guy Le Moing by his publication in 2003 of *La Bataille Navale des 'Cardinaux' 20 November 1759*. With these new resources and with additional work by myself in the naval intelligence papers, it is appropriate, in this the anniversary year, to tell the story again with the broader context in mind.

List of Illustrations

C Plan of Dunkirk, published by J Gold, 103 Shoe Lane, London, 26 February 1807. *Naval Chronicle*, pl. 480.

D View of Dunkirk, engraved by T Rickards after a painting by F Gibson, published by J Gold, 28 February 1806. *Naval Chronicle*, pl. 172.

Plate 4 A Etienne François de Choiseul Duc de Choiseul-Amboise, engraving by Fèchard.

B A New Chart Exhibiting the Seat of War in the Mediterranean Sea, by T Kitchin, Geog., printed for R Baldwin at the Rose in Paternoster Row. *London Magazine* 1756, p. 264.

C Edward Lord Hawke, Admiral of the White Squadron and Vice Admiral of Great Britain, engraved by Ridley after a painting by Francis Cotes, published by J Gold, late Bunney and Gold, 30 June 1802. *Naval Chronicle*, pl. 90

D A Plan of Rochefort and Rochell with the Islands of Ree, Oleron, Aix &ca. By T Kitchin, Geog. *London Magazine* 1757, p. 472.

E Rt Hon Richard Earl Howe, K.G., engraving by Ridley and published by J Gold, 31 May 1803. *Naval Chronicle*, pl. 74.

Plate 5 A Le Havre-de-Grâce, a strong town and port of France, published by Joyce Gold, 31 August 1815. *Naval Chronicle*, pl. 443.

B A Flat-Bottomed Boat, as it appeared (at Havre-de-Grâce Road) in going from Le Havre to Honfleur. *London Magazine*, 1759, p. 452.

C Detail of Plymouth from Thomas Jeffreys' 'A New Hydrographical Survey of the British Channel, with Part of the Atlantic Ocean as far as Cape Clear,' 1770, in *A complete channel pilot*.

D Marine View from Spithead, engraving by F Cheshance after a painting by Nicholas Pocock, published by J Gold, 30 April 1804. *Naval Chronicle*, pl. 149.

E View of Berry Head, Torbay, engraving by Wells after a painting by Nicholas Pocock, published by Bunny & Gold, April 1799. *Naval Chronicle*, pl. 8.

Plate 6 A Coast of France from L'Orient to the Isle of Rhé, published by Joyce Gold, 1 May 1813. *Naval Chronicle*, pl. 387.

List of Maps

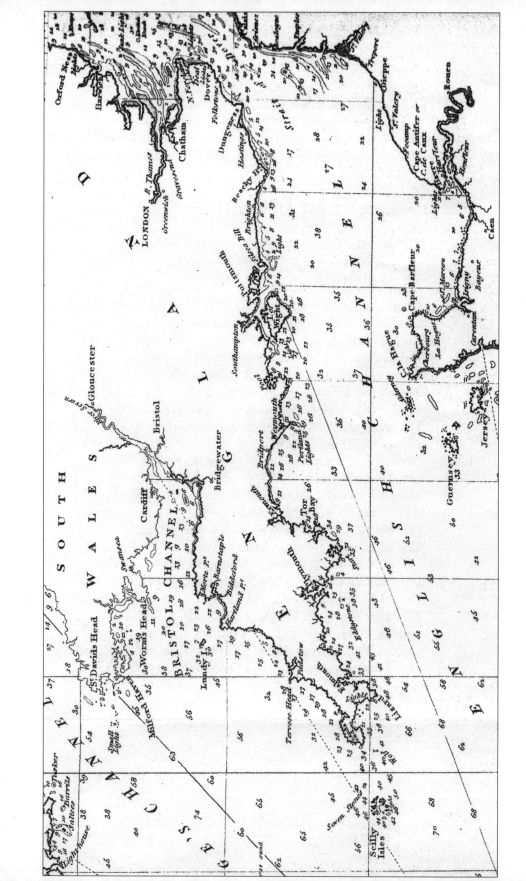

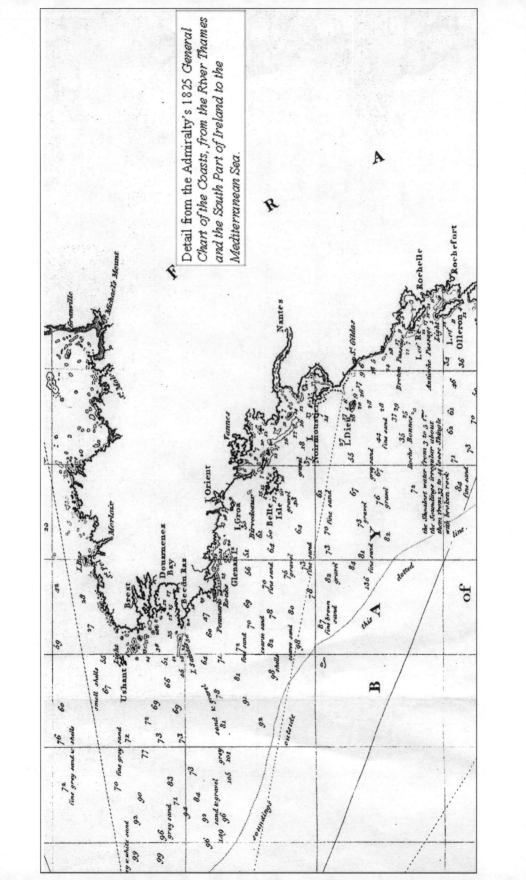

Detail from the Admiralty's 1825 General Chart of the Coasts, from the River Thames and the South Part of Ireland to the Mediterranean Sea.

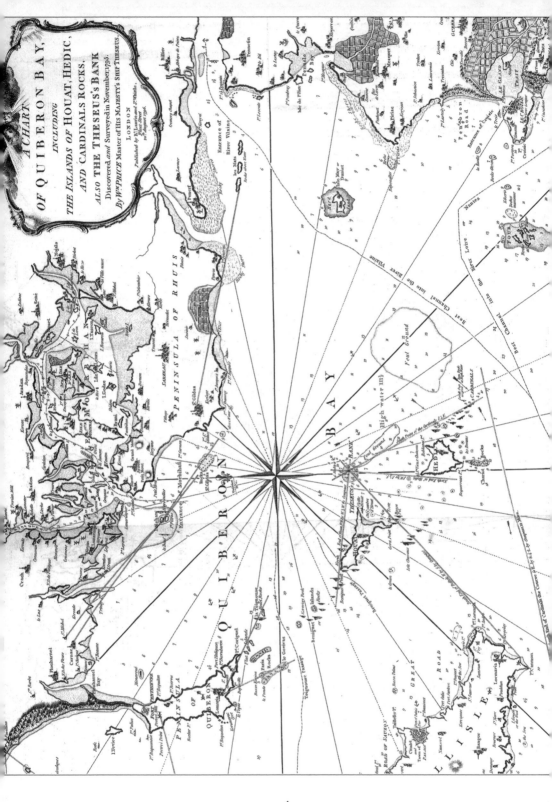

A CHART OF QUIBERON BAY, INCLUDING THE ISLANDS OF HOUAT, HEDIC, AND CARDINALS ROCKS. ALSO THE THESEUS's BANK. Discovered and Surveyed in November 1795. By Wm. PRICE Master of His Majesty's Ship THESEUS.

LONDON Published by R. Laurie and J. Whittle, 10 August 1796.

Chapter One

Context

The Seven Years War was the first truly 'world' war, a great power struggle between Britain, Hanover and their ally Prussia against France and her ally Austria, joined in 1762 by Spain, with Russia an ally of Austria. Its beginning was a continuation of the War of the Austrian Succession between 1744 and 1748 when, in the forests of North America, both the British and the French used Native American warriors to raid homes and farms. After a period of hostile peace, in 1754 there occurred a clash between the French, seeking to enforce their dominance in Ohio with a string of forts, and settlers from Virginia encroaching on Native American lands. King George II's First Lord of the Treasury, Thomas Pelham-Holles, First Duke of Newcastle, sought to respond with a graduated show of force. Whether that would have worked to calm the situation cannot be known. Newcastle, however, was manoeuvred by George II's younger son William Augustus, the Duke of Cumberland, into sending a considerably larger force under the command of Major General Edward Braddock with orders to destroy not only the French forts in Ohio but all those south of the St Lawrence and on the Nova Scotia border of Acadia. William Pitt, as Paymaster of the Forces, played a part in ensuring that Braddock was given aggressive instructions. French intelligence heard something of this plan in December and Louis XV sent his ambassador, the Duc de Mirepoix, hurrying to London. Before he had even left France, however, the king had also approved the dispatch of two small troop convoys to New France to counter Braddock's army.[1]

Admiral George Lord Anson, First Lord of the Admiralty, was the dominating mind controlling the British Royal Navy during the Seven Years War. He had been on the Admiralty Board under John Russell, the Fourth Duke of Bedford, from 27 December 1744, and John Montagu, Earl of Sandwich, from 26 February 1748, and became First Lord himself on 22 June 1751. He had established his reputation for seamanship, navigation and command authority in a voyage round the world between 1739 and 1744 during which most of the men in his squadron died of disease, reducing it to a single ship of the line. He also made his fortune by capturing a Manila galleon, *Nuestra Señora de Covadonga*. Many of the men who were to become leaders in the fleet in the second half of the eighteenth century had begun their careers under Anson during the circumnavigation. To wealth and reputation Anson added political connection through his father-in-law Philip Yorke, Earl of Hardwicke, who was the Lord Chancellor from 1737 to 1756. Anson was ousted from office in November 1756 but returned in July 1757, and remained at the head of the Admiralty until his death in June 1762.[2]

Questions have been asked about the adequacy of Anson's leadership of the Admiralty prior to the outbreak of war. Admiral Sir Edward Hawke was later to write, when he himself was First Lord and having to deal with decaying ships hastily built during the war, that

> by the economy adopted after the peace of 1748, the supplies [of money] assigned to the Navy had been by no means adequate to the necessary repairs; [and] that in 1755 the Admiralty had been so sensible of it that they had increased the number of shipwrights by every means in their power, and had set up in the King's and Merchant Yards as many ships as could be admitted.[3]

Anson's management of wartime problems was much more effective. He was to err on the side of exerting too much control from the Admiralty, and may have been too cautious during the crisis of 1756, but his leadership at the Admiralty in 1759 was an effective partnership with Hawke, who commanded the British fleet blockading Brest and defeated the French fleet in a full gale amongst the rocks, shoals and tide rips of Quiberon Bay.

When intelligence was received in London in January 1755 of the French plan to reinforce their army in Canada, a fleet had been prepared under the command of Vice Admiral Edward Boscawen to pursue the French. The Inner Cabinet agreed on 22 April to his instructions, and his force got away to sea on 27 April, a week before the French sailed from Brest. On 8 June off the coast of Newfoundland Boscawen intercepted three scattered ships from the French convoys.[4] Capturing two 64-gun ships, he returned with them and 1,500 prisoners to the British fleet anchorage at Spithead in the Solent outside Portsmouth. Boscawen was one of the Lords of the Admiralty, suggesting that his actions were what the government wanted. Parliament voted him their thanks. But in fact he had not succeeded in preventing the reinforcement of New France, and had only managed to ensure there would be war. The captain who fired the first precipitant broadside at the French, Richard Howe, was later to play an active part in the Battle of Quiberon Bay.

On 9 July Braddock's army was surprised and destroyed as a fighting force by a smaller number of French regulars, Canadians and Native Americans, and despite the reinforcements that were hurried out to America on 10 August 1756 the British fort at Oswego was captured. News of that defeat brought the fall of the Newcastle administration. William Pitt was asked by the king in November 1756 to form an administration as Secretary of State for the Southern Department, with William Cavendish Duke of Devonshire at the Treasury.

Pitt had come into politics in opposition to Sir Horace Walpole, Britain's first prime minister. He had become a confidant of the Prince of Wales, which ensured that he fell out of favour with the king, and then he also broke with the prince in opposition to Britain's commitment to the Electorate of Hanover. He is known for advocating a war policy based on the 'long forgotten people of America' and 'our proper force', the navy.[5] His search for political connections had led him to amend his anti-Hanoverian attitude, but he was never a favourite of King George II, who had only accepted him into ministerial circles because of his influence in the House of Commons, where he acquired a reputation as an orator and a 'patriot'. His personality was aggressive and unstable; he was a life-long sufferer from depression and possibly bipolarity.

It was Pitt who ousted Anson from the Admiralty, replacing him with his brother-in-law, Earl Richard Temple.

The Pitt–Devonshire administration did not last long. Pitt was politically isolated, and Cumberland was unwilling to take command of the army in Hanover while Pitt controlled policy. In April 1757 he was dismissed, and Temple was at the same time removed from the Admiralty, which was given to the incompetent Daniel Finch, Earl of Winchilsea. So strongly did the public indicate support for Pitt, however, that in June George II was obliged to sanction his return to power in harness with the Duke of Newcastle. With the return of Newcastle, Anson was brought back to the Admiralty.

Pitt's plan was to put an end to the conflict in America by the capture of Quebec, the capital of New France, but he also abandoned his opposition to supporting Britain's allies on the continent. Although Canada was not economically important to France, because the fur trade was by the middle of the eighteenth century of limited value, it was of strategic importance to the French empire because it contained the military potential of the British colonies, and was valued for its missions to the Native Americans. Quebec could be approached from New York up Lake Champlain, or from the Atlantic up the St Lawrence River, past the fortress at Louisbourg on Île Royale, the present-day Cape Breton Island. Louisbourg was the guardian of the Gulf of St Lawrence; a base from which a French fleet could threaten the rear of any seaborne expedition against Quebec. Île Royale also served French interests as a base for the French fishery in Newfoundland and on the Grand Banks, and as such it was both profitable and believed to be vital to the French Marine. The French navy, like the British, regarded the Banks fishery as the 'nursery of seamen' that supplied the trained manpower needed by the ocean trades, which in turn trained the topmen needed by the navies of both countries.[6]

A plan to capture Louisbourg in 1757 was frustrated because the covering naval force sent under the command of Vice Admiral Francis Holburne proved to be too small to support a landing against a squadron of sixteen French ships of the line under the command of Lieutenant General of the Fleet du Bois de la Motte. They had sailed in three sections from Brest, Toulon and Rochefort without being brought to action, and only the outbreak of typhus prevented the fleet once united seeking action with Holburne.

In the end, nearly half the 12,000 officers and men under la Motte's command died of disease, with very serious long-term consequences for the French navy. Another 2,500 or so French sailors were captured by British cruisers, and the British government capitalized on its advantage by putting a stop to the exchange of prisoners. At the end of 1757 there were 60,000 men serving in the British navy, and the French Marine could only muster 35,000. But the greatest difficulty for the French navy was a financial one, which both limited the number of men who could be paid, and also limited the purchase of stores. It is remarkable that France, despite these difficulties, was for so long to hold its own in America and India, although to do so it had to be very much on the defensive in European waters.

The shortages were to prove decisive when the following year Britain again mounted an expedition to reduce Louisbourg under the command of Major General Jeffrey Amherst. The French government ordered sixteen ships of the line to guard Louisbourg, sailing them individually or in small squadrons as they were ready for sea, but losses to the enemy, equipment failure, further outbreaks of typhus and shipwreck left only six ships of the line under the command of Capitaine de Vaisseau Jean-Antoine Charry, Marquis des Gouttes, at Louisbourg to defend the fortress from the sea. This number was far too little to be able to seek battle with the twenty-three ships of the line that Britain was able to concentrate in Nova Scotia waters under the command of Boscawen, who had been promoted to Admiral of the Blue. Once Amherst's 14,000 soldiers were ashore it could only be a matter of time before Louisbourg's garrison of nearly 4,000 regulars, marines, gunners and militia, with most of the 3,500 sailors brought ashore, was forced to capitulate. But the delay – Louisbourg did not fall until 26 July – was enough to save Quebec for another year. This was the second time in thirteen years Louisbourg had been captured by British forces, it having fallen in June 1745 to a force from Massachusetts, and then been returned to France as part of the Treaty of Aix-la-Chapelle in 1748.

Boscawen was not enthusiastic about proceeding immediately into the St Lawrence, because he lacked river pilots and necessary stores. A year is a long time in war, especially as a British assault on New France from New England had been defeated.

The administration of the French empire was the responsibility of the French navy, with governors filling a place in the chain of command similar to that of port commandants, supported by a civilian intendant to manage finances. Lieutenant General of the Fleet Pierre de Rigaud de Vaudreuil-Cavagnal, who had been born in New France, travelled to Quebec in the 1755 convoy as the new governor general. Major General Louis-Joseph, Marquis de Montcalm de St-Véran, was sent to Quebec in 1756 as his field commander, but the chain of command was confused. Vaudreuil had not been given authority over the soldiers, and Montcalm was supplied with a private cipher for reporting his own opinions. Despite the successes against General Braddock and at Oswego, and his own successful defence of Fort Carillon in July, he believed that New France must inevitably fall to the British. Indeed, by the end of November the British had captured Fort Frontenac on the north-east corner of Lake Ontario, due largely to having detached the Iroquois from their support of the French, and forced the abandonment of Fort Duquesne on the site of modern Pittsburgh. To express properly his views, Montcalm sent the future Pacific explorer Louis-Antoine Comte de Bougainville as an emissary to Versailles, where he arrived on 20 December 1758. Vaudreuil was convinced that the Canadian irregulars could stand up to British regulars using guerrilla tactics, but Montcalm was promoted to Lieutenant General, giving him complete authority to conduct the campaign of 1759.

In March 1759 a convoy was able to slip out of Bordeaux with 350 recruits and 17 merchant ships escorted by privateer frigates. Most of these made it to Quebec, along with two frigates of the French navy and a supply ship from Brest and Rochefort. The French government committed thirty million livres to support New France in 1759, ahead of the expected British assault, but in France it was believed that the fate of New France depended on what happened in Europe.

In 1759 ten regular British battalions and auxiliary American forces commanded by Major General James Wolfe were committed to the direct attack on Quebec, escorted up the uncharted and treacherous St Lawrence River by twenty-two ships of the line, thirteen frigates and numerous small craft that sailed from Spithead on 17 February under the command of Vice Admiral Charles Saunders. James Cook, whose three voyages into the Pacific were later to set the highest standard for navigation and science, served in the expedition charting a route up the river. Vaudreuil and Montcalm had both regarded the river as impassable to a hostile fleet, and not until it was too late did they make any attempt to construct batteries to oppose it. The British force was to reach Quebec in late June and open batteries across the river to bombard the fortifications. Another six battalions under the direct control of General Amherst, who was now Commander in Chief of all British forces in North America, would attack northward from New York into the Lake Ontario region.

The view from Versailles was darkening in every direction. A British attempt to capture Martinique in January 1759, with 4,500 to 5,000 soldiers under Major General Hopson and Commodore John Moore with ten ships of the line, had been beaten off, but they had compensated for their failure by capturing Basse-Terre, the capital of Guadeloupe. The French governor, Capitaine de Vaisseau François V de Beauharnais, had retained a position above the town, and Hopson died before he could discover a way of dealing with it. His successor, Major General John Barrington, was more effective and brought the French to sign a capitulation. Nevertheless, the British position was in fact fragile because of the decimating effects of disease, and the French might have reversed their defeat. After extended delays, a force of nine ships of the line under the command of Chef d'Escadre Maximin Comte de Bompar had got away from France on 21 January, and reached Martinique on 8 March. Any hope of a successful recapture of Guadeloupe, however, was defeated by the indolence of Governor Beauharnais. Having swept up the small French islands of Désiderade, Petite Terre, Marie Galante and the Saintes, Moore then returned to England with eight of the line as an escort for a large convoy.

In the mercantilistic economics of eighteenth-century Europe, control of the sugar-producing islands in the West Indies was of the first order of importance. Sugar provided France, and Britain, with a high-value commodity that could be re-exported to European markets. That trade alone accounted for a large proportion of the money economy upon which depended the ability of states to make war effectively. But France was at a disadvantage because the costs of her landward defences precluded the scale of expenditure on her navy that the British administration was able to persuade parliament to pay. And the relative weakness of the French navy was not compensated for by French resources in the American theatres. The British population of the Atlantic colonies was too large and wealthy for New France to survive in wartime without constant resupply from Europe.

The situation of France in India seemed more hopeful. General Thomas Arthur, Comte de Lally, Baron de Tollendal, invested the British-controlled city of Madras (the modern Chennai) in the spring of 1759, and there were hopes in France that the British could be driven out of the south. In the previous war the French capture of Madras had helped to offset the loss of Louisbourg. The French naval commander Chef d'Escadre Anne-Antoine Comte d'Aché was reinforced. But he failed to provide effective support, and in a dramatic shift of fortune, the siege of Madras had to be lifted following the appearance of the British East Indies Squadron commanded by the more energetic Vice Admiral George Pocock. News that the French had abandoned their lines before Madras reached London on 12 October, and in November the British took the offensive against the French post at Pondicherry. In 1760 Lieutenant Colonel Sir Eyre Coote would defeat the French at the Battle of Wandiwash, and in 1761 Pondicherry would be forced to capitulate.

Her colonies were important to French aspirations, and their defence vital to French prestige, but their importance was inevitably outweighed by French interests in Europe, and Britain had her own vulnerabilities in the European continent that France could exploit. British conquests in America during the War of the Austrian Succession, including the capture of Louisbourg, had necessarily been restored to France at the conclusion of the peace treaty of Aix-la-Chapelle as a quid pro quo for French abandonment of its conquest of the Austrian Netherlands, modern Belgium. This exchange had caused great anger among the public in Britain and America, but had been unavoidable. It was obvious policy for France to return to that strategy. The editor of the *Annual Register* for 1759 was to write that

The affairs of France and England were partly connected with the general system, and partly distinct and independent. France perceived that the strength of the English, and the exertion of that strength, increased continually in America; she knew from the natural inferiority of her colonies, and the feeble state of her navy, that she could not in reason hope for great success in that quarter; for which reason ... her great efforts were to be made in Europe; she had two objects, the recovery of Hanover, and the invasion of these islands; in either of which if she succeeded, there could be no doubt, but that it would prove a sufficient ballance [sic] for all that she had suffered, or had to apprehend in any other part of the world.[7]

It was necessary to mount an effective defence against the perils of losing Hanover or the Flemish ports, or worse, of being invaded, if Britain were to retain her American conquests when eventually a peace treaty were negotiated. Newcastle, however, was to become sceptical that even a successful defence in Europe, coupled with victories in Canada and the Caribbean, would be enough to bring about the peace he believed was essential.

Louis XV's first riposte to British aggression in America was in fact a naval and military assault on the British fortress at Port Mahon on the Balearic Island of Minorca, hoping that would bring Britain to negotiate a peace settlement. Minorca eventually fell to France, but that did not have the intended results; rather it proved counterproductive as it was important in the fall of the pacific Duke of Newcastle, and Pitt's formation of an administration. At the time it appeared that nothing more could be undertaken in Europe by the French navy, so it was left to the army to rescue France. The only question was whether British interests should be threatened by France again seizing the Austrian Netherlands, or by military action against Hanover. The Austrian Netherlands were of infinitely more direct importance to Britain because control of the harbours of Ostend and Nieuport would significantly improve the French ability to invade England, but the British government could not ignore the fate of Hanover because it was the hereditary duchy of the reigning British monarch, George II. In the previous war, George II had actually commanded a British and Hanoverian army in the field, for the last time in British history, at the Battle of Dettingen on 27 June 1743.

9

In 1755, desperate to neutralize the continent so that Britain could deal with the crisis in America, the Duke of Newcastle had blundered into an agreement with Frederick the Great of Prussia to respect each other's territories. A previous agreement with Empress Elizabeth of Russia to provide an army to defend Hanover had been used, successfully, to obtain Frederick's signature. The Convention of Westminster concluded in January 1756 contained an unfortunate clause binding each to resist the incursion of hostile forces into Germany. Both Russia and Austria, the heart of the Holy Roman Empire, had quarrels with Prussia, and this led both to seek an understanding with France despite the traditional rivalry between France and the Empire in northern Italy. In the circumstances, faced with a difficult defensive war in America, Louis XV was eventually persuaded, and expressed indignation that Frederick should have concluded a treaty with a country with which France was at war in all but name. He denounced the long-standing but in any case fragile Franco-Prussian alliance, and in May concluded with Maria Teresa a neutrality agreement known as the First Treaty of Versailles, which included a defensive alliance should either be attacked by a 'third party', Prussia. Maria Teresa, who was Queen of Hungary and soon Empress by virtue of the election of her husband as Emperor, was careful to limit the scope of the agreement to conflict in Europe.

In theory the treaty with Austria should have protected France from the prospect of Britain using German troops against her, as had been done in the War of the Austrian Succession, and for Louis it might have bought time for the Minorca operation to bring Britain to serious peace negotiations. But it was immediately followed by negotiations leading to a more offensive alliance with Austria. Empress Elizabeth of Russia was most eager to go to war against Prussia, but was dependent on Austria for a subsidy, as Austria was dependent on France. The Austrians offered Louis a sweetener in the form of the Austrian Netherlands for Louis' favourite daughter Marie-Louise-Elizabeth, and his son-in-law Don Philip, who were pinching pennies as Duchess and Duke of Parma. France was also offered free use of the Austrian ports of Ostend and Nieuport during the war with Britain.

Frederick's intelligence network had concluded that Prussia was to be attacked in 1757, and he moved quickly to forestall

10

his enemies. No one had anticipated that he might view it as in his interest to precipitate war simultaneously against all his three great neighbours, Russia, Austria and France. In August 1756 he launched a pre-emptive and successful attack on neutral Saxony preparatory to a move into the Austrian territory of Bohemia. Diplomatically this was a blunder that ensured France would take an active part in the European war. In turn, it forced Pitt to align British policy more closely with that of Prussia, and to undertake to create an army for the defence of Hanover. This realignment of alliances, bringing the rivals France and Austria together, and Britain and Prussia, came to be known as the Diplomatic Revolution.

The offer to establish in the southern Netherlands Don Philip, who was the heir presumptive to the Spanish throne as well as Louis XV's son-in-law, was most particularly threatening to Britain. Madame de Pompadour, once Louis' mistress but laterally his procuress, had successfully persuaded the king in 1755 not to take direct action to seize the Netherlands, as had been done in 1744, and instead to come to terms with Austria against Prussia. But the realization of a dynastic ambition to find a better home for Marie-Louise-Elizabeth would equally threaten Britain. The prospect that the harbours of Flanders might come under the control of France, directly or through a son-in-law of Louis XV, had to be taken very seriously. It gave Britain a very real reason not to quarrel with Maria Teresa, and in fact British military action in Germany was to be directed entirely against France, with support for Prussia being limited to the payment of subsidies.

It is not surprising that the French calculated Prussia would be easily defeated, as Russia joined the coalition in January 1757 and Sweden in March. In June Frederick, having failed to occupy Prague, suffered a defeat at Kolin. It appeared to the French that they could honour their commitment to Austria and defeat the British at the same time. The difficult transatlantic war in America might be won indirectly by aggressive military action in Hanover. Potentially, any colonial territory France lost to Britain during the war might be recovered in a peace treaty, in exchange for restoring Hanover to George II, should French armies succeed in capturing it. Having settled the terms of the Second Treaty of Versailles, it was signed on 1 May 1757.

Whether the alliance with Austria could have saved New France had Louis concentrated on the task cannot be known for certain. Unwisely, however, he allowed himself to be persuaded by de Pompadour to disgrace his experienced army minister, Pierre-Marc de Voyer, Comte de Argenson, and his experienced Navy Minister, Jean-Baptiste de Machault d'Arnouville, at the outset of the continental campaign. Machault was succeeded in rapid succession by François-Marie Peyrenc de Moras, who struggled to meet the needs of the fleet until May 1758, when he was replaced by Lieutenant General of the Fleet Claude-Louis d'Espinchal, Marquis de Massiac, and then on 1 November 1758 by Nicolas-René Berryer, Comte de La Ferrière. Massiac had been port commander at Toulon and was appointed Secretary of State for the Navy, but was not a member of the Council of State, which reduced his effectiveness in controlling the senior officers of the fleet, and in securing the necessary state funds. The exclusion of army and navy secretaries of state from the Council of State was consistent with an attitude that their departments existed solely to implement strategies devised by the king and his great friends. Berryer succeeded as Secretary of State, and was not called to the Council until October 1759. He owed his power to his friendship with de Pompadour, who had had him appointed Lieutenant Général of the Paris Police so that he could guard her against public slander. Jonathan Dull, historian of the French navy in the mid-eighteenth century, described him as 'suspicious, bad-tempered, and caring nothing about popularity, he was the perfect person for the thankless job of reducing the navy's expenses'. Guy Le Moing, whose recent account of the Battle of Quiberon Bay fills an important gap in French naval scholarship, regards him as having been ignorant of maritime affairs. Locked in a struggle with the naval officers to impose bureaucratic and fiscal control, Berryer let a naval campaign be planned by army officers who worked diligently to perfect plans that were fundamentally un-sound, and gave orders for them to be carried out with inadequate forces. The fault was endemic in the French service where those promoted for their competence and seniority were despised by the aristocratic *officiers rouges* of the *grand corps* of Toulon, Rochefort and Brest.[8]

12

The French sent two armies into Germany, and in the summer of 1757 these closed a trap on the Duke of Cumberland, commanding his father's 'Army of Observation' in northern Germany. Louis-Charles-César Le Tellier, Comte d'Estrées, with 60,000 men, defeated Cumberland's 35,000 at Hastenbeck on 26 July. His successor in command, Louis-François-Armand Vignerot du Plessis, Duc de Richelieu, Marshal of France, pursued Cumberland to the coast, and in September forced him to sign a convention at Kloster-Zeven to abandon Hanover to the French and to intern his army. Had Richelieu realized in what a demoralized condition was the Army of Observation, he might have destroyed it altogether. The convention was vaguely enough worded that it was not to be relied upon should circumstances change, but Cumberland was recalled to England, and treated by his father with contempt, upon which he resigned both his command and his office of Commander in Chief of the army. The second French army, under the command of Charles de Rohan, Prince de Soubise, with 21,000 men, was intended to reinforce the Austrian army and was concentrated at the end of August in Thuringia, 100 miles from Hanover.

Cumberland's defeat was partly the result of Pitt's insistence on using the British soldiers Cumberland had requested for the army in Hanover to mount an attack on Rochefort, hoping to divert French resources away from the German theatre. It failed in this respect, but Frederick's Prussian army soundly defeated a Franco-Austrian army at Rossbach on 5 November, and then against the odds but with superior generalship defeated the Austrians at Leuthen a month later in one of the most strategically important battles of the eighteenth century. This persuaded George II as Elector of Hanover to denounce the convention of Kloster-Zeven, which had not been ratified, and Pitt undertook to ask parliament to supply the money needed to support an allied army under the command of Ferdinand, Duke of Brunswick, to reconquer Hanover.

Louis virtually withdrew from the Prussia war at that point, and concentrated French military action against Ferdinand's Army of Observation. It appeared that Pitt was throwing a good army after a bad one. Such was the optimism in France that Prussian peace feelers at the end of 1757 were rejected, and there was discussion of sending back to France some of the military units in Germany for refitting.

In reality, however, the French army of Westphalia had been reduced to less than half strength as a result of Richelieu's corrupt practices, and its new commander, Lieutenant General Louis de Bourbon-Condé, Comte de Clermont, began a strategic withdrawal on 18 February towards the Rhine, on the very day that Ferdinand began a surprise attack well before the usual campaigning season. Reinforced by Prussian cavalry, he drove Clermont and Soubise west of the Rhine, inflicting losses on the French of 15,000 men, mostly captives. The catastrophe led to the appointment of Marshal of France Charles Louis Auguste Fouquet, Duc de Belle Île, as war minister, a position he felt was well below his dignity as one of the highest of French nobility. This was by no means the end of the fighting in Hanover in 1758. Ferdinand crossed the Rhine on a bridge of boats and threatened the Austrian Netherlands, which led Louis XV to send garrisons into Ostend and Nieuport. Newcastle and George II wanted to attack them there, but Pitt disagreed with any step that might lead to hostilities with Austria, and instead agreed to send British soldiers to join Ferdinand's army, which Soubise threatened from the rear. By the end of the year Ferdinand was back in Hanover.

Frederick's offensive into Austria had proved a failure, but the enemies of Prussia had also failed. In a dreadfully bloody battle at Zorndorf, which cost the Russians forty per cent casualties and the Prussians thirty per cent, Frederick saved Berlin from Russian occupation, although the Russians occupied Königsberg. Logistic difficulties and lack of field artillery forced the Swedes to withdraw from their own offensive. But Frederick was so short of money he was only able to stay in the field because of the renewal of Britain's subsidy. French finances were almost as strained, and there seemed to be no prospect of ending the stalemate. Louis XV's foreign minister, Abbé François-Joachim de Pierre de Bernis, had realized after Leuthen that France had little to hope for, and now urged that France conclude the best peace treaty it could.[9]

Louis was not willing to contemplate a move that would be contrary to his personal relationship with Maria Teresa, who viewed Frederick the Great as 'a monster'. Peace was opposed by de Pompadour, and would have made it impossible to provide a better kingdom for Louis's daughter and son-in-law. In any case, Bernis had annoyed de Pompadour by his attempts to reduce the expenses of the court and Louis by his political manipulation. He had sought to bring into the Foreign Ministry as his deputy Etienne-François, Comte de Stainville, elevated to Duc de Choiseul and made titular foreign minister. Louis complied, but also banished Bernis from court. Choiseul took full control of French strategy. He was no more in favour of continuing the continental struggle than had been Bernis, but his idea was to cut the Gordian knot and defeat at a stroke Britain's armies in America, India and Hanover by a direct invasion of the British Isles.

Choiseul had been Louis XV's chief minister in all but name for a dozen years. Dull writes that 'Like William Pitt and Frederick II, Choiseul was arrogant, astute, ruthless, manipulative, sarcastic, and charismatic.'[10] His strategy was devoid of solid operational possibilities, but had to be taken seriously nonetheless. It was he, rather than Berryer, who presented the final plan to the Council of State in July 1759.[11]

Choiseul's first requirement was to reduce France's obligation to Austria, so that funds would be available for the invasion campaign. That proved to be the easy part. By the Third Treaty of Versailles, negotiated between December 1758 and March 1759, France renounced its interest in the Austrian Netherlands and reduced the financial subsidy she was committed to paying Austria by 25 per cent, although she agreed to field a French army in Germany of 100,000 men. It was also agreed that France would never make a treaty with King George II that left Britain free to support Prussia, and in return Austria agreed not to make any peace with Prussia that left Frederick free to support Britain.

The idea of invading Britain had first been floated to the Austrians in December 1757, and Newcastle had been concerned that the French occupation of Ostend and Nieuport presaged an assault on England. Once Choiseul moved into the Foreign Ministry he set about promoting the attack, although the details of the military operations were in the hands of Marshal of France, Belle Île, with the co-operation of Berryer, whose appointment to the Naval Ministry on 1 November 1758 was supported by Choiseul and Belle Île. The underlying motive behind the proposed invasion was to undermine London's financial credit, for which purpose even a convincing threat never carried into effect could be useful. The difficult part was to make the threat convincing.

In March Newcastle received secret intelligence from one of his own agents pointing to an invasion, and he ordered General Sir Joseph Yorke, who was the British ambassador to the United Provinces, to make enquiries from the embassy at The Hague. Yorke was unable to corroborate this intelligence, although he had learned that 'several battalions are order'd to Brest among which are the Irish Reg[iment] that were quartered in Normandy and those Parts. That twenty-five ships of war are there ready to take Troops on Board. That Ireland is the place talked of ...' Newcastle became increasingly impatient, writing on 3 April that 'these things are not given out to frighten us, but are under their serious consideration – You know, I suppose, that flat bottomed boats are preparing all along the French coasts; & that it is said, that there are great numbers of French troops upon the Coasts – I shall soon expect', he added, 'to have some particular account from you relating to them.' Yorke was too professional to be stampeded, and answered firmly: 'Your Grace seems to have a great contempt for all my intelligence ... I am following the French Coasts as well as I am able ... people must have time to make their tour; I have in the meanwhile had all the masters of vessels who come in from the French Ports examined, and from their unanimous Reports, no preparations of the nature you mention appear; the want of ships & seamen seem to be great.' He tried to soften the rebuff by adding that he would not 'pretend to contradict your grace's positive intelligence without strong proofs ...' Newcastle was not to be dissuaded: 'They have now 40 men of war of all sorts great & small in Brest. They are fitting out 14 large ships of the line at Toulon, and, if they happen to join, God knows what strength we may be able to bring against them.'[12]

The *Annual Register* reported at the beginning of June the scale of the preparations:

Ten thousand workmen are employed at Le Havre-de-Grâce, in building 150 flat-bottomed boats, 100 feet long, 24 broad, and 10 deep. 100,000 livres are paid to them weekly. These boats are to have a deck, and to carry two pieces of cannon each, and to use either sails or oars, as occasion may require. Some will carry 300 men, with their baggage, and others 150 horses with their riders; 150 more are building at Brest, St. Maloes, Nantes, Port L'Orient, Morlaix and other ports of Brittany.[13]

The French threat was magnified by the anger expressed in Denmark and the Netherlands at the depredations of British privateers. Newcastle eagerly welcomed a Danish proposal that ships brought in by British cruisers and privateers for condemnation should be granted bail so that they could continue their voyage. Newcastle remarked to William Murray, First Earl of Mansfield, the Lord Chief Justice, that 'by this Proposal, the Danes give up their Pretence of covering, or protecting, the French property, and clearly admit the Right, or Power, of Visitation, and bringing their ships into port for Examination, and giving Security &ca.'[14] The Dutch were not to be so easily accommodated. On 23 March Yorke learned that the States General were sending a commission to London to consider the question of belligerent rights and free trade, but on 1 April he remarked that it was dangerous for an Englishman to travel in Holland: 'their Hatred and malice against us, and the injuries We receive are inexpressible – They call us in general a Parcell of Pirates, Thieves, &ca.' Worse followed. He learned that 'Twenty five ships of War are getting ready here with all Expedition.' If the Dutch decided to convoy to Brest ships laided with naval stores, and perhaps even go into Brest, the balance of naval power could be decisively tipped against Britain.

'Is this a time', Newcastle asked Yorke, 'for Holland to be Equipping a Squadron (as they are actually doing) against England?' But even Pitt recognized the need to placate the Dutch. Pressure was put on the Appeals Court to overturn the condemnation of some Dutch ships, and on 3 April Yorke was informed that the new Privateers Bill would certainly be put to the Commons, restricting the numbers of privateers and requiring more convincing bonds for good behaviour.[15]

Foremost among Choiseul's difficulties was the rapidly dwindling strength of the French Marine. In 1758 the French lost thirteen ships of the line, nine attempting to reach New France, and decommissioned another, taking delivery of only two new ships built at Toulon, and purchasing two sixty-four-gun ships from the French East India Company. Only fifty-four ships of the line were available for sea duty, and of those only twenty-five were actually commissioned because of manpower shortages. British cruisers had captured 9,000 prisoners during the year, and another 3,000 had been captured at the fall of Louisbourg. At the end of 1758 some 20,000 French sailors were in British prisons. In contrast, there were 70,000 British sailors serving in the Royal Navy, and only 3,000 in French prisons. Underlying the shortages of ships and crews was the falling ability of the French government to raise loans. The weakness of crews was a partial explanation of why so many ships had been lost to the elements and to the enemy. In 1758 no attempt was made to fit out a fleet at Brest or Rochefort for service on the French coasts.[16] In those straitened circumstances, the cost of building the flatboats and the broad flat-bottomed praams was a serious consideration. The *Annual Register* had understated the scale of the preparations: 225 to 275 flat boats were to be built to carry the troops, and 12 praams to provide close escort. Twenty-seven million livres were earmarked for the construction, but the first praam was not launched until late in December 1758.

Among the assets that could be drawn upon in planning for the 1759 campaign was the 'Young Pretender', 'Bonnie Prince Charlie', who could be used in Scotland and might find a few supporters in England. It was only fourteen years since France had last succeeded in landing him in Scotland, and the Duke of Cumberland's draconian Highland Clearances following Charles's defeat and flight were the strong basis for continued anger, and might be the basis for another uprising. But there was a difficulty. When Choiseul met Charles Stuart on 7 February 1759 the no longer very Bonnie prince was intoxicated, and Choiseul concluded he was indiscrete and rather stupid. It was also a problem that the Dutch had no use for a Stuart restoration, and Choiseul needed Dutch financial support. Charles had earlier embarrassed his French hosts following his defeat at Culloden and flight back to France by referring with pride to Rear Admiral Hawke's triumphant action at Finisterre in October 1747 as a victory by 'my country's fleet'.[17] Nevertheless, some use might be made of him.

The first plan was to make a landing of French soldiers in Ireland, while an army of Swedes and Russians was concentrated at Gothenburg and sailed to Scotland. These two assaults were in fact to be feints. The main assault force would be directed at the Thames estuary, and would be escorted by the Brest fleet.

A weakness in this concept was that Empress Elizabeth of Russia failed to be interested in participation, and the Swedes could not even afford to concentrate troops at Gothenburg, let alone transport them to Scotland. An even more serious defect was the Duc de Belle Île's lack of experience with naval operations. The underlying intention was that the escort fleet would be able to carry out its ferrying operations without first defeating the British fleet.

Plan 'B' was then devised, eliminating the Irish landing, and sending 10,000 French soldiers from Ostend to eastern Scotland in August 1759. The Swedes were to follow in October, and be compensated by cession of the island of Tobago. The main invasion force would sail from Dunkirk, Calais and Boulogne, and be landed at Dover. Naval cover would be provided by the Brest fleet passing north about Scotland, and by employing privateers to make a diversion. Later, the feint to Ireland was reinstated.[18]

Plan 'B' was replaced in May 1759 by a plan 'C', which called for the Scottish landing to be launched from Brittany. By the end of July a departure date of 10 September had been decided on, so as to enable the invaders to complete the inevitable siege of Edinburgh before winter set in. This strike force was increased to 20,000 men, and was to be escorted by 4 ships of the line. In August the proposed landing site was switched to western Scotland, because it was believed it would be easier for the army to forage there for provisions. It was then to march east to besiege Edinburgh, opening communications across the North Sea. The proposed Swedish landing was put back to November, and in fact never took place. The Brest fleet would escort the Scottish expedition clear of the land, but would then turn back, rather than make the diversion around northern Scotland. Entering the English Channel it would cover the passage of the second army, of 20,000 French soldiers, to southern England. Marshal Soubise was to be its commander. A diversion force was to be assembled at

Dunkirk, under the command of a Franco-Irish smuggler captain François Thurot, which was to raid Ireland.

The technical problems for the French Marine were greatly increased by the decision to muster the soldiers for the Scottish landing in the ports along the north shore of the Bay of Biscay, in the enclosed water of the Morbihan in Quiberon Bay, and to muster those for the English landing at Ostend, with their invasion transport constructed at Le Havre-de-Grâce. Should the Brest fleet succeed in getting to sea it would have to double back to collect the transports in the Morbihan before escorting them clear of the land. However, concentrating the army at Brest would have posed impossible difficulties with supply over inadequate roads. There would also have been a danger of the army being affected by the typhus that still persisted in Brest. In the towns around Quiberon Bay the soldiers could be supplied by water from the fertile area around the River Loire.[19]

The idea of sending the Brest fleet north of Scotland was abandoned, but it would still be challenging for it to collect the invasion barges at Le Havre, escort them to Ostend, stand by while the army was embarked, and then escort them to their landing site at Maldon in Essex.[20] It was not to be supposed that the Royal Navy would be passive during these extended and difficult manoeuvres. Maldon was chosen because it was close to London, and apparently because the choice was thought likely to catch the British off guard. With British land forces concentrating on the Isle of Wight, a successful landing at Maldon would certainly have created great difficulties for the defenders. However, the prospect of the French successfully pulling off a coup at Maldon was remote. The approach through the Thames estuary is very difficult. The Wallet channel off the only beach near Maldon where men could be put ashore, at Clacton, would have been very confined for a fleet, with little room for the deep draft ships of the line to manoeuvre. Approaching Maldon up the Blackwater would have been even more problematic, because of the narrow, twisting channel. The odds against a large and cumbrous invasion fleet safely traversing the complicated sands and channels of the Thames estuary and putting an army ashore late in the year were very long.

There was a fundamental contradiction to this planning: that it depended on deception, but was on a large scale, and had many moving parts that all had to work together. It was to be another half century before General Carl von Clausewitz wrote his famous observation that 'Everything is very simple in War, but the simplest thing is difficult. These difficulties accumulate and produce a friction which no man can imagine exactly who has not seen war.'[21] But any experienced military planner would have recognized that truth. The fact that Choiseul, Nicolas-René Berryer and the Duc de Belle Île committed the lives of two armies and two fleets to such a dangerous gamble exposes them and the structure of the French *Ancien Régime* to the gravest criticism. Sir Julian Corbett, in 1907 Admiralty historian and strategic advisor, wrote in his account of *England in the Seven Years War* that 'the design ... was, as Newcastle said, "extremely well laid". So far as it was possible for such an enterprise to succeed without previous command of the sea, every chance was taken. Nothing could be better devised for confusing the enemy and concealing from them what the real line of operation was.' But he then continued: 'If the French fleet was capable of defending an expedition of twenty thousand men against an attack by [the Channel Fleet] still more was it capable of dealing with [the Channel Fleet] if it had no convoy to encumber it.' Corbett thought that Belle Île had overlooked the role of Britain's flotilla of frigates and sloops patrolling the French Channel coast.[22] Indeed, the naval commander, Maréchal Hubert de Brienne, Comte de Conflans, found that his expert advice on how the fleet should be deployed was not welcome: '*Messieurs les ministres ne m'ayant jamais fait part d'aucun project,*' he complained on 15 August 1759, '*je ne puis sur cela suivre que les orders que le Roi me donera.*'[23]

The French plan was not kept secret for long. Newcastle risked betraying his source to stimulate a strong response. On 14 June he more or less broadcast the intelligence by informing the Duke of Devonshire that France had acquainted 'the ministers of the Republick of Holland in Form with their Design of making a Descent in England; that the Pretender is to have no share in it; and the Protestant Succession not to be attacked ... After this tho' a very odd Declaration, there can be no Doubt of the Design, for which they are making Preparations with Utmost Expedition.' He was quoting Anson when he wrote that the plan was 'extremely well laid'. 'It is generally said', wrote Newcastle in a second long letter on the same day, that the invasion force would be 30,000 men. Alarmed as he was, Newcastle had faith, he said, that 'our little Light Squadrons in the Downs, and Spithead, will prevent their Landing'. His faith, however, was razor thin: 'otherwise if 30,000 men should land, I don't see where we can get 30,000 to oppose them'.[24] Newcastle may well have been the source for the report in the *Annual Register* later that month.

Having studied the documents, Anson concluded that the government had several months' warning, which could be put to good use in preparing defences. The French had requested a supply of cannon from the Swedes, ones suitable for use in the invasion attempt, and it was unlikely they could be delivered until late in the summer. Anson recommended sending frigates to the Skagerrak to intercept them, and applying diplomatic pressure on the Netherlands to prevent the use of their ports for reception of the contraband munitions.[25] At first Pitt refused to consider the invasion threat as serious, believing it was intended only as a bluff. He refused to alter the offensive plans in North America and the Caribbean, and confined military preparations in England to the camp on the Isle of Wight, which was intended as a counter-bluff, threatening an attack on Brest. Anson and the king were persuaded to order a fleet of transports to form at Spithead, and a second fleet was assembled at the Nore in the Thames, probably to threaten Flanders and thereby support Ferdinand's army.[26] But eventually Newcastle, Hardwicke and the Duke of Bedford, who was Lord Lieutenant of Ireland, prevailed so far as to obtain agreement that the Channel Fleet should be brought forward for service. On 21 June orders were issued to send out press gangs to gather in every available seaman, 'without regard to any protection whatever except those granted in pursuance of Acts of Parliament'.[27]

Newcastle's personal agent at Versailles and Yorke's official correspondence from The Hague were not the only sources of intelligence of the progress of French plans. The Consul at Rotterdam, Robert Wolters, had established a network of agents inside France and Spain, and made effective use of reports by neutral ship masters when they entered Rotterdam. On 4 June he reported that, besides the 150 boats being built at Le Havre-de-Grâce, batches of 50 were also ordered to be built at Dunkirk, Calais and Boulogne, and the chaloupes were being built at Rouen, Dieppe and Honfleur.

Troops were being trained at Le Havre in amphibious operations. At Bordeaux 200-ton merchant ships were being taken up for naval service, and sent to Bayonne and La Rochelle to be equipped.[28] On 4 July Wolters's agent in Brest reported the arrival of Maréchal de Conflans: '*il a reçu de la Terre et de la Mer les Honneurs dus à son Rang, et le Soir toute la Ville a été illumine.*'[29] His admiral's flag had been hoisted on board his ship, *le Soleil Royal*. To fill out his crews, it was reported that 1,500 Normandy coastguards had been pressed into service. He believed that the soldiers were going on board the transports, but also reported the presence of the Royal Navy squadron off the entrance to the harbour.[30] On 27 July Wolters's Paris agent sent in the first report of the preparations at Dunkirk for Thurot's raiding force, but was unable to provide any solid information concerning its destination: '*Le Secret de cette Expedition est impenetrable*,'[31] but there was word it might be intended against Scotland. He was also able to report that the Brittany towns of Vannes and Morlaix were the rendezvous for the invasion army being assembled from the Biscay region.[32]

Meanwhile, in Germany, Ferdinand had again launched his campaign early, but Soubise's replacement, the Duc de Broglie, proved able to stop the Army of Observation at Bergen outside of Frankfurt. Ferdinand was able to retreat eighty miles, but de Broglie and Louis-Georges-Erasme, Marquis de Contades, who had replaced Clermont in command of the French army on the lower Rhine, attacked Ferdinand in June from the south and west, pushing him back to the border of Hanover. Contades, now in supreme command, paused to capture the Hanoverian fortresses of Minden and Lippstadt, before dealing with Ferdinand's army, which he outnumbered two to one. But Ferdinand threatened his supply lines, and Contades was provoked into a premature attack on 1 August. Against the odds, the allied force of British, Hanoverian, Hessian and Prussian soldiers inflicted a stunning defeat, largely because of mistaken orders that advanced a British infantry brigade supported by the Hanoverian Guards and by British and Hanoverian artillery against massed French cavalry. Despite heavy losses, they drove off repeated French cavalry charges with musket fire, and inflicted serious casualties on the French horsemen. The soldiers had picked white roses from the hedgerows and worn them on their hats, adding to the rich traditions of the British army. The French fled back almost to the point of their departure before Frankfurt. Only the cowardice of Lord George Sackville commanding the British cavalry limited the extent of the victory. But for Ferdinand's victory, Corbett wrote, 'Hanover must have been lost, and the efforts of Saunders and Wolfe, of Boscawen and Hawke, would have been of little avail. If the navy was able in the end to secure the object of the campaign, it was because Ferdinand kept the ring intact at Minden.'[33]

That left only the invasion plan to pluck victory from defeat, but in June 1759 the French fleet only contained forty-seven ships of the line, the largest of which were five ships of eighty guns. On the same date, the British battle fleet possessed 111 ships of the line of which one, the *Royal George*, was of 100 guns, and ten were of 90 guns. Both fleets were divided among several ports, but with forty ships of the line in or approaching home waters, and fifteen based on Gibraltar, Britain could expect to contain the thirty-three ships of the line of French home forces more widely dispersed between the Atlantic ports of Brest, L'Orient and Rochefort, and the Mediterranean fleet base at Toulon. That left forty-three British ships of the line in North America and the West Indies to pursue the war against nine French ships of the line in the West Indies, and thirteen British ships of the line in or en route to the East Indies against only five French ships of the line.[34]

But if the odds were long against the French invasion plan, they were also long against Pitt's strategy. In preparing notes on the 'State of Foreign Affairs' on 17 April 1759, Newcastle wrote that

the worst Remark I can make from the present State of Things is; that there is not the least appearance of any Disposition in Either the court of France or that of Vienna towards Peace ... If there is no Inclination in the Enemy to Peace, the next consideration is, what means we have of forcing them to it this Campaign? I am afraid none; and experience shows that it will be impossible for this Nation to support this Expence another year ... I flatter myself that, with the Blessing of God, we may have very good Success this year in N. America; But to think of being able to extirpate the French from N. America; or, if we could, that our business was done by so doing; or that such a nation as France, would sit down tamely under it, is to me the idlest of all imaginations. If providence should bless us with some signal success in Germany [he concluded], that would contribute more to Peace than any other thing, which I can forsee.[35]

He feared that it might even be necessary to suspend payment of the course of Admiralty, with serious consequences for British credit. Three weeks later he was more sanguine about money, his attention having turned to political matters, but the strategic dilemma was never solved.[36]

Chapter Two

Britain's Naval Strategy

In the eighteenth century the principal operational commitments for the British navy were control of the English Channel, access to the Baltic and an ability to influence events in the Mediterranean. Secondary commitments were in North American, Caribbean and East Indian waters. Only if the British government were able to meet these requirements could it keep intact the house of cards of an empire based on sea power. Given the vast distances involved in naval warfare and the relatively limited resources of even the most powerful navy, operational strategy was generally offensive in character, even when the objective was defensive. Years later, when in 1902 the Admiralty prepared a memorandum for the Imperial Conference, it expressed the fundamental reality that had to be central to operational planning:

> the primary object of the British Navy is not to defend anything, but to attack the fleets of the enemy, and, by defeating them, to afford protection to British Dominions, supplies and commerce. This is the ultimate aim. To use the word *defence* would be misleading, because the word carries with it the idea of a thing to be defended, which would divert attention to local defence instead of fixing it on the force from which attack is to be expected. The traditional role of the Royal Navy is not to act on the defensive, but to prepare to attack the force which threatens – in other words to assume the offensive.'[1]

Historically, the oldest and most decisive mechanism by which navies have been used to determine the course of affairs ashore has been by the transport of armies to invade hostile states, or to defend against the threat of invasion. In his great study *Some Principles of Naval Strategy*, published in 1911, Corbett wrote: 'Since men live upon the land and not upon the sea, great issues between nations at war have always been decided – except in the rarest cases – either by what your army can do against your enemy's territory and national life or else by the fear of what the fleet makes it possible for your army to do.'[2] It was the French plan to invade the British Isles that was central to the naval campaign of 1759, but the possibility that British naval forces could influence events in Europe by the transport of armies to critical theatres by way of the Mediterranean, the North Sea or the Baltic was fundamental to the leverage Britain had in world affairs.

Important as that strategic capacity was, however, invasion was becoming a secondary aspect of Britain's maritime strategy, which increasingly was one of economic warfare. The outcome of the Seven Years War was to be influenced to a far greater extent by the economic resources Britain, France and other countries acquired from seaborne commerce, and from colonial empires that were multipliers of trade. Naval forces served that end by their action against the commerce of the enemy, and by playing their part in forwarding the imperial interests of the powers. 'The undoubted Interest of England is Trade,' wrote an anonymous pamphleteer in 1672, 'since it is that alone which can make us either *Rich* or *Safe* for without a powerful Navy, we should be a Prey to our Neighbours, and without Trade, we could neither have sea-men or Ships.'[3]

A classic statement of the relationship between naval strength, trade and power was made by Robert, Earl Nugent, during the parliamentary debate in 1745 on the need for courts martial following the Battle of Toulon:

> Let us remember that we are superior to other nations, principally by our riches; that those riches are the gifts of commerce, and that commerce can subsist only while we maintain a naval force superior to that of other princes. A naval power and an extended trade reciprocally produce each other; without trade we shall want sailors for our ships of war, and without ships of war we shall soon

28

discover that the oppressive ambition of our neighbours will not suffer us to trade.[4]

The two strategies of invasion and trade control met in the struggle for colonial control, and at the coastal towns of Europe where naval forces could intercept trade, and could also use shipboard firepower to attack military positions and shipping.

The Mediterranean, the middle sea of the ancient world, was and remains the theatre in which naval forces can have the most direct influence on European affairs. English use of naval forces to control logistics in the Mediterranean had such powerful local effects that its tactical results produced systemic, strategic, results. Eighteenth-century armies had come to depend on elaborate commissariat arrangements in order to facilitate control of the soldiery. At the same time, the improvement of fortification meant that armies depended increasingly upon their siege train. The heavy guns had to be transported by water, and water transport was preferable for bulk stores. In the Mediterranean area, it was often necessary to make use of the sea for the supply ships because there were few major rivers, and this gave navies the opportunity to influence, or even determine, the outcome of campaigns ashore. Admiral of the Fleet Edward Russell defeated a French assault on Barcelona in 1694 by interception of French supply ships moving along the Spanish coast. Twelve years later Admiral Sir John Leake defeated another French attack on Barcelona by the same means.

This latter operation was a small part of a larger example of the role of naval power in continental conflict when the English fleet was deployed to the Mediterranean during the War of the Spanish Succession in support of the army commanded by the Duke of Marlborough. The immediate cause of the war had been the death in 1700 of Charles II of Spain, leaving as his heir Philip, Duc d'Anjou, who was a grandson of Louis XIV. The prospect of a near-universal monarchy, under the King of France, was enough to make Britain and the Netherlands, among other states, support the rival claim of Emperor Leopold I for the Habsburg dynasty. The first necessity for British and Dutch forces was to protect the Netherlands, but that would do nothing to defeat a French thrust into Bavaria towards Vienna. In 1704 Marlborough secretly marched an army of 70,000 across the French front to the upper Danube to support Austria, and Admiral Sir George Rooke was sent into the Mediterranean to support the independent Duchy of Savoy, and seek with the help of the Savoyards to capture Toulon. This proved an effective diversion. The French could not ignore the loss of their Mediterranean naval base. French soldiers that might have reinforced their army in Bavaria instead marched south to Provence, allowing Marlborough to fight and win the Battle of Blenheim. In 1705 Marlborough continued the strategy of diversion in the Mediterranean, and in 1707 a second attempt to capture Toulon succeeded in so far as the French Mediterranean fleet was sunk at its anchorage.

This strategy was only possible because in 1703 naval pressure had been put on Portugal, which joined the allies and permitted Rooke to use the Tagus as a staging base. In the course of 1704 Gibraltar was occupied, and remained a British naval base until 1982. Gibraltar was better located than was the Tagus for supporting Mediterranean operations, but its harbour was never entirely secure in the eighteenth century, and it was too far from Toulon for it to be satisfactory for a force blockading the French. The only really good base for such purposes was Minorca, and in 1708 it was captured by the British navy. British ownership was confirmed under the terms of the Article XI of the Treaty of Utrecht. A dockyard had been established at Port Mahon, and the harbour defended by the 800 guns of the fortress of St Philip.

Minorca remained in British hands until the French attack in 1756. Command of the army that laid siege to Fort St Philip was Marshal Richelieu's first war assignment, before being given command of French forces in Germany. In order to delay any British naval force being sent to the Mediterranean, Louis XV had ordered the Duc de Belle Île to mass an army of nearly 70,000 men in western France. The threat of invasion of England at that time, however, was only a feint, no effort being made to secure transports.[5]

The Baltic provided access to the north coast of Germany. Fearing Russian and Swedish attacks from seaward in 1757, Frederick tried to persuade the British to send a fleet into the Baltic, but Pitt refused. A Baltic operation would have had to confront seventeen Russian ships of the line, or eleven Swedish, at a time when the French occupation of Ostend and Nieuport presented the danger of a French attempt to invade England. Furthermore, Britain had no interest in opening direct hostilities with Russia, Sweden or Austria.[6] The preeminent significance of the Baltic in the naval strategies of the great powers, however, was a result of the naval stores that were needed to maintain their fleets. In the Northern War, which continued until Charles XII's death in 1718, the Dutch and, for the first time, the British had sent fleets into the Baltic to protect their shipping. Especially important were the supplies of hemp grown in southern Russia and coming through the ports of the Baltic states that had been captured by Russia.[7]

Of greatest importance to Britain was control of the narrow seas dividing England from the Continent. This was important both because they provided to shortest invasion route, but also because they funneled trade. The commerce of the Baltic and North Sea states mostly passed through the Strait of Dover to avoid the stormy passage around Scotland, and trade into the port of London took the same route. Control of the Strait was needed both for defence and for the exercise of sea power. The port of Calais had been in English hands for 300 years, until 1558, but it was then lost to France. In the following three and a half centuries Britain was to attach the highest strategic importance to ensuring that the harbours of the southern Netherlands were not controlled by any great maritime power. In the seventeenth century Britain fought three wars with the Netherlands, partly over control of the 'British' sea. Following the Glorious Revolution of 1688 and the accession of the Dutch King William III to the throne of England with his Stuart wife Mary, England was an ally of the Dutch and sought to ensure their continued independence from France, and as allies to prevent hostile use of the ports of Flanders.

The Dutch – following their revolution against Spanish suzerainty – had closed, for commercial reasons, the Sheldt River leading to the port of Antwerp, and for commercial and strategic reasons the British continued to insist that Antwerp be kept closed until the formation of modern Belgium in 1830. The only time Antwerp was opened as a naval port was during the period Napoleon's brother Louis Bonaparte controlled the Netherlands, followed by Napoleon's direct rule of the Netherlands when he quarrelled with his brother, between 1806 and 1815. To frustrate Napoleon's naval plans the largest amphibious operation to leave from England was to be launched in 1809. The port of Ostend was very nearly as important. When in 1722 an East India Company was founded with a Royal Charter from the Holy Roman Emperor, Charles VI, based on Ostend, the British government reacted strongly. The heavily armed ships of East India Companies constituted navies in embryo, and were frequently attached to state naval forces. An East India Company based on Ostend was regarded as creating the potential for a seagoing battle fleet in the hands of a hostile naval power directly across the English Channel from the Thames estuary, and near its narrowest point. To prevent this, Horace Walpole's administration sent a fleet in March 1726 under the command of Vice Admiral Francis Hosier to the West Indies to stop the Spanish flota of treasure ships carrying to Europe the specie that could have made it possible for the Emperor to fight a war against Britain. Spain had been separated from the Holy Roman Empire since the establishment of the Spanish Bourbon dynasty in 1700, but the wealth of the Spanish empire continued to finance Habsburg, Bourbon and Napoleonic wars until into the nineteenth century. Hosier had orders not to attack unless the Spaniards fired first, and he maintained a blockade of Porto Bello, Vera Cruz and Havana for over a year, at a cost of 4,000 dead from disease, including his own death. Richard Glover published in 1740 a versified attack on Walpole entitled 'Admiral Hosier's Ghost': 'See these mournful spectres sweeping, Ghastly o'er this hated wave, Whose wan cheeks are stained with weeping: These were English captains brave.' But the clear demonstration of purpose by Walpole's administration had led the Emperor to suspend his charter for an Ostend East India Company in May 1727, and in March 1731, by the Second Treaty of Vienna, to terminate it altogether. The bishop and politician Benjamin Hoadly wrote at the time that 'no man who is the least conversant in the affairs of Europe can make any doubt but that this incident has been the only thing that has hitherto prevented a war in Europe, by depriving the Courts of Vienna and Madrid of the means of putting in execution the dangerous schemes they had projected.'[8] This was the beginning of the Anglo-Austrian alliance that survived until 1756.[9]

European concerns were central to British security, but naval wars cannot be fought without money, and that ensured much of the fighting would take place in distant theatres. The maintenance of naval forces in North American, Caribbean and East Asian waters was important to support British trade in goods from those areas, and to protect the colonists. This role acquired offensive significance from the importance of trade in financing British naval forces, and enabling Britain to subsidize continental allies. Consequently, naval warfare in the two Indies, East and West, was vigorously conducted, and the struggle for control of the Ohio, Île Royale and New France was a product of sea power. Operationally, however, power projection across the Atlantic and into the Indian Ocean was a by-product of successful control of the English Channel.

*   *   *

With the development in the sixteenth century of seagoing sailing warships, naval powers sought to perfect the means of employing their fleets to influence events ashore by disrupting the trade of hostile states in cycles to maximize the economic returns of national trade. Nicolas Magens, a German financier in London, wrote in 1775 in his *Essay on Insurance*: 'when we examine to the bottom of the thing, it appears very evident, that sea battles are fought not so much to kill people, as to be masters of trade, whereby people live; and by stopping their supplies, to compel our enemies in the end to live in friendship with us.'[10] Economic blockade in the modern sense of denying an enemy access to the commodities available through international trade was not generally practical in the age of sail. Fleet movements were too greatly affected by weather conditions for it to be possible to prevent cargos arriving by sea to any extended coastline. Hawke's blockade of Brest in the summer of 1759 was all but unique in the eighteenth century, and was only made possible by an unprecedented effort. As a result, economic warfare was primarily directed at the direct seizure of wealth, and at the mercantilist objective of using naval action to injure the commercial prospects of the enemy, in order to maximize the ability of the belligerent to make war-inflated profits by trade. Profits would be funneled into the national Treasury through taxation and used to support the cost of maintaining the navy, and also the cost of subsidizing the military forces of allies.[11]

Admiral Hosier's mission to blockade the Spanish treasure fleet was only one episode in a three-century-long strategy directed at the interception of bullion being transported from the Spanish mines in Central and South America. Queen Elizabeth's Treasurer of the Navy, John Hawkins, the Earl of Essex, Admiral William Monson and Sir Walter Raleigh, to name the most important, had established the strategic idea of making war by attacking bullion shipments. Fifty years later it was accepted by Cromwell's Commission of Admiralty as good doctrine.[12] In the seventeenth century, economic thinking developed crude bullionism into the more sophisticated mercantilism. Economic warfare, however, often retains use for otherwise outdated practices. While this has been especially true of mercantilist trade war, it was also true of bullionism. There was a penalty to be paid for making war by intercepting the Spanish treasure ships because the loss of liquidity played havoc with European markets for English goods. Attack on trade also led to trouble with neutrals. But the short-term advantages outweighed any long-term difficulties, at least in the minds of the men who stood to make a direct profit.

The Spanish decision in 1701 to ally themselves dynastically to France had presented England with a chance to use attacks on the Spanish treasure fleets as a means of disabling the French army. In 1702 Admiral Rooke burned a flota with its French escort in Vigo harbour, and was thanked for his exploit by the House of Commons: 'France has endeavoured to support its ambition by the riches of the Indies: your success, Sir, hath only kept them the burden of Spain and stripped them of the assistance of it.'[13] In fact, the advantage to England was illusory, and led to Spanish reprisals against Dutch and English mercantile interests.[14] Nevertheless, the direction of maritime strategy against the treasure fleets continued to find strong advocates in England. In 1708, Admiral Wager met the Spanish treasure galleons at sea, captured three, and drove the rest into Vera Cruz. In a 1712 pamphlet 'The Conduct of the Allies', the Church of Ireland Dean Jonathan Swift complained that not enough emphasis had been placed on maritime operations: 'I have sometimes wondered how it came to pass, that the Style of *Maritime Powers*, by which our Allies, in a sort of contemptuous manner, usually couple us with the *Dutch*, did never put us in mind of the Sea.' By failing to blockade bullion shipments, Dean Jonathan Swift wrote, the English had enabled the King of France to make war: 'the Supplies he hath received from the *Spanish West Indies*, which in all are computed, since the War, to amount to Four hundred Millions of Livres, (and all in *Specie*) have enabled him to pay his Troops.'[15] When in 1760 it looked in London as though Spanish bullion shipment might be used to support the tottering finances of the French government, Pitt was all for making a pre-emptive attack on the Spanish flota.

Mercantilism was a system of power that sought the impoverishment of the enemy only in so far as it contributed to the increase of the belligerent's own wealth, which in turn multiplied the belligerent's power. It was more sophisticated than bullionism because it saw that the wealth a state needed for the purpose of war was derived from all trade, including trade in low-value products. Indeed the volume, not the value, of trade goods determined the scale of investment in the merchant shipping fleets that were an index of national trade, and also provided the technical infrastructure for naval forces. Seaborne trade was therefore doubly valued as the source of naval power. Even during the years of peace the mercantilist struggle between Britain and France was continued until the advent of *laissez faire* economic principles in the last quarter of the eighteenth century began to draw distinctions between the strategies for wealth and those for security.

The principal means of conducting trade warfare were the privateer fleets of the belligerent states. Trade war could be, and was, conducted by the officers and men of the state navy, but navies are expensive, and privateers provided the necessary multiplier of state effort. Privateers accounted for forty per cent of the prizes taken by British ships in the five wars between 1702 and 1783, although in the Seven Years War regular naval forces accounted for the greater number of captures.[16] The French, after the defeat at La Hogue in 1692, went so far as to lay up their battle fleet altogether and depend entirely upon their privateers, which took a great toll of English shipping. Swift believed that King Louis 'is at no Charge of a Fleet, further than providing Privateers, wherewith his Subjects carry on a Piratical War at their own Expense, and he shares in the Profit; which hath been very considerable to *France*, and of infinite Disadvantage to us, not only by the perpetual Losses we have suffered to an immense Value, but by the general Discouragement of Trade, on which we so much depend.'[17] Privateering was not necessarily a very remunerative undertaking, but the return was evidently enough to keep the raiders at sea throughout the wars of the sixteenth to eighteenth centuries.[18]

Originally, privateers had been private traders who had suffered injury from foreign pirates, and consequently applied to their governments for letters of marque authorizing them to conduct private warfare against the nationals of the state harbouring the pirates until they had recovered the amount of their loss. From 1357 letters of marque were generally issued in England by the Lord High Admiral in the High Court of Admiralty.[19] An application for a letter of marque contained a statement of the grievance, and an account of the monetary value to be recovered. To ensure that the privateersmen conformed to international norms, the High Court of Admiralty sitting as a prize court had to judge the validity of captures, employing Roman Law, which was itself based on the 'Law Merchant' of the ancient Mediterranean. No purely national enactment could apply to the ships of different nations on the high seas beyond national jurisdiction. The publication in 1494 of the Provençal *Consulato del Mare* describing the rights and duties of belligerents at sea had provided a statement of legal norms upon which the law of prize subsequently depended. Prize courts were supposed to ensure that belligerents did not exceed their rights according to the laws of nations, and over time their decisions modified the law of war at sea, establishing in that way what is known as the 'course of Admiralty'. But the matter inevitably became more complicated when states began to view privateers as low-budget force multipliers, and justified the issuance of letters of marque on the wrongs supposedly suffered by the state.[20]

Governments tended to observe what they believed were the laws because they believed in the value of law, but also because the principle of reprisal could be invoked by an enemy, or more dangerously, by an injured neutral. As recently as 1916 during the First World War and before the United States became a belligerent 'associated' with Britain, the British Judicial Committee of the

House of Lords hearing the *Zamora* case was at pains to maintain the independence of prize courts from the British government.[21] The danger of lateral escalation by the alienation of neutrals is a very potent force; interception of neutral trade had and has a strong track record for turning neutrals into enemies.

Sir Julian Corbett wrote his account of *England in the Seven Years War* in 1907 at a time when the delegates at the Second Hague Conference were trying without success to establish the concept of an international prize court to minimize disputes over belligerent rights at sea. 'The prolonged exercise of belligerent rights,' Corbett wrote, 'even of the most undoubted kind, produces an interference with trade that becomes more and more oppressive.'[22] There was a danger in 1758 and 1759 that the Dutch, Danes, Swedes and Spaniards, who claimed that neutral ships were entitled to carry on their trade without molestation whatever cargo their ships were carrying, would combine to escort their convoys. Having passed down Channel, the fleets of the northern states might even go into Brest and combine forces with the French.

The needs of government to ensure that the exercise of sea power would support the national war effort while minimizing conflict with neutral states, some urging vigorous action and others urging restraint, inevitably clashed with the more commercially motivated privateer interests. In the first half of the eighteenth century the latter were in the ascendency in England. The view of the political philosopher John Locke, that the right to private property was the only control over despotism, was so generally believed in England that no restriction was possible on the right of the captors to 'their property'. In 1708 Queen Anne's government enacted the Cruisers Act allotting the whole value of prizes to the captors, abandoning the crown's previous claim to a share, and this provision was renewed by an act of 1739, the Prize Act of 1756 and the Privateers Act of 1759.[23] A result was that privateers became increasingly independent, with damaging consequences for relations with neutrals. At the beginning of the Seven Years War, the Duke of Newcastle felt unable to alter the law so as to restrain the privateers, or even to act decisively to oblige them to conform to their instructions. Before he was brought into the government, William Pitt vigorously defended the privateer interests in parliament. When France attempted to circumvent the

British cruisers by opening the trade of the French West Indies to neutral shipping, Lord Chancellor Hardwicke decided to interpret belligerent rights as enabling privateers to capture neutral ships which were undertaking trade as a service for the enemy. 'The Rule of War of 1756' unleashed the cruisers and privateers against Dutch and Spanish shipping. Three years later, even Pitt recognized the need to accommodate the complaints of the Dutch about 'divers outrageous acts of piracy and robbery'. The Privateers Act sought to reduce the threat to neutrals by giving the Admiralty the right to refuse letters of marque to vessels under one hundred tons and with fewer than twelve four-pounder guns, and by tightening up the rules about sureties.[24]

Apart from the protection to trade provided by the Royal Navy, the mercantile community employed privateers not just to raid enemy shipping, but also to protect British shipping. Ships that were taken by the French had a good chance of being recaptured by a British privateer before they could reach French ports. In that event, the ship owners would be required to pay 'prize salvage' to the owners of the privateers, but they were able to insure against the risk of loss, or of having to pay prize salvage. The relatively small insurance premiums charged on British shipping even in wartime indicates the extent to which business could accommodate itself to war. The wine trade from London to Madeira paid six per cent premiums during the Seven Years War, reduced to three per cent if the ship sailed in convoy. The larger freight rates shippers could charge in wartime, and the greater wartime demand, appears to have more than offset the costs and possible risk of losing a ship to the enemy.[25]

Historians, with the advantage of hindsight, do not rate highly the strategic value of injuring French commercial profits from trade. The capacity of France to fight the Seven Years War was to be seriously affected by the inability of the government to obtain enough revenue through taxation or loans, but it does not appear that the depredations of British privateers were a major cause of the financial crisis. The combined value of imports and exports to the French colonies in the years before the outbreak of war, 1753 to 1755, had risen well above thirty million livres, and after the outbreak of war fell below eight million in 1758 and 1759 and below four million in 1760. However, in 1761 the figure rose to nearly seven million, and in the last year of the war almost touched fifteen million. Richard Pares, still regarded as an authority on trade war, concluded that the Seven Years War demonstrated 'the impotence of blockade and colonial conquests to break the will of France'. French colonial trade did not slowly decline until in 1762 it reached vanishing point, and obliged the French Government to make peace. 'On the contrary, it collapsed quickly in the spring and summer of 1757, and in the last two years of the war it was reviving a little. The colonial merchants simply went out of business, and contented themselves with getting home their old debts if they could.' Despite vociferous complaints from the corporations of seaport and manufacturing towns, Choiseul was able to ignore the loss of colonial trade, and continue the war long enough to restore to France at the Peace of Paris an important number of her colonies. 'If she made peace in 1763 on terms not unworthy of her, it was because her Minister would not yield to a form of pressure which only touched the circumference of her economic life.'[26] Corbett's judgement was similar: 'we are inclined to forget how impotent [seapower] is of itself to decide a war against great Continental states, how tedious is the pressure of naval action unless it be nicely coordinated with military and diplomatic pressure.'[27]

Statistics showing the sudden drop in trade movement at the outbreak of the war exaggerate the toll on France of British naval and privateer attacks on French shipping. French businessmen had learned how to compensate for the dangers of predatory activity. In anticipation of war, trade would be artificially expanded in order to secure a stockpile; on the outbreak of war, merchants would withdraw their assets from the sea; but with the return of peace they would again rush to build up stocks and to fill over-due orders. France did lose large numbers of merchant ships to *guerre de course*. Marseilles records show that 716 Marseilles and Provençal ships were lost in the period 1755–1763. During the Seven Years War, marine insurance for Marseilles shipping rose from two to four per cent to as high as fifty to sixty per cent. The incidents of bankruptcy amongst the merchants of Marseilles, however, indicate that the economic problems of maritime war could be supported by the community. In fact, bankruptcies at Marseilles peaked in 1730 and 1774, years of peace. After a high in

1755 before the Seven Years War reached the Mediterranean, the rate of bankruptcy continued to decline during the war. Because of French invisible earnings, French balance of trade remained favourable throughout the war. Throughout the eighteenth century the volume of French trade grew steadily, perhaps at a faster rate than did that of Britain.[28]

One reason for the continuance of French trade during the war, despite the losses at sea, was that English business maintained a lively wartime trade with the enemy. Eighteenth-century constitutional thinking and administrative practice placed severe limits upon the ability of government in Britain to impose its laws. There was no customary law about trade with the enemy, and such prohibitions as were made by royal proclamation did not have the same force. A merchant trading with the enemy stood to have his goods condemned as a lawful prize if taken by a privateer or warship, but so long as the goods were not contraband weapons of war he was only held to be guilty of a 'high misdemeanour', which incurred little penalty. Furthermore, convictions were almost unobtainable, especially in the colonial courts, which had jurisdiction over misdemeanours. The difficulty was increased by the need to prove that a merchant had actually completed a trade transaction; it was not enough to prove that he intended to undertake trade with the enemy for in English law the intention to commit a crime was not itself a crime. Besides the legal pitfalls, the government was faced with the collusion of colonial officials in those colonies that could profit by trading with the enemy.

London insurers had learned how to balance risks from different trades, and in the eighteenth century they were so efficient that they not only kept the British merchant marine at sea, but also that of France. There was some feeling that it was unpatriotic to send compensation to the enemy owners of ships taken by British naval forces, but there were no second thoughts about accepting the wartime premiums. In 1747 Corbyn Morris published *An essay towards deciding the question, whether Britain be permitted by right policy to insure the ships of her enemies?* in which he criticized the practice. Acceptance of insurance on enemy vessels was made illegal in 1748. But 1748 was the last year of one phase of the Anglo-French war, and although Morris reprinted his pamphlet in 1758, the legislation was not renewed until 1793.[29]

The result was that wartime maritime predation not only lost any strategic function of denying the enemy cargoes, but also lost the capacity to drive enemy traders out of business. British insurance kept the French merchantmen at sea, and British naval forces served British interests by keeping insurance premiums high. The capture and condemnation of a French ship lost it to its French owners, but their financial suffering was limited by the insurance they had purchased, and they could use the payment made by the London insurers following the condemnation of their ships to purchase other ships, which in their turn might be captured by British cruisers and privateers. French shippers could instruct agents in London to buy back from their captors the captured ships, the cost of which might be depressed by a glutted market. Together with the practice of privateers of ransoming captives while still at sea, so as to minimize the danger they would be recaptured before they could be brought into port, the marine insurance system ensured that war operations against shipping became a sophisticated system designed to funnel the profits of a lively international commerce into the pockets of the merchants of the more successful state.[30]

Britain was more vulnerable to the effects of commerce raiding than was France, because of the strong political connection between its mercantile interests and its parliamentary government. The Comte de Broglie, French ambassador in London in 1731, believed that trade attack should be the central focus of French naval strategy: 'A captured vessel belonging to a merchant or to one of the English companies makes the nation cry out more than does the loss of ten battles.' He urged that the French fleet be broken up into cruising squadrons which could be deployed in support of the privateers. After the unsatisfactory Battle of Toulon in February 1744, Comte de Maurepas, the Minister of the Marine, did just that with the naval forces in the Mediterranean.[31] In 1707 the English parliament actually passed into law an act 'for the better securing the Trade of this Kingdom by Cruisers and Convoys', requiring the Royal Navy to commit forty-three ships to the needs of trade defence. This might have disastrously limited the ability of the Admiralty to use offensive means to defeat the enemy. But in fact, British maritime and naval resources were large enough that defensive and offensive actions could be undertaken simultaneously. In the Seven Years War between 1756 and 1763, no doubt in part because of improvements in convoy organization, there was little protest in Britain at merchant shipping losses.[32]

Whatever the statistics on British and French losses at sea, assessment of the value to Britain of the trade war has to concentrate upon the British bottom line. The British government had little incentive to stop Britons trading with the enemy when contemporary mercantilist economics suggested that making an exaggerated wartime profit out of sales to the enemy was in the national interest, provided the items sold were not contraband war materials. Mercantilist trade war was a strategy rooted in the instincts of people who had not yet learned to find value in injuring an enemy unless the result was at the same time of direct profit. It was high treason to 'aid and comfort' the king's enemies (25 Edward III) but that was not an adequate deterrent because selling goods to the enemy on favourable terms was held to injure the enemy. It was the insurance profits, and those enjoyed by ship owners charging wartime rates, and the profits made by British merchants able to undersell those of France, who had to meet the higher costs of being on the losing side of the maritime war, that made the strategy a valuable one for Britain. Successful businessmen liked to lock in their wealth and status by purchasing estates, and the land tax, supplemented by customs tariffs collected on imports, paid for the war. Not only did it pay for the cost of maintaining the Royal Navy, but it also paid for the army, and for subsidies paid to foreign governments. In effect, British trade war paid to maintain the Army of Observation in Hanover, paid to keep Frederick the Great in the field against France, and also paid for the campaigns in North America, the Caribbean, and in India.

* * *

There was an exception to the rule that trade warfare was directed to maximizing profit rather than to starving the enemy, because naval stores needed to maintain battle fleets were bulky enough that they could only be transported by sea, and had to be taken directly to the dockyards of the enemy. With a relatively small number of ports to watch, ports that were being watched in any case for tactical reasons, and with a major incentive for a naval power, that of eroding the enemy's naval strength, it was worthwhile intercepting ships carrying naval stores to the enemy. That objective, however, posed a very serious risk of expanding the war. Mercantilist objectives could be furthered simply by capturing the merchant ships owned by nationals of the enemy, although the Rule of War of 1756 did extend the threat to neutrals serving the enemy on routes closed to them in peace time. That rule increased the danger of lateral escalation, and the danger had to be managed by limiting the scope of privateer activity. No such limitations could be imposed on efforts to intercept naval stores if enemy battle fleets were to be eroded in their harbours: Britain had to be ready to stop and condemn all and any neutral ships carrying cargoes of naval stores even when they were nominally owned by neutral businesses. This inevitably put Britain into conflict with the Baltic countries from which came much of the naval stores needed by Britain and France for their navies, especially masts, hemp and tar, but also Swedish ironwork, including cannon.

During the seventeenth century a concept of contraband gradually developed, and the right of belligerents to intercept neutral ships carrying it was promoted. The great Sir Leoline Jenkins established in the English High Court of Admiralty many of the precedents that make up the course of Admiralty, permitting the use of statistical evidence to determine whether cargo was or was not the property of neutrals who nominally 'owned' it, and putting the onus of disproof on the victim, who usually presented his transaction books if he were honest. The court was interested in evidence of the ultimate destination of the cargo, wherever it may have been captured.[33] In the late seventeenth century the domestic supply in England and France of masts and timber became difficult and the High Court of Admiralty began to condemn cargoes of naval stores. It was able to do so because relatively few neutral states were injured commercially by the inclusion of naval stores in contraband lists, and those that were injured were not able to mount an effective naval resistance. Nevertheless it remained British policy to purchase the stores at invoice price plus ten per cent and freight. The inclusion of food on contraband lists was no more consistent, although victuals and drink such as cheese and beer which could be used to supply ships of war were more often found by courts to be lawful prize. Grain which might be used to feed armies was less certain to be considered contraband. The definition of contraband, however, depended less upon pervasive law than upon treaties between different states which had different interests, and upon the military potential of the nations.

* * *

Even had transports been available at the time, invasion was beyond the means of the French navy in 1756. Amphibious assault across a tidal channel, control of which is contested by an enemy fleet, is the most difficult of all military operations. When in the nineteenth century the French navy began to build steam-propelled ships there was to be serious concern in Britain that 'steam had bridged the Channel', but that proved to be an exaggeration. Before the invention of steam engines, the limitations of sailing fleets, the predictability of wind patterns and the hard realities of geography had dictated how any invasion fleet would have to operate, and how the British navy would frustrate its efforts.

The pattern had been set when Spain tried to invade England in 1588, using a fleet assembled at Cadiz and an army in Flanders. The only harbour in southern England where the Spanish Armada might have been able to find refuge from the sea, and a secure place to defend itself, was the Solent behind the Isle of Wight. But that would have made it impossible to provide cover for the Spanish army crossing in the Straits of Dover. Subsequent to the Glorious Revolution of 1688 when the Dutch King William III came to the throne of England, and France became the hereditary enemy, the English navy had developed the means to operate a strong squadron, and eventually its main fleet, in the approaches to the English Channel to counter the threat of a French invasion. These were to be brought to perfection in 1759 under the direction of Lord Anson at the Admiralty and Admiral Sir Edward Hawke commanding the Channel Fleet.

In the western approaches to the Channel wind direction is between northwest and southwest about sixty per cent of the time, and only in the late spring, between March and May, are north-easterlies frequent enough to be relied upon. It was then that the ocean trades made their passages down Channel.[34] The French had no safe and adequate harbours east of Brest for their largest ships, providing they could not acquire control of Antwerp. If the

French battle fleet entered the Channel without first defeating the British fleet it risked having nowhere to find shelter in a hard westerly blow, or if they should suffer battle damage and be unable to beat their way back to Brest, harried in their retreat by a Western Squadron operating in 'the chops of the Channel'. Following the Battle of Barfleur in 1692 French first-rate battle-ships were unable to get into any defended harbour and were destroyed in Cherbourg and La Hogue bays.

At the beginning of the eighteenth century it was still thought to be too dangerous to send the main British fleet down Channel as far as Plymouth, and in any case, there was little provision there for its support. The first experiment took place in 1705 when Rear Admiral George Byng, First Viscount Torrington, mounted a watch on Brest, but the threat then was not seen as one of invasion. Byng was there to guard the rear of an Anglo-Dutch force that had been sent to the Mediterranean. When the objective was more strictly defensive, as it was in 1702 and again in 1708, the fleet was kept further to the eastward. Later in the century, however, when the Western Squadron was expanded virtually to be the Channel Fleet, it would have been suicide for the French fleet to run into the Channel with an undefeated enemy behind them.[35]

If the French were to concentrate the forces they would need to defeat the English Channel Fleet, they might try to bring the Toulon fleet north to join the Brest fleet. But a strong Western Squadron detached from the main Channel Fleet was well placed to defeat the Toulon force in detail as it approached Brest. This was pointed out to King William III by Sydney Godolphin, one of the English Treasury Commissioners, in 1693.

A strong Westerly Squadron was also well placed to pursue the Brest fleet if it were employed aggressively to the west or south. In 1702 Admiral Cloudesley Shovell urged the importance of a strong Western Squadron stationed south-west to west-south-west of the island of Ushant off the western tip of France because it could intercept the Brest fleet if it tried to interfere with an English attack on Cadiz under the command of Sir George Rooke. A Western Squadron could also intercept French fleets going to or returning from the West Indies or New France, and it could provide a response to any French attempt to land an army in Ireland.

Among the papers published following the condemnation of
Vice Admiral John Byng, fourth son of Admiral George Byng,
after the Battle of Minorca is one, probably by Anson, justifying
the priority given to maintaining a strong Western Squadron
as the means of protecting British colonies and trade, as well as
for defence against invasion: 'the best defence . . . for our colonies
as well as our coasts, is to have such a squadron always to the
westward as may in all probability either keep the French in port,
or give them battle with advantage if they come out.'[36] When
fully developed at the end of the eighteenth century, the Western
Squadron of the Channel Fleet was the *place des armeés* from
which squadrons could be deployed in pursuit of any French
forces that escaped from Brest, L'Orient or Basque Roads. In 1799
the fleet commander, Admiral Lord Bridport, was to be instructed,
in the event of an enemy detachment escaping the blockading
force, 'to direct the officer commanding the squadron' sent in
pursuit 'to follow the enemy to any part of the world to which it
may go as long as he is able to obtain information on which he
may certainly depend of the route it has taken'.[37]

And a Western Squadron was essential to provide for the safety
of British trade. As Anson put it in 1756:

> All our trade, except that to the northward and the coasters, comes
> in between Cape Clear [on the south of Ireland] and Ushant, a
> station where the French cruisers and privateers might do infinite
> mischief if they were suffered to go out or return in safety. During
> the last rebellion [i.e. the Jacobite rebellion of 1745], when the
> western cruisers were called in to defend our coasts, the number of
> captures and mischief done to our merchants were incredible.
> These are the benefits of which a western squadron is productive.

A small Western Squadron had been based on Plymouth from
1650 during the Anglo-Dutch wars for commerce raiding and
protection, but during the Dutch wars the main British fleet had
been able to work out of maintenance facilities in the Thames at
Deptford and Woolwich, and in the Medway at Chatham. These
together possessed three double and five single dry docks. With
the manufacturing and storehouses of London immediately in
their rear, the problems of maintaining a fleet off the Dutch coast

were minimized, although the problems of preserving food and drink were still significant. At Portsmouth at the beginning of the eighteenth century there was one double dry dock capable of taking the smallest first-rate ships of the line, and there was a relatively small dockyard to service the fleet. At Plymouth there was only a careening hulk for heaving down ships to clean their hulls, and a Victualling Board agent working out of a rented room. The consequence was that when on 1 May 1689 the British fleet was severely damaged in the Battle of Bantry Bay on the west of Ireland it had to put all the way back to Portsmouth for repairs, and during the two months it took to get the fleet back to sea, the French dominated the Channel. The need to develop the infra-structure for the British fleet in the Channel, at Portsmouth and particularly at Plymouth, was clear. The fact that the Glorious Revolution of 1688 had brought to the English throne William III, whose credentials as a Protestant hero were in line with the will of parliament, ensured there would be funds made available. A dry and a wet dock were built at Plymouth, and at Portsmouth two new dry docks and two wet docks. The dry docks were built of stone, with the intention that they should last.

The larger effort at Portsmouth reflected in fact that the great battles to prevent France restoring the Catholic Stuart dynasty in England were fought in the English Channel at Beachy Head in 1690 and at Barfleur and La Hogue in 1692. With Portsmouth as the main *operational* base, the fleet could still be made ready in the Thames each spring. Once brought forward for service, it was easier to supply the fleet at Portsmouth than at Plymouth because of the shorter distance from London for the supply ships, and because of the more productive farms in the vicinity. Portsmouth also enjoyed a safer anchorage for the fleet, at Spithead off the Isle of Wight, where ships could lay in safety, and could get to sea on a southwest wind, or proceed through the Needles channel on an easterly wind. At Plymouth there was little shelter until the break-water was built across the sound in the nineteenth century. By 1711 Portsmouth was the largest English dockyard, with Plymouth remaining the smallest. Half the entire dockyard force remained concentrated in the Thames and Medway yards.

But there were dangers associated with operating the main English fleet out of Portsmouth. It was the last good English harbour in the Channel, which then rapidly narrowed and turned north. Just as the French understood the dangers of entering the Channel with their only adequate dockyard behind them, and to windward, so the English realized the danger of operating the main fleet in the Straits of Dover where, in the event of a westerly gale, they might be driven ashore, or have to drive northward into the North Sea. The Downs anchorage north of Dover provided shelter in most circumstances, but could be dangerous during a strong southerly blow. If a fleet were forced to sail then, the northerly exit from the Downs, the Gull Stream, was narrow and potentially dangerous. Once driven north from the Downs, a fleet might have to wait weeks for an easterly wind to take them back into the Channel – and during that time the French would be free to land an invasion force on the south coast. This threat was particularly seen during the period 1744 to 1759.[38]

The development of Portsmouth as the main operational base also, paradoxically, served to reduce its utility for that purpose. Once it became possible for the British fleet to be maintained at Portsmouth, it became unacceptably dangerous for the French fleet to enter the Channel, with their only refuge at Brest a hard beat to windward. In fact, the main French Atlantic fleet only returned to the Channel after the defeat at Barfleur three times in the eighteenth century, in 1744 when it enjoyed an element of surprise, and in 1779 and 1781 when alliance with Spain provided them with dominating numbers.

The circumstances led the French to concentrate on operations to windward of Brest, where they could threaten British trade, and threaten invasion of Ireland where they could hope for a friendly reception from the Catholic population, and from which beachhead they might be able to move against England across the Irish Sea. Brest was also well placed for maintaining connections with New France, and with French establishments in the West Indies and India. If the British were to protect their own colonies, their trade and Ireland, they needed to expand the capabilities of the Western Squadron. For all these reasons it became necessary for the English to develop Plymouth into a base capable of supporting the main fleet. In 1719–1722 a second dry dock was constructed in Plymouth, and gradually the number of ships deployed to the

Western Squadron increased to twelve third rates and smaller under William Martin in 1745.

Apart from the need for developed dockyard facilities to support an enhanced Western Squadron, there needed to be developments in naval architecture to enable the fleet to keep the sea in the western approaches. In the seventeenth century it was the accepted practice to retire the first- and second-rate battleships into safe anchorages in early September and not to bring them out until May. With the introduction of fore-and-aft sails on the stays and reduction of the mizzen lateen to a spanker, ships came to have more ability to hold their position in a strong head wind, or at least tack across it to a refuge. With the improved rig, increases in the size of ships made them steadier in a high sea state, and able to carry supplies for a more extended cruise. A first rate rebuilt in 1692, the *Royal William* of 100 guns, measured 1,568 tons. The *Victory* of 1737, also with 100 guns, measured 1,921 tons, and the *Queen Charlotte* (100 guns) of 1790 measured 2,286 tons. In the same period third-rate battleships increased in size by seventy per cent and sixth-rate frigates by one hundred per cent.

But even with these improvements, fleets could not hold the sea in all weather, even in the summer months. As early as Rear Admiral George Byng's watch on Brest in 1705, mounted to guard the Channel when the Anglo-Dutch fleet sailed to the Mediterranean, use was made of Plymouth, Dartmouth and Torbay for shelter – but Plymouth was not safe for a large fleet, and Dartmouth had too constricted an entrance for a fleet to enter in a hurry in squally weather. Falmouth in Cornwall was inaccessible to a fleet off Brest in the event of a westerly gale, and the harbour was believed to be too shoal for it to be used by a fleet with safety. George Byng finally took shelter from an August storm in Portsmouth, but in doing so he left Brest completely open for the exit of the French fleet. When in 1759 Admiral Hawke mounted his watch on Brest to guard against the threat of invasion, he was ordered not to bring his ships eastward of Plymouth or Torbay. Given Plymouth's limitations, Torbay was adopted as the usual refuge for the fleet watching Brest. It was dangerously exposed should the wind back suddenly from south west to east, as it did on 13 February 1795, but it was the best anchorage available. Because it was impossible for the French to get out of Brest during a westerly or southwesterly blow, it was possible, but not certain, that the British fleet could return to its station off Brest before the French could get out.

Experience showed that ships supplied for more than three months' service were too deep in the water to perform well. In 1758 Anson made that recommendation. At the same time, strategic flexibility required that ships have a reserve which would enable them to be sent in pursuit of the enemy if circumstances enabled them to leave harbour. Hawke was ordered in 1759 to keep two months' reserve of victuals in his ships.[39] The only way these requirements could be met while keeping the fleet on station off Brest was to organize a system of afloat resupply.

Barrelled stores had to be kept at Portsmouth and Plymouth: salted fish, beef, pork, beer, biscuit, oatmeal, butter and cheese. More demanding was the provision of fresh meat and vegetables to prevent scurvy. Until the middle of the eighteenth century this requirement prevented the fleet staying at sea for more than six weeks, and the sheer scale of the fleet's needs prevented them being met in the west of England. Admiral Russell's command in 1692 numbered 24,000 men, while the town of Exeter numbered only 14,000 men. When on 6 June 1759 Hawke put into Torbay and requisitioned nearly 50,000 pounds of beef according to a standing contract stating that supply would have to be filled in 48 hours, the Exeter contractor Richard Cross was unable to do so, and paid the penalty bond.[40] Provision of fresh vegetables on twelve hours' notice was an even more exacting requirement.

When the fleet did have to seek shelter it was important to make use of the opportunity to take on board stores, but there was a great danger that the enemy would be able to take advantage of the circumstance should the fleet be unable to resupply without returning to port. With the advantage of hindsight, and without a full appreciation of the realities of naval operations, it appears obvious to make arrangements to take supplies to the ships at sea, and this was first undertaken to support Rear Admiral George Byng's watch on Brest in 1705. Victualling ships were laided in the Thames, and at Portsmouth and Plymouth, and were dispatched by two resident victualling agents sent out to Plymouth for the purpose.

The result was successful enough that Byng was sometimes driven off station by bad weather, but not by illness. Progress in establishing proper hygiene and nutrition to the fleet was anything but continuous. In 1755 Hawke was to be driven off his station watching Brest by the ravages of disease, but learning from that experience he and Anson were to insist on the highest possible standards during his long watch in 1759. His fleet had only 20 men sick out of 14,000 when he fought the Battle of Quiberon Bay.[41] Hygiene was as difficult to maintain as a nutritious diet. Scrubbing the decks and hammocks with sea water, or even with vinegar, was found to be counterproductive unless a system was devised to dry them afterwards, as the immune system of the men was compromised in the damp and confined spaces. In the middle of the century, several devices were developed for ventilation of the lower decks, the best of them by a system of stoves and ducts. Anson's desperate experience struggling with scurvious crews during his voyage around the world inspired a new professionalism about naval medicine. When the physician to the Royal Hospital at Haslar, James Lind, published his *Treatise on the Scurvy* in 1753 he dedicated it to Anson.[42] The successful management of the health of the British fleet in 1759, in contrast to the disastrous typhus epidemic that had more than decimated the French fleet in 1757, was enough in itself to explain Hawke's victory.

It was a highly demanding task, however, to manage a continuous succession of supply cycles, requiring laided hoys to make offshore voyages to meet the fleet, which had to be on station to meet them. Weather could affect the movements of either, as could the actions of the enemy. The successes of 1705 and 1759 were unique to the first half of the eighteenth century, and were not to be repeated until the nineteenth century.

For most of the eighteenth century, the Western Squadron was only able to resupply when it entered a fleet base at Portsmouth, Plymouth, or the anchorage at Torbay. The inevitable result was that admirals kept their fleets on station just as long as they could, and their crews paid the price in sickness and death. It was important, therefore, for the navy to make provision for hospitalizing the sick so that they would not be lost forever to the service. But it was remarkably slow to do so. A hospital for 1,200 patients was finally built at Stonehouse near Plymouth in 1762, and it was to be 1800 before a 300-bed hospital was built at Paignton to serve the fleet at Torbay.

To maintain effectively the Western Squadron on station it was necessary to address the management culture of the Royal Navy. This was, perhaps remarkably, highly centralized. Decisions were made in London about quite trivial matters. The impact of this centralization on operations had been manageable during the Dutch wars, when Samuel Pepys had been Secretary of the Navy. But it was a serious problem during the French wars. It was one reason the fleet continued to base its operations on Portsmouth, which was within a day's ride of London. Plymouth, by contrast, was six days' ride from London. It took half a century to find ways of dealing with the problem. In 1745 Admiral Anson requested the Admiralty issue a standing order to its agents that the fleet should be cleaned and refitted whenever it entered port.[43] In 1759 the Admiralty Board, Navy Board and Victualling Board sent representatives to Plymouth so that decisions could be made locally. Three months after the start of the campaign, on 23 July, Admiral Hawke had complained about 'the want of a Commanding Officer at Plymouth to see all orders executed with the dispatch and punctuality necessary'. The Admiralty, belatedly, provided a base commander in the person of Captain Thomas Hanway, who had fought under Hawke's command in 1747. The Victualling Board sent one of its Commissioners, Robert Pett. The Navy Board already had a Yard Commissioner, Rogers, at Plymouth, but it also sent one of its Commissioners, Digby Dent, to back him up.[44]

The ships engaged in commerce protection were a major commitment of the Plymouth yard, because they could only do their job if they were kept in good repair and cleaned regularly to give them the needed speed. The conditions in the exposed western approaches exacted a high toll on spars, rigging and sails. To meet these demands, manpower at Plymouth increased between 1756 and 1763 such that it became the second-largest yard in the navy.

The crisis of 1759 showed that Plymouth was adequate to meet the needs of the fleet, but at least in part that was because Hawke was able to manage the movements of the fleet to ensure the dockyard was not swamped by more work than it could handle. Hawke had sufficient ships under his command that he was able to release them in succession to return to Plymouth for cleaning and repairs to hull and rigging. It is also true that he was fortunate not to suffer any major weather damage that might have forced him to take shelter, which to some extent is an indication that his officers' ship handling was of an adequate standard. He did bring the whole fleet into Plymouth in October 1759 to resupply for three months, and Hanway was able to complete the work in six days despite bad weather. Nevertheless, Hawke was constantly concerned by the inability of Plymouth Victualling Yard to supply enough beer in good condition, and he warned that Plymouth was unable to handle first-rate three-decked ships.

The construction of the breakwater at Plymouth between 1811 and 1848, at a cost of £1,446,963, and the Royal William Victualling Yard between 1825 and 1834 was a final affirmation of the value to Britain of its strategic control of the western approaches to the Channel. Its role was supplemented by the construction of a fortified harbour at Bre on Alderney to watch Cherbourg, the construction of landward defences around Portsmouth, and the development of Portland and Dover harbours. It was also supplemented by the maintenance of British naval stations on Gibraltar and Malta, and later by control of Suez, and stations at Aden, Bombay, Trincomalee, Hong Kong, Halifax and Esquimault. But in the long term the development of Japanese and American naval power put an end to the unique geographical advantage Britain enjoyed.

Close blockade was not a panacea solution to Britain's problems because it was exhausting, and because the best-conducted blockade sometimes failed. In practice, close blockade was only mounted at times when there was an immediate threat of invasion: 1759, 1800–1801 and 1803–1805. In 1800 the Spanish fleet under Admiral Gravina had joined the French in Brest, and their combined force Admiral St Vincent, First Lord, viewed safer kept in harbour. But when the enemy did escape from the blockade forces stationed offshore an opportunity was created to transform a static defence into active defeat of the enemy.

The best-known instance of this was when in 1805 Vice Admiral Villeneuve escaped Nelson's watch on Toulon, and Vice Admiral Sir Robert Calder was detached from off Brest to intercept him on his return from the West Indies. Admiral Lord Barham, the First Lord of the Admiralty, regarded this as an opportunity to defeat the Franco-Spanish allies in detail, and so make it impossible for them to plan any major naval action. Destruction of Villeneuve's squadron would also increase the effectiveness of the blockade by discouraging further attempts to break out. In a personal memorandum he wrote that it would 'damp all future expeditions, and would show to Europe that it might even be advisable to relax in the blockading system occasionally for the express purpose of putting them in our power at a convenient opportunity'.[45] Calder did indeed damage Villeneuve's squadron, and deflect him from Napoleon's plan that he should join the Brest fleet and together dominate the English Channel long enough to make invasion possible.

Less well known are the events of November 1759 when Maréchal Conflans did escape from Hawke's blockade, with a fleet worn down by the difficulty of getting stores through the blockading force, by the shortage of credit due to the losing war at sea and in the colonies, by the shortage of seamen, many of whom had been captured by British cruisers, and by the inability to provide sea training for those seamen scraped together to man the ships. Hawke was able to seize the opportunity to destroy the Brest fleet in the most dramatic sea battle in the age of sail.

Chapter Three

Admiral Sir Edward Hawke

The watch on Brest during 1759 and the battle in Quiberon Bay were to be very much the masterworks of one of Britain's greatest admirals.

According to a later account by William Locker, who was to serve under him during the 1759 campaign as a lieutenant in the *Sapphire* frigate, Admiral Hawke was 'the founder of that more gentlemanly spirit, which has since been gradually gaining ground in the Navy. At the period when he first went to sea, a man of war was characterised by all the coarseness so graphically described in the novels of Smollett ... His gentlemanly deportment and propriety of conversation effected a salutary improvement among his officers.'[1] Locker, in turn, was to be one of Horatio Nelson's patrons, and to pass on to him Hawke's ruthless determination as well as his civility.

Born in 1705, probably in London, Edward Hawke had joined the navy in 1720 with the help of his Yorkshire mother's brother, Colonel Martin Bladen, who was a Commissioner of Trade and Plantations. His father, Edward, was a barrister of Lincoln's Inn, but died in 1718. In 1725 the future admiral passed for lieutenant, and served in North American and West Indian waters. He served as first lieutenant of the *Kingston* of sixty guns, the flagship of Commodore Sir Chaloner Ogle, who promoted him master and commander of the ten-gun *Wolf* on 13 April 1733 and, on 20 March 1734, to captain of the frigate *Flamborough* of twenty-four guns, which established Hawke in post rank. Two years later he was married, to Catharine Brooke, Colonel Bladen's seventeen-year-old niece, and was on half pay when in 1739 war broke out with Spain. For the next three years he commanded an aged fifty-gun ship in the West Indies, the *Portland*, accompanied by his wife, and in August 1743 he commanded the seventy-gun *Berwick* in the Mediterranean. There, on 11 February 1744 at the Battle of Toulon, he firmly established his reputation for moral and physical courage, and for skill at arms.[2]

The Battle of Toulon was remarkable for displaying all that was wrong with the early eighteenth-century navy and with the tactical tradition that had developed from the time of the Second Dutch War, with the use of line of battle tactics to maximize the effectiveness of the broadside armament of warships. The problem with line tactics was that they were of greatest value for a fleet standing on the defensive, and posed great difficulties for a fleet seeking to attack. The ship of the line is the only weapon system ever developed that could not direct the weight of its fire along the line of advance of the weapon carrier. Any sort of engagement depended upon the admirals manoeuvring their fleets so that they crossed the danger area where they could be fired on, but could not return that fire. Once able to engage, the attacking admiral then had to deploy a crushing fire upon part of the enemy line by doubling it, or by cutting it. Doubling was the act of bringing part of the enemy fleet into action from both sides. Cutting the enemy line disorganized the enemy so that the ships astern of the cut would be forced out of formation, bunching so that firing arcs were closed, or exposing their vulnerable sterns to fire. The official fighting instructions to the British fleet mandated that admirals were to form a close-hauled line of battle to windward, and seek to overwhelm the enemy from to windward, and the consequences of ignoring that requirement could be severe.

At Toulon Admiral Thomas Mathews attempted to bring on a general action by steering directly for the Franco-Spanish fleet, under the command of Admiral Le Bruyère de Court, when it emerged from Toulon and sought to avoid action. But the movement of the two fleets, and observance of the traditional requirement that the Vice Admiral lead the fleet when on the starboard tack, forced the British fleet to redeploy when a shift of the wind brought them on to the port tack. The van commanded by Vice Admiral Richard Lestock had to pass through the Centre to take up position, and the van and centre had to pass through the rear commanded by Rear Admiral William Rowley. In the process the order of the ships within each squadron also had to be reversed. Inevitably the British line was not well formed, and Mathews confused his subordinates by leaving the signal for line of battle flying despite his approach nearly in line abreast. Lestock's insistence on working to rule was probably also motivated by his personal dislike of Admiral Mathews, which the latter had exacerbated by his rude and curt response when the night before the battle Lestock had come aboard asking if there were any orders for him. Once the ships around Mathews' flag were engaged with the Spanish flagship, Lestock obstinately maintained the fleet formation even though the Spanish line had sagged far to leeward, and despite repeated signals and orders sent by boat.

It was then that Hawke first distinguished himself. *Berwick* was stationed two astern of Rowley's flag in the rear. While admirals and captains were working to rule, or shirking their duty, Hawke bore down on his own initiative much as Nelson was later to do at the Battle of Cape St Vincent, engaged the Spanish *Poder*, and forced her to strike her colours. Article 21 of the Fighting Instructions ordered that 'none of the ships in the fleet shall pursue any small number of the enemy's ships until the main body be disabled or run'. Hawke disregarded this order. He had been obliged to fill up *Berwick*'s crew with landsmen and weaklings, but so effectively had he trained them that their gunnery dominated the engagement. Broadsides aimed at the enemy gun decks could rapidly degrade the rate of return fire. Hawke fought at 'pistol shot', about fifty yards, at which range it was possible for lower deck guns to be elevated to fire upwards through the enemy deck, dismounting guns and killing gunners. The initial broadsides could be decisive, loaded with double shot, or even triple shot. Later in an engagement it would be unwise to attempt that, as the heated guns might burst, perhaps because an excited loader might put two powder bags down the barrel. For that reason, and also to forestall any reluctance to come to close quarters, the most effective captains refused permission to open fire until the range was down to at most a few hundred yards. With *Berwick*'s gunners having aimed their opening broadsides well and then having served their guns rapidly, the Spaniards suffered 200 dead and wounded, compared to only 6 wounded on board *Berwick*. *Poder* was the only ship to surrender that day.

Mathews might have used the confused moment to come to close action, but instead ordered the fleet to tack out of battle. *Poder* was retaken by the French even before Hawke could withdraw his prize crew, some of whom succeeded in escaping in the yawls to other ships. But the following day the French were obliged to abandon her again. Hawke would have secured his prize but for Mathews' order she should be burned, which was carried out by Captain Robert Norris, who had demonstrated the most abject cowardice during the previous day's action, but now took the plunder for himself.[3]

At a subsequent court martial of one of the 'shy' captains, Robert Pett, Hawke was asked about his actions. 'How soon did the *Berwick* engage the *Poder* after the admiral bore down? And did the *Berwick* engage nearer than the *Princessa* and *Somerset* had done?' Answer: 'We engaged the *Poder* about two hours. We had her fire half an hour before we bore down close to her. We began to engage her close about 2 o'clock or a little after, and continued to engage her till about 1/4 after 4 before she struck. When she first fired at us, she was nearer than the *Princessa* and *Somerset* had done. The *Princessa* appeared to me to engage her very near, but whether as near as us, I can't say. We engaged her very close at last ...' Question: 'What ship of the enemy might be opposed to you before you engaged the *Poder*?' Answer: 'The *Neptune* as I took her to be.' Question: 'Did you never engage with her or any other ship but the *Poder*?' Answer: 'Yes, we engaged with the *Neptune* ahead of her and had part of the fire of a French ship ahead of her. When we first brought up, we had the *Neptune* abreast of us and the French ships ahead of us upon our bow, and as they shot ahead the *Poder* came up ...'[4]

Mathews was cashiered by the Court Martial and Lestock used apparently perjured evidence to obtain an acquittal. Only Hawke came out of the affair with an enhanced reputation, but all the same he was nearly passed over for promotion in 1747. It was the king, George II, who insisted on Hawke's promotion to Rear Admiral of the White Squadron. Hawke's disregard of Article 21 in the heat of action was held against him by some, and perhaps especially by those who had lacked the courage to do so themselves.

Admiral Sir John Jervis, Earl of St Vincent, victor of the Battle of Cape St Vincent in 1797, was to expostulate to a brother officer and naval historian, Captain Edward Pelham Brenton, that 'Lord Hawke when he ran out of the line [at the Battle of Toulon] and took the *Poder*, sickened me of tactics; the Admiralty wanted to disgrace him for it, but George the Second saw his merit and rewarded it.'[5] This expression of what was to become known as the 'go at 'em school' is paradoxical; battle without central planning and control could only be entertained by a fleet that was composed of ships, officers and crews that were individually significantly superior to those of the enemy. In fact, the Royal Navy was to spend much of the second half of the eighteenth century developing superior tactics that would enable it to deal with those of the French navy. Admiral Nelson's victory at Trafalgar in 1805 was viewed by some as a demonstration of the value of dispensing with tactical norms. But in fact Nelson's dispositions at Trafalgar were carefully worked out tactics that exploited surprise and the limitations of his enemy – and they also proved to be so risky that the Admiralty made certain they did not become embedded in the Fighting Instructions. What Hawke had shown at the Battle of Toulon was not so much that the science of tactics can be ignored as that tactics exist only to make it possible to bring crushing force against the enemy, with an afterthought of ensuring that the enemy cannot do so against your own fleet.

Hawke was himself to promulgate innovative tactics in August 1747 that were to become standard throughout the fleet. The concept probably originated with Vice Admiral Anson in 1746, or following his convoy battle off Finisterre in May 1747 when he met a French convoy escort under Rear Admiral de la Jonquière, Governor General of New France.[6] These were to be embodied in 'Additional Instructions', which admirals were free to add to the standing Fighting Instructions, and which might become standard if subsequent admirals retained them for their own use. Article 8 of Hawke's 1747 Additional Instructions was truly remarkable in the degree of initiative given to junior captains commanding smaller ships who were permitted, if the fleet were in action with a less-numerous enemy force, to fall out of the line without waiting for a signal from the flagship and manoeuvre to rake the enemy van or rear. Articles 11, 12 and 13 provided individual captains with a signal to other captains that they could use to help in station keeping. Articles 9 and 10 gave even more initiative to individual captains, in the particular circumstance of the pursuit of an enemy fleet that was unwilling to give battle. Anson had encountered this circumstance in his action off Finisterre. Not only could deployment from order of sailing to order of battle take so long that the enemy would have time to retreat, but the line of battle once formed could only advance at the speed of the slowest of the ships from which it was composed. The signal ordering 'general chase', which permitted ships to leave the order of battle to pursue the enemy, was on its own only suitable if the enemy force were disorganized. Anson introduced the idea of an emergency line of battle to be formed by the captains of the faster ships as they came up with the enemy, the furthest advanced taking the lead without regard to seniority. This *ad hoc* line was to engage the rearward ships of the enemy and to try to pass on to the enemy van.

Anson also introduced into British tactics the 'bow and quarter line', which was a line of bearing formation that had been introduced in the French fleet fifty years earlier as the 'First Order of Sailing' by the innovative French tactician Père Paul Hoste.[7] Again, the only surviving indication that English use of this tactic originated with Anson is that when Hawke issued it in his own Additional Instructions during the Seven Years War he attributed it to Anson.[8] This innovation was intended to enable an admiral to deploy his fleet from a patrol line into a close hauled line of battle with the minimum of delay. As with the later versions of Hoste's order, the axis of the patrol line could be any bearing ordered by the admiral, but if it were to be immediately transformed into a close hauled line of battle, the axis would have to be seven points off the wind. The course set for the fleet could be anything the wind permitted. The term 'Starboard' or 'Larboard [Port] Line of Bearing' was used to indicate lines of bearing that could be made into a close-hauled line to windward on the starboard or port tack by ordering the ships to change course. If it was wanted to change the line of bearing, as opposed to the ships' heading, it was usually necessary to deploy into line ahead, and pay off on the new bearing, before returning to the intended heading.

During his brief period in command of the Western Squadron in 1758 Anson issued an instruction that if he found his ships were unable to engage the enemy while maintaining line discipline he would haul down the signal for the line. Every ship was then to engage the ship opposite it in the enemy line. The next year Rear Admiral Hawke amplified the same instruction.[9]

Hawke was not to employ Anson's tactical concept of an emergency line forming while chasing when he brought his command into action on 14 October 1747 at the second convoy Battle of Finisterre. Perhaps it was a little too radical even for him at that stage in his career, although it is more likely that the circumstances did not suggest to him its utility. Far from dispensing with central direction of the battle, he remained in control throughout. But he had communicated his ideas effectively with his captains. This was of the utmost importance, because the system of signals used at the time only provided for an admiral ordering his captains to carry out previously promulgated tactical movements. It is evident that they understood his intention that the fleet should fight at pistol-shot range.

Finding the enemy convoy was itself a consummate tactical action. Having hoisted his flag at Plymouth on 9 August in the *Windsor* of sixty guns, Hawke's instructions were to cruise between the latitudes of Belle Île outside Quiberon Bay, on the southern coast of Brittany, and Ushant, keeping about a hundred miles west of Ushant. But despite his junior rank and subordinate command under Admiral Sir Peter Warren, he so far ignored his instructions as to cast south to appear off Cape Finisterre, and then, having given a false scent to the enemy, stood out to sea to avoid encounters with coast-wise traffic and used the variation of the winds to narrow the likely route the enemy would take. As Nelson was to do before the battles of the Nile in 1797 and of Trafalgar in 1805, he took his captains into his confidence, discussing with them the course to be steered.

The engagement began when the British fleet of two 70-gun ships of the line, one 66, two 64s, seven 60s, two 50s and a 44 sighted a large French convoy to the south-west, covered by a squadron of eight powerful ships of the line, an 80, three 74s, two

64s, one 58 and a 50, each of which was much stronger than any British ship of equal number of guns, and a 60-gun East Indiaman, commanded by Admiral des Herbieres de l'Etrenduere. The wind was about south-east with Hawke slightly to leeward. He at once signalled 'general chase' and after only about three hours, due to his ships having recently been cleaned, he was up to within four miles of the French warships. He stopped chasing and signalled for the line ahead on the port track so that his ships could proceed straight ahead on the shortest course towards the enemy. This manoeuvre, unfortunately, took nearly an hour to execute, the heavier sailers having dropped astern during the chase and at least one of the leading ships having to shorten sail and tack so as to fall into station at the rear of the line.

While this was going on, de l'Etenduere sent his convoy ahead on a course a little south of west, accompanied by his frigates and the Indiaman. Having followed them so far with his eight of the line in line abreast, he now formed his squadron in line ahead rather closer to the wind, probably with the hope of drawing Hawke away from the convoy, now crowding sail to leeward. If Hawke decided to ignore him and steer directly for the convoy the French would be to windward and capable of giving trouble. At about 11.00 am Hawke signalled 'general chase' again, in place of the line, judging that the enemy was trying to escape him. As a result his fleet came up with the French rear in a loose irregular formation, three ships managing to scrape round on to the weather side of the French and the remainder attacking from leeward. Arguably, de l'Etrenduere should have formed his fleet into line abreast, which would have forced the leading British ships to risk a cross fire if they engaged any of the retreating enemy. But this did not occur to him, and instead it was the French rear, which included three of the weaker ships, that was taken between two fires. It fought magnificently, but by 1.30 pm two of the stern-most French ships had surrendered. Two more, including the *Neptune* of fifty-eight guns and the *Monarque* of seventy-four, held out until 3.30 pm. Meanwhile the British ships, following the same procedure as in the first battle, were gradually working up the French line. A French account states that the British began the action with case shot so as to disable the French masts and rigging, and that the French ships were issued with only four charges of case shot per gun.

A pell-mell ensued. The leading French ship, the *Intrepide* of seventy-four guns, having been less heavily engaged then the rest, tacked and worked her way back to support the French admiral in the *Tonnant* of eighty guns, which, though badly damaged in masts and rigging, was holding her own. These two ships eventually withdrew to leeward and, though pursued, made good their escape to Brest; all the rest surrendered. In the closing stages of the battle several of the leading British ships had tacked or worn, like the *Intrepide*, and had thus been able to help in forcing the surrender of those French ships still holding out. Not all Hawke's captains had shown an equally aggressive spirit, however, and Hawke repeatedly signalled *Kent* to engage the enemy more closely.[10] Captain Thomas Fox repeatedly failed to do so, and was later court martialed and dismissed from active service. The capture of six French warships effectively ended the ability of France to employ naval force for the rest of the war, but the French convoy was saved by their sacrifice, since Hawke's fleet was too damaged to pursue.

It is worth printing Hawke's dispatch reporting the battle, dated 17 October from the *Devonshire*, to which he had transferred his flag before meeting the enemy. Hawke's secretary, John Hay, later claimed to have been its author.[11]

Sir,

At 7 in the morning of the 14th of October, being in the latitude of 47.49 N. longitude from Cape Finisterre 1.2 W., the *Edinburgh* made the signal for seven sail in the SE quarter. I immediately made the signal for all the fleet to chase. About 8, saw a great number of ships, but so crowded together that we could not count them. At 10, made the signal for a line of battle ahead. The *Louisa*, being the headmost and weathermost ship, made the signal for discovering eleven sail of the enemy's line of battle ships. Half an hour after, Captain Fox in the *Kent* hailed us and said they counted twelve very large ships.

Soon after, I perceived the enemy's convoy to crowd away with all the sail they could set, while their ships of war were endeavouring to form in a line astern of them, and hauled near the wind under their topsails and foresails, and some with topgallant sails set. Finding we lost time in forming our line while the enemy was standing from us, at 11 made the signal for the whole squadron to chase. Half an hour after, observing our head most ships to be within a proper distance, I made the signal to engage which was immediately obeyed. The *Lion* and *Princess Louisa* began the engagement and were followed by the rest of the squadron as they could come up, and went from rear to van.

The enemy having the weather gauge of us and a smart and constant fire being kept on both sides, the smoke prevented my seeing the number of the enemy or what happened on either side for some time. In passing on to the front ship we could get near, we received many fires – at a distance till we came close to the *Severne* of fifty guns, whom we soon silenced and left to be taken by the frigates astern. Then, perceiving the *Eagle* and *Edinburgh* (who had lost her fore topmast) engaged, we kept our wind as close as possible in order to assist them. This attempt of ours was frustrated by the *Eagle* falling twice on board us, having had her wheel shot to pieces and all the men at it killed, and all her braces and bowlines gone. This drove us to leeward and prevented our attacking the *Monarque* of seventy four and the *Tonnant* of eighty guns within any distance to do execution. However, we attempted both, especially the latter. While we engaged with her, the breechings of all our lower deck guns broke and the guns flew fore and aft, which obliged us to shoot ahead, for our upper and quarterdeck guns could not reach her. Captain Harland in the *Tilbury*, observing that she fired single guns at us in order to dismast us, stood on the other tack between her and the *Devonshire* and gave her a very smart fire.

By the time the new breechings were all seized, I was got almost alongside the *Trident* of sixty-four guns, whom I engaged as soon as possible and silenced by as brisk a fire as I could make.

Just before I attacked her, observing the *Kent*, which seemed to have little or no damage, at some distance astern of the *Tonnant*, I flung out Captain Fox's pendant to make sail ahead to engage her, as I saw it was within his power to get up close with her, she being somewhat disabled, having lost her main topmast. Seeing some of our ships at that time not so closely engaged as I could have wished and not being well able to distinguish who they were, I flung out the signal for coming to a closer engagement. Soon after I got alongside within musket shot of the *Terrible* of seventy-four guns and seven hundred men. Near 7, she called out for quarter.

Thus far, I have been particular with regard to the share the *Devonshire* bore in the action of that day. As to the other ships, as far as fell within my notice, their commanders and companies behaved with the very greatest spirit and resolution, in every respect like Englishmen. Only I am sorry to acquaint their Lordships that I must except Captain Fox whose conduct on that day I beg they would give directions for inquiring into at a court martial.[12]

Having observed that six of the enemy's ships had struck, and it being very dark and our own ships dispersed, I thought it best to bring to for that night; and, seeing a great firing a long way astern of me, I was in hopes to have seen more of the enemy's ships taken in the morning. But instead of that I received the melancholy account of Captain [Philip] Saumarez being killed, and that the *Tonnant* had escaped in the night by the assistance of the *Intrepide* [74 guns] who, by having the wind of our ships, had received no damage that I could perceive. Immediately I called a council of war, a copy of the result of which I send you enclosed.

As to the French convoy's escape, it was not possible for me to detach any ships after them at first or during the action, except the frigates; and that I thought would have been imprudent, as I observed several large ships among them; and to confirm me in this opinion, I have since learned that they had the *Content* of sixty-four guns and many frigates from thirty-six guns downwards. However, I took a step which seemed to me the most probable to intercept them, for as soon as I could man and victual the *Weasel* sloop, I detached her with an express to Commodore [the Honourable Edward] Legge [Commander in Chief Leeward Islands station].

As the enemy's ships were large, except the *Severne*, they took a great deal of drubbing and lost all their masts, excepting two who had their foremasts left. This has obliged me to lie by these two days past in order to put them in a condition to be brought into port, as well as our own, which have suffered greatly.

I have sent this express by Captain Moore of the *Devonshire* in the *Hector*, and it would be doing a great injustice to merit not to say that he signalised himself greatly in the action ...

Hawke brought his prizes under jury rig into Portsmouth on 29 October and was rewarded by being made a Knight of the

Bath and Member of Parliament for the Admiralty borough of Portsmouth. He chose 'Strike' as the motto on his coat of arms.

On 30 July 1748 Hawke, promoted to Vice Admiral of the Blue, was given command at Portsmouth in Warren's place. By then, however, the war was all but over. The Peace Treaty of Aix-la-Chapelle was concluded in October, following which the navy was drastically reduced in size. The bulk of the fleet was laid up, 'in ordinary', and some were scheduled for major repair. Economy in peacetime was essential if the government were to protect its ability to fight the next war on credit, but the small size of the fleet had implications for trade protection and preparedness. From a low point of 8,000 men in sea pay, the administration of Henry Pelham with Anson at the Admiralty increased the vote in 1752 under pressure from William Pitt, but even then only to 10,000 men. By contrast, between the Seven Years War and the end of the eighteenth century the number was never to drop below 16,000.

Although a few ships were kept in active service to maintain a presence on key stations at home and abroad, the most important work was the maintenance of guardships that could be manned and sent to sea should there be an emergency. These were cleaned annually in the spring, carried part of their stores and armament on board, and were given a complement of 150 men. The annual expense of a squadron of twenty guardships in the early 1750s was an estimated £33,814.[13] They were principally intended as a security against a sudden mobilization of the Bourbon fleets, and were theoretically moored at Plymouth, Portsmouth, Chatham and Sheerness, although they also served as a ready reserve of ships to reinforce other squadrons or to transport troops. When it was felt possible to reduce the number of guardships, several might be sent into dockyard hands for a long refit, without being replaced. By keeping on the books more guardships than the international situation required it was possible to expand the squadron quietly should a crisis occur in international affairs, or be anticipated, without endangering the peace by announcing the mobilization of ships in ordinary. Similarly it was possible to increase the number of men in the guardships, thus shortening the notice required before the squadron could go to sea. Hawke commanded those in Portsmouth from 1748 to 1752, and was to be confronted by the difficulties of maintaining the guardships and bringing them forward for sea duty on the outbreak of war in 1756 and again in 1770 at the time of the Falkland Islands crisis, when he was First Lord of the Admiralty.[14]

Chapter Four

Hawke in Command

After his term in command at Portsmouth, Hawke spent several years ashore without duties, as was common at the time. In January 1755, however, when the government ordered Boscawen to pursue the French troop convoys to New France, Hawke was asked to resume his command at Portsmouth. Hawke and Boscawen, and their wives, were close friends. War appeared to be inevitable, but the French government had not at once declared war in response to Boscawen's unprovoked attack, hoping to buy time for the French merchant marine to return home.

Hawke's most immediate task was to find the crews to man fully the guardships and other ships brought out of the ordinary reserve, to make up a fleet of seventeen ships of the line. Eleven of these were to be sent under Boscawen's command, and six under Rear Admiral Holburne, after which Hawke had to bring forward for service another seventeen ships of the line, sixteen of which he was to take into the Channel himself. That amounted to 20,000 men brought in by recruiting parties and by the press. The process had not been entirely smooth because press gangs from ships based at Plymouth met the homecoming trade, leaving nothing for the Portsmouth gangs. Men had to be transported from other bases to Portsmouth. The Admiralty order on 7 May that seamen be pressed regardless of any protections they had been granted, apart from those authorized by parliament, imparted some sense of urgency.[1]

The Admiralty set about finding in the Channel Islands pilots familiar with the French coast. But as late as 29 June, according to a memorandum by the Duke of Newcastle, a cabinet presided over by the Duke of Cumberland decided that it would be 'advisable that Sir Edward Hawke's sailing with the whole; or any part, of the Fleet, should be suspended, till such time as proper Instructions can be settled; – Especially, as Lord Anson apprehends – that, upon the Meeting of the English and French fleets, Hostilities might probably happen.' On 1 July the framing of instructions were again deferred.[2]

The Duke of Cumberland was in favour of ordering Hawke to anticipate the war and cripple the French Marine by capturing French shipping, but Newcastle hesitated. Anson then suggested a compromise, and on 22 July Hawke was instructed 'to take under your command Rear-Admiral West and sixteen of His Majesty's ships of the line, with such frigates as shall be directed by the Lords Commissioners of the Admiralty, and proceed immediately to sea, and cruise between Ushant and Cape Finisterre.' He was to provide protection for British trade, and 'in case you should meet with the French squadron, or French men of war of the line of battle, you are to intercept them, making use of the means in your power for that purpose, and to send them under a proper convoy directly to Plymouth or Portsmouth.' The intent was clearly provocative, but until the French government and armed forces had shown their hand by acts of force, Hawke was to be careful 'that every person belonging to all ships so intercepted be well treated, and that no plunder or embezzlement be made of any effects on board'. The French sailors were to be held, and should this action lead to war, they would be confined as prisoners of war. Hawke was to establish a rendezvous for the fleet, and send a dispatch to London every ten days.[3]

In a separate letter, Anson personally warned that there was no doubt the French were determined on war, and he provided Hawke with somewhat Delphic advice: 'you will hear of their having taken our ships, and that our Channel will be full of their privateers; but you will be very well satisfied that they have seized some of our ships before you fall upon their trade.' Anson apparently hoped that evidence would be speedily forthcoming, and although the French were careful to avoid provocation, eight days after Hawke sailed he was sent orders to capture privateers and merchant ships. He received his orders on 23 August, and they were extended to the rest of the British fleet on 27 August.[4] Possibly as many as 300 French merchant ships were seized without declaration of war, and 7,500 seamen and apprentices were brought to Britain in 1755.[5] This aggressive policy was to have important consequences for the manning of the French navy, and in particular was to be of very great importance in Hawke's victory at Quiberon Bay over four years later. But the unprovoked belligerent acts, the war that followed and the victorious battle were also to set in train a disastrous sequence of events that kept Britain at war with France for more than half of the next sixty years.

This was the beginning of the long watch on Brest that was in 1759 to become a model for later British practice, but the full development of the victualling system that permitted the fleet to remain on station without returning to Plymouth or Portsmouth for supplies was not yet in place. Hawke was sensitive about the criticism he received for his decision to lift the blockade in September 1755 so that he could resupply in harbour, and wrote to John Clevland, the Admiralty Secretary, that he was

> extremely sorry to find that their Lordships think any of the ships of my squadron could have stayed out longer. I hope they will be of another opinion when they reflect that most of the men had been pressed after long voyages, cooped up in tenders and ships at Spithead for many months, and the water in general long kept in new casks, which occasioned great sickness, beside the number of French prisoners and the men spared to navigate them into port. For my part, I should not have come in had it been possible for me to have continued longer out.

So many of the crews were sick that delay in coming into port could have left too few to handle the ships: 'I am morally certain that, had I stayed out longer, the ship's companies had been totally ruined.'[6]

In 1756 Brest was watched in succession by Admirals Henry Osborn, Hawke, Boscawen, Francis Holburne and Charles Knowles. In February 1756 Hawke sailed again in command of the Western Squadron, and after an uneventful cruise passed command to Boscawen and returned to Spithead on 8 May. His

71

instructions were detailed as to which ships should be handed over to Boscawen, to join the nine he brought with him, and which should be sent in as 'it is necessary for the health and refreshment of the officers and seamen that the ships cruising to the westward should be relieved as frequently as may be.'

It was problematic to extend this degree of control over fleet commanders, but it was to be important in enabling dockyards to plan the rapid cleaning and repair of ships and to enable the victualling authorities to know what ships were where and which needed resupply. The full development of fleet management was to be established by Earl Spencer at the time of the blockade of Brest at the end of the century. Important as it was to have a system of central control, with a capacity at Portsmouth and Plymouth to act without further authorization from London, it was also recognized that circumstances could require fleet commanders to deviate from orders framed days or weeks before far away from the scene of action. Hawke might need to remain off Brest with the entire force, and he was left 'at liberty to continue out therewith'.[7] In the event, he did not need to exercise that latitude.

Hawke was scarcely back in Portsmouth when he was called on to attempt to restore Britain's position in the Mediterranean. Following the news of Boscawen's action and the withdrawal of the French ambassador, London had become aware of a possible French plan to commence military action against Britain by operations to capture Port Mahon on Minorca. But the success of the French bluff had delayed any response until it was clear there was no real danger of an invasion of England being attempted. In January 1755 the Duke of Cumberland had called for naval reinforcements for the Mediterranean, but Anson had resisted, believing that it was the threat to Minorca that was the French feint. 'I think it would be a dangerous measure to part with your naval strength from this country which cannot be recalled if wanted, when I am strongly of opinion that whenever the French intend anything in earnest their attack will be against this country.'[8] Finally on 9 March the cabinet agreed to send a squadron of ten ships of the line to provide a seaward defence of Minorca, under the command of Vice Admiral John Byng. But its sailing was delayed because of the difficulty of raising men.

A total of 95 ships had been manned with 29,278 seamen by November 1755, but many of those were to be stricken with typhus. In the course of the season 1,227 men were discharged as unfit and 2,162 were 'discharged dead'. At the beginning of 1756 there were 168 ships ready for service, but apart from those on distant service, and cruising in defence of trade, the remaining 71 ships were little more than half manned. Byng was kept cooling his heels for twenty-nine days, because priority was given to manning the Channel Fleet, and when he sailed on 6 April many in his ships' complements were Irish landsmen or men discharged from hospital, and his marines had been replaced by soldiers.[9] He passed through Hawke's fleet en route to Port Mahon, with orders to touch at Gibraltar to ensure the Toulon fleet had not sailed into the Atlantic to support the invasion of England.[10]

The French army had already landed on Minorca and were besieging Fort St Philip by the time Byng arrived on 20 May. He immediately engaged the French fleet commanded by Vice Admiral Roland-Michel Barrin, Marquis de La Galissonière, off Minorca, but the British fleet suffered heavy damage and Byng returned to Gibraltar. In his absence, the British garrison was forced to capitulate.

At the Battle of Minorca a lucky shift of wind had given Byng the windward position, passing the French on opposite courses. A crossing action, however, could never achieve decisive results, as only protracted concentration of fire could destroy ships. Byng had to devise a means of bringing his fleet to close action on the same heading as the French. But he was very limited in his means of doing so, because of the limitations of British signals, and because this was the situation governed by a virtually mandatory Article 17 of the official Sailing and Fighting Instructions that required him to tack the fleet, beginning with the rearmost ship. This he did, although his timing would have been better had not La Galissonière ordered the French fleet to back their sails. Once tacked, the two fleets were on slightly converging courses that would have permitted the British to ease down on the French line without exposing themselves to unacceptable damage. This was a long-established tactical idea, recommended in 1688 by Lord Dartmouth. Unfortunately, Article 19 of the Fighting Instructions required the leading ship, the *Defence*, to seek to engage the leading ship of the enemy. Her captain, Thomas Andrews, judged that he could not get up with the French leading ship if he continued on his course, so he bore up, setting a course parallel to the French line of advance. This could not have helped much given the relatively clean hulls of the French ships, but repeated signals to bear down a point did not serve to correct the situation. Byng was too far back in the line to be able to see exactly what was required, Andrews was too unimaginative to understand the intent behind Byng's approach, and there was no way of communicating them to him because of the inadequacy of British signals. In desperation, Byng hoisted the signal to engage, and the entire fleet bore down on the French in a loose line of bearing. In doing so they were exposed to heavy fire without being able to reply, and suffered so much damage that they were unable to press home their attack. As Audibert Ramatuelle observed in *Cours Elémentaire de Tactique Navale*, published in 1802, Byng's attack became a down-wind run on which point of sailing it was impossible to ensure good station-keeping by backing the topsails of the faster ships.[11]

But it was the French who broke off the action, and Byng's abandonment of the Minorca garrison to its fate was a serious strategic mistake. Given the preponderance of the Royal Navy, Byng should have risked the loss of the most damaged ships rather than risking the loss of the fleet base.

Anson warned Newcastle on 31 May about having received a letter from Byng, 'who arrived at Gibraltar the 2nd Instant and left it the 8th in the morning with a fresh and fair Gale. He had with him 13 sail of the Line and 3 Frigates. I think', he continued, 'you won't be much pleased with his letter, and less with the Governor of Gibraltar who has sent no troops for the relief of Port Mahon, and for a very extraordinary reason *Viz* because he would then have had fewer at Gibraltar.' The cabinet based its decision to relieve Byng of his command at least in part on intelligence sent to Newcastle from Versailles on 1 June reporting that 'there was an action the 20th past between the two fleets near Minorca'. The correspondent had not 'heard any reason why Admiral Byng should choose to retire; for he had the wind of us, and his fleet suffered less than ours'.[12] For this failure, Byng was condemned 'for not having done his utmost' against the enemy, and shot. The

French hoped that the capture of Minorca would lead Britain to seek a negotiated peace, but the bellicose British public blamed Newcastle for the loss, and he sacrificed Byng to save himself.

How much Hawke was to be influenced by Byng's failure, and his fate, when he encountered the French Brest fleet in Quiberon Bay over three years later is not known, and the tactical circumstances of the two battles were very different. The immediate effect on his life was to put a sudden stop to his leave. On 18 May Britain had declared war on France, and on 8 June Hawke was given instructions 'to repair without loss of time to the Mediterranean to supercede Admiral Byng in the command of His Majesty's ships there'. These included an additional five ships of the line that, too late to save Minorca, had been hurried to Gibraltar on 6 May.

He was directed to take passage in a frigate, *Antelope*, with Saunders, who had been one of Hawke's more aggressive captains in the Finisterre battle and was now promoted to rear admiral, apparently on the recommendation of the king.[13] They were directed 'not to lose a moment's time in proceeding to Gibraltar'.[14] Having superseded Byng and arranged for him to be returned under arrest to England, Hawke hoisted his flag on *Ramillies* of ninety guns that was to serve as his flagship later before Brest and made his way to Minorca, where he arrived too late to prevent the fall of the fortress. He established a blockade of Port Mahon, but the French had left only a small garrison there that could survive on the stores available. He hoped to tempt the French to sortie from Toulon, but they refused to do so, and eventually Hawke was obliged to return to Gibraltar.

It was during this frustrating cruise that Captain the Honourable Augustus Hervey first served under Hawke. First impressions seem not to have been good ones, as he noted in his 'journal', which was not written up from rough notes until over ten years later. He was right about Hawke's unfortunate choice of a secretary: 'we all knew Sir Edward Hawke was totally governed by a damned interested Scotch secretary, a fellow without a grain of understanding who had been bred up to business in a shop and had the impudence to show his ascendancy over the Admiral to the whole Fleet.' John Hay was a trouble maker. But Hervey's other criticism of Hawke was misplaced, and may only have reflected his loyalty to Byng, on whose behalf he was to go to great lengths by publishing pamphlets critical of the government. Hawke's practice was to bring his subordinates together, just as Nelson was to do half a century later, and to ensure that they understood his aggressive intentions. This practice Hervey mocked:

> The 3rd at daylight there was a signal for Flag Officers, and soon after for all Captains, when the Admiral told us that he had intelligence by a Dane that the French fleet lay with their topsail sheets hauled home at Toulon and were determined to come out and fight us. Then he made us a fine speech that he was determined to run close up to them, and that the honour of our country required we should do our very utmost to destroy these ships and he did not doubt that we should, with a great deal of all this sort of stuff.[15]

In fact the French did not put to sea, but that was because la Galissonière fell seriously ill. Hervey's bitchiness was set aside when he was ordered home to appear at Byng's trial, and Hawke, Hervey noted, entrusted him with his dispatches.

Hawke was exasperated, not only by the inability to fight the French, but with the government's failure to support him properly, as his dispatch of 12 September did not hide:

> My orders of the 8th of June say I am 'to clean them [i.e the ships under his command] as often as necessary either in some port of the King of Sardinia's dominions or at Gibraltar, as I shall find to be most convenient.' What port in Sardinia can be convenient? What port there can furnish us with a sufficient quantity of provisions, or what certainty have I of even being received there at all? At the time I received these orders, I foresaw all these difficulties, but on account of the exigency of the times made no objection, flattering myself that their Lordships would soon send me more explicit orders on these heads. I have now been near ten weeks out and own I am sensibly mortified at not having heard from England.
>
> Tis true I can go to Gibraltar, and must. But I cannot clean or repair any above a fifty or sixty gun ship there; neither should above a sixty be left in a bay so open and exposed to wind and weather during the winter ...[16]

The Admiralty agreed to Hawke bringing the larger ships home with him, leaving a small squadron in Gibraltar for the winter under Saunders's command. When Hawke arrived with the rest to Spithead on 14 January 1757 he found that his much-loved wife, Catherine, had died in his absence.

The French navy had lost three ships during the year, but captured one, and launched five others. French naval finances were in such poor shape, however, that most of the Toulon and Brest fleets were laid up during the winter of 1756–1757 so that sailors could be released from service. Only two more ships of the line were ordered from the French dockyards, and there was a great shortage of naval stores and guns. Contracts were agreed with Swedish gun founders for the manufacture of 400 guns, but these did not start being delivered via the Netherlands until 1759. In June 1756 the supply of masts and timbers to Rochefort dockyard dried up, and in July a fire destroyed 1.2 million livres worth of stores.[17]

* * *

Following William Pitt's formation of an administration in November 1756, Hawke found that his services were again needed, this time for the amphibious attack on Rochefort intended to divert French attentions from the German theatre. His instructions came directly from King George II, although they were drafted by Pitt. His opponents, who included the Duke of Newcastle, characterized his strategy as 'breaking windows with guineas'. For diversionary attacks on the French coast to be effective, they would need to be on a large enough scale that they could not be contained by the garrisons maintained along the French coast, and they would need to threaten a target the French valued. The naval dockyard at Rochefort was indeed such a target, and the means for its reduction was adequate. Lieutenant Robert Clerk, of the Royal Engineers, had visited Rochefort before the war and was able to report on its weakness. He was promoted Lieutenant Colonel and appointed Chief Engineer of the expedition. But it was not only the French who found the technical requirements of amphibious operations challenging.

Hawke's instructions included a formula that became standard during Pitt's administration. Aware of how many combined operations had been frustrated by disagreements between the army and navy commanders, a paragraph was inserted emphasizing that

> whereas the success of this expedition will very much depend upon an entire good understanding between our sea and land officers, we do hereby strictly enjoin and require you, on your part, to maintain and cultivate such a good understanding and agreement, and to order the sailors and marines, and also the soldiers serving as part of the complements of our ships, to assist our land forces, if judged expedient, by taking post on shore, manning batteries, covering the boats, securing the safe re-embarkation of the troops, and such other services at [sic] land as may be considered consistent with the safety of our fleet ...

Hawke was ordered 'immediately upon the receipt of these our instructions' to 'repair to Spithead where we have ordered a squadron consisting of at least sixteen ships of the line and a proportionate number of frigates to rendezvous, together with transport vessels for our troops (who are to embark from the Isle of Wight) and also the vessels with the artillery and stores, which squadron and transports you are to take under your command; and so soon as the troops shall be embarked, you are to proceed without loss of time to the coasts of France.'[18]

Hawke persuaded the Admiralty to increase the tonnage of transport intended to carry the soldiers, and he communicated with Lieutenant General Sir John Mordaunt, commanding the expeditionary force, and Major General Henry Seymour Conway to ensure their needs were met.[19] The Portsmouth Office for Sick and Wounded, with Admiralty approval, provided a supply of dried apples and dehydrated soup as an experimental dietary supplement for the sick. Hawke recognized that successful opposed landings needed to be carried out with dispatch, before the enemy could bring its defences into action. In a memorandum for the fleet he noted that he intended to 'consider with the flag and general officers which will be the properest place to attempt; to settle this in going along; and to fix upon the ships and troops that are to make the attack, which, if done at all, must absolutely be done upon the first going in, or otherwise they will be prepared to make head against you; no time must be lost upon these occasions.'[20] He planned to cover the landing with gunfire from several small frigates, firing grape and partridge shot. In another memorandum written as the fleet approach the entrance to Basque Roads outside the shoal entrance to the Charente River, on 20 September, he wrote that 'As it is more than probable that the disembarkation will only be opposed by militia which may be easily dispersed, it is earnestly recommended to all the marines and soldiers, when directed to attack, to march up vigorously, preserving their fire till they come very near, so as to do certain execution and, whenever their General orders, that they run in with their bayonets.' The men were to be quickly followed by guns, ammunition, provisions, supplies, scaling ladders, and all the other requirements to ensure military success.[21]

But intelligence was inadequate. The Admiralty did not have any good charts of the Charente River where the landing would have to be made, and was wrongly advised by a Huguenot pilot, Joseph Thierry, that there was adequate depth of water for the transports and covering ships. In fact, these could not approach the coast nearer than a mile and half, with the result that it would only be possible to row the soldiers ashore if the wind were calm, or blowing onshore. But if the latter, a heavy surf could be expected, which would have made heavy losses probable, and would have made withdrawal of the soldiers impossible should their attack miscarry. For this reason the Rochefort expedition proved a fiasco; it sailed too late in the year, and the soldiers lost heart.

In a private letter to Pitt, Hawke later described the frustrating proceedings:

> I sailed with the squadron entrusted to my command, with the transports, from off St. Helens on the 8th September, resolutely determined to execute my part in the destined enterprise. Being by His Majesty's instructions of 5th August ordered to return at or about the last of September and contrary winds having detained us so long in England, and even a little while upon our passage, the Generals Mordaunt and Conway before we reached the place of our destination began to think it too late to undertake anything. The consideration of our detention in England, the warning the enemy had to prepare for our reception, and our almost total ignorance of the coast we were to attack, confirmed them in their

opinion that it was most advisable to return to Britain without risking any attempt and in consequence they urged me to assemble a council of war for that purpose.[22]

That first council eventually decided to continue, but on arriving at Basque Roads the generals became increasingly discouraged about their prospects, about landing safely, and about being able to get off again should they meet strong opposition and the weather turn bad.

About the only concrete result of this operation was a spirited attack Captain Howe made when Hawke ordered Vice Admiral the Honourable Charles Knowles to silence the fort on the Île d'Aix so that its guns could not interfere with the landing. Howe brought his ship, *Magnanime*, on which was Thierry who had at least some knowledge of the area, to within sixty yards of the fort, holding his fire until anchored – and reduced the fort in a thirty-five-minute bombardment. Although considered an act of reckless courage, Clerk later noted in a pamphlet he wrote on 'The Secret Expedition' that

it is clear that if the Governor of the fort had done his duty he could have destroyed not only Lord Howe's ship, but the other four ships of the line, if they had bore down and come to an anchor in as proper a manner as Lord Howe; and that might have been done without the least danger to anybody in the fort ... [However, he added] five Governors out of six in such places, and with the same circumstances, will surrender in the same manner. Distant places and places upon the coast have not commonly the best Governors or the best artillery officers and engineers.[23]

During the night of 23–24 September a landing beach was surveyed from the boats of the fleet, and according to Clerk Captain Matthew Buckle found two suitable bays where the transports could be beached at low tide. But General Mordaunt refused to order the landing to go forward without first convening a council of war, as he was entitled to do. That imposed another day's delay. 'Early in the morning of the 25th', Hawke reported, 'we were doubting but the council of war would come to a resolution to land. I ordered the transports inshore that no time might be lost. Instead of landing, it took a very different and to me unexpected turn. As to the first precarious reason of winds and weather, I could not, as a seaman, when the question was urged, say I could bring them off in a storm and a great surf.' Clerk wrote that 'there is seldom finer or more moderate weather in the Bay at any time of the year than [during] the ten days we were upon the French coast'. At the Council he urged an immediate landing, but he was easily outranked by the generals who were discouraged, and even went to so far as to consult Hawke about the practicability of taking the French fortress by escalade, a matter hardly in an admiral's purview.

Yet another council of war was assembled on 28 September, before which Hawke again ordered the transports moved into position, and at one o'clock on the morning of 29 September the landing operation was begun, only to be aborted when the generals found that it could not be accomplished in a single tide. This final exasperation led Hawke to demand formally of the military whether they had any 'further military operations to propose, considerable enough to authorise my detaining the squadron under my command longer here'. If not, he continued, 'I beg leave to acquaint you that I intend to proceed with it for England without loss of time.'[24] The fears prevailed, and the expedition returned home with nothing accomplished.

Hawke dryly added that 'a proposal having been made on the evening of the 26th or 27th to land on the island of Oléron, I frankly own I opposed it with all my might. For I could perceive that nothing could derive from landing against defenceless peasants and their salt pits, while the enemy must be on the continent.' In this judgement, however, Hawke may have been at fault. He certainly was at odds with Pitt. A lodgement on Île d'Oléron poised to make a landing anywhere in the Bay of Biscay could have tied up a considerable French army.

Perhaps the frustration of this failed operation was important in Hawke's steely resolve when later he was to sweep into Quiberon Bay before a gale, to seek action amongst the rocks. 'In my opinion,' he wrote, 'a council of war can neither excuse nor exculpate a commanding officer in breaking his master's orders.' For his part, Anson expressed to his father-in-law, the Earl of Hardwicke, his dismay that Hawke had not found a way to overcome the general's reluctance.[25] Rochefort had in fact been almost defenceless, its garrison numbering only 3,000, of which only 200 were regular soldiers, while Sir John Mordaunt's army numbered 8,500. Clerk was to visit Rochefort in 1766 and wrote to Pitt: without doubt 'we might have been masters of this place, if we had landed even seven or eight days after we were in Basque Roads, and destroyed the great naval magazines there with a great part of the French navy, without perhaps the loss of a single man.'[26]

* * *

Hawke spent the last part of the year in command of a squadron ordered to attempt to intercept a French effort to reprovision the garrison at Fortress Louisbourg. For this cruise he issued his squadron on 21 October with copies of the printed fighting instructions that included an amendment to clarify his intentions in situations such as he had dealt with on a personal level in the Battle of Toulon. Article 13 requiring captains to maintain the order of battle prescribed by the admiral had those words crossed out, and not only crossed out, but done so in such a way, as Hawke's biographer Ruddock Mackay has pointed out, that captains could clearly read the words that he wanted eliminated. In a hand-written addition to Article 13 he also dealt with the prohibition in article 21 to captains pursuing 'any small number of the enemy's ships'. The wording now ran: 'As soon as the Admiral shall hoist a Red Flag on the Flag Staff at the Fore Topmasthead, and fire a gun, every ship in the fleet is to use their utmost endeavour to engage the enemy as close as possible, and therefore on no account to fire until they shall be within pistol shot.'[27]

Hawke's tactical initiative was innovative, because admirals of the calibre of Mathews had been content simply to use the printed Fighting Instructions, but it was not out of line with the under-stood duties of commanders. Anson himself was to issue additional instructions in August 1758 clarifying Article 13 when command-ing in the Channel. Boscawen was to make a similar change to Article 13 when he was commanding in the Mediterranean in 1759.

On 14 December Hawke was back at Spithead having achieved nothing but the exhaustion of his ships and men, but three months later he was again ordered to sea with 'the utmost dispatch'

in order to intercept French convoys believed to be preparing
to sail from ports in the Bay of Biscay to India and New France.
His instructions indicated that he had been given command in
'the Channel, Soundings or wherever the services shall require'.
In effect, he was to be Commander in Chief of the Channel
Fleet. Perhaps because he lacked powerful political connections,
however, Hawke was not sent a formal commission, which would
have entitled him to a Commander in Chief's share of prize
money. He was to have the responsibility, but not the honour or
the emolument. There had not been a Channel Fleet commander
since the end of the previous war. The overall direction of
operations had been retained by the Admiralty, and it continued
to exercise detailed control of operations in home waters until the
end of the war.[28]

Clearing from Plymouth on 13 March, he split his force to pass
both sides of Belle Île so that any convoy inside Quiberon Bay
could be sighted, and on the 3 April passed the Île de Ré making
for Basque Roads. There he encountered a convoy escorted by
three frigates, but it was to windward of him, and successfully got
into the protection of St Martin-du-Ré. Bearing away again for
Basque Roads Hawke surprised a convoy at anchor preparing to
sail with 3,000 soldiers and supplies to the relief of Louisbourg.
It, and its escorting squadron made up of a 74, three 64s, a 60 and
six or seven frigates, cut their cables and fled for shelter in the
Charante. Hawke's account is more than a little confusing, but the
outcome was that the French ran in among the shoals and many
grounded on the mud, leaving the British squadron anchored
offshore close to the Île d'Aix.

> At 5 next morning, saw them all aground, almost dry, about five
> or six miles distant from us. They had a whole tide of flood which
> would have carried them up under shelter of the guns of Fouras, if it
> had been possible for any ships of burthen either to get up or down
> from thence, except when they are light and on top of a spring tide.
> Many of the merchant and several of the ships of war were on their
> broadsides, and then I could not help regretting the want of
> fireships and bomb vessels.
>
> As soon as the flood made, I put the best pilots on board the
> *Intrepid* and *Medway* and made the signal for weighing. They got

about a gun shot farther in, come to an anchor and, sounding a little ahead of them at high water found but five fathom, of which the tide rises eighteen foot.

By this time all the boats from Rochefort and the adjacent places were employed in carrying out warps to drag them through the soft mud, as soon as they should be waterborn. In the meantime they threw overboard their guns, stores, ballast, and were even heaving water out of their ports, all of which we could plainly discern. By that means some of them got that day as far up as the mouth of the Charente; but the *Florissante* was not got above Fouras [to the north of the river] on the Thursday afternoon [6 April], and the greatest part of their merchant ships left aground in towards the Isle Madame [south of the river] when we fell down to Basque Road. The frigates' boats cut away about eighty buoys laid on their anchors and what they had thrown overboard.[29]

Having sent an officer ashore on the Île d'Aix to see what progress the French had made in restoring the fortifications Howe had defeated the previous year, Hawke landed a party of marines to destroy the new work. Learning from a neutral trader that the convoy sheltering in St Martin was loaded with provisions and stores for the French posts in North America and the Caribbean, with another convoy expected out of Bordeaux similarly laided, all of which were to have been escorted by the squadron now without their guns and in the mud of the Charante, Hawke left six ships to cruise for them should they sail, and himself returned to the Channel. Although frustrated by the lack of fireships and bombs to destroy the beached ships, Hawke had prevented supplies reaching Louisbourg.

*   *   *

There then occurred one of those emotional scenes that sometimes characterize very senior officers at the end of their patience. The government had decided to follow the aborted Rochefort expedition with another diversionary raid on the French coast. In a misguided effort at preserving secrecy, and possibly also because Pitt continued to attach some blame to Hawke for the failure at Rochefort, Hawke was not informed of the plan. He was simply ordered to have all the ships effectively under his command back at Portsmouth by 15 May, and he was denied leave.[30] At

Portsmouth he was waited on by Captain Howe, who showed him orders from the Admiralty Board. Unfortunately, Hawke hastily concluded that Howe had been sent to take over responsibility for the convoys in Basque Roads, and he was infuriated that he appeared to be directed to provide Howe with the resources he himself had lacked. 'I have been kept here, and even now have their Lordships' directions, at least in terms, to obey him. He is to judge of what he wants for his expedition. He is to make his demands and I am to comply with them!' The prominent part Howe had taken in the reduction of the fort on Île d'Aix the previous year, and the subsequent publicity, lent some basis for the misunderstanding, but in fact Hawke was mistaken. In June Howe, commanding a four-ship escort of an amphibious assault force, was to lead the first British squadron ever to sail through the tidal race between the French coast and Alderney, in order to attack shipping at St Malo and Granville. By then, however, Hawke had already taken the drastic step of striking his flag in protest. The incident may in part have been precipitated by Hawke's secretary, John Hay. Hawke's exasperation may also have been stoked by the appearance in 1758 of an anonymous satire, *The state farce: or, they are all come home.* In it a thinly disguised Hawke was made to share the blame for the failure of the Rochefort expedition, and the only credit was given to Howe.[31]

Without even a fleet 'in being' that summer rigged and ready for sea inside Brest Road, the French Marine was not able to pose any threat to these operations. Nevertheless, the St Malo raid, and two subsequent raids, again demonstrated the limitations of British amphibious abilities. It had been intended that St Malo would be occupied, but the army commanders, the Duke of Marlborough and Lord George Sackville, were not an effective team, and the fortifications proved too strong. A second raid was made a month later with a new army commander, Lieutenant General Thomas Bligh, Cherbourg successfully seized, and its harbour razed. At the end of August Bligh and Howe, who had succeeded to the viscountcy when his elder brother, George Augustus Howe, was killed at the Battle of Ticonderoga, made another attempt on St Malo, but were beaten off by the French Commandant of Brittany, Emmanuel-Armand de Bignerod du

Plessis de Richelieu, Duc d'Aiguillon. As a direct consequence of his stellar performance, d'Aiguillon was subsequently put in command of the ground forces to be used in the Scottish invasion. He tried to persuade Versailles to alter the muster for the invasion army to Brest, but the impossibility of supplying them there prevented any change of the plan. Thirty years younger than Maréchal Conflans, the two were not on good terms.[32]

Howe took personal command of the boats in the last stages of the evacuation, during which the brigade of guards suffered heavily. Hawke bore Howe no personal ill-will, and was to find him a very valuable officer in the action before Brest and in Quiberon Bay. Howe's second in the June St Malo raid, Captain Robert Duff, was also to play a notable part in the blockade and Battle of Quiberon Bay.

Hawke had been called up on the carpet at the Admiralty, although the whole affair was kept very quiet. He explained that he thought Howe's orders constituted 'a slur upon his reputation and that he thought he might have been represented to the king as an unfit person for such a command, which affecting his credit he hastily determined to strike his flag'. He said he later realized his mistake. The conclusion of the Board was 'that Sir Edward Hawke's striking of his flag without order is a high breach of discipline. Therefore notwithstanding the acknowledgment contained in the said minute, the Lords do not think proper to restore him to the command of the ships in the Channel, although in consideration of that acknowledgment and of his past services they have not proceeded to any further censure.' Anson, who must bear some responsibility for his failure to keep Hawke informed of actions planned for the forces under his command, was ordered to fill the vacancy, for the moment, with Hawke serving under him.[33] Anson undertook this task rather grumpily and took charge of the covering operations during the raids. Hawke soon fell ill and was given leave for the winter. But he was to be put to good use the following summer, when the French made the attempt to solve their strategic difficulties in central Europe, India and North America by invasions of England and Scotland.

Chapter Five

The Watch on Brest

The pace of operations was to mount in 1759 as it became apparent that France was planning an invasion. King George informed both houses of parliament of the danger on 30 May. In the Commons Journal it was recorded that: 'Mr. Secretary Pitt acquainted the House, that he had a message from his Majesty to this House, signed by his Majesty: and he presented the same to the House; and it was read by Mr Speaker; all the Members of the House being uncovered ... his Majesty acquaints this House with his having received repeated Intelligence of the actual Preparations making in the French Ports to invade this Kingdom, and of the imminent Danger of such Invasion being attempted.' The Members prepared an address thanking him, and assuring

> his Majesty, that this House will, with their lives and fortunes, support and stand by his Majesty against all attempts whatever; and that his faithful Commons, with Hearts warm with Affection and Zeal for his Majesty's sacred Person and Government, and animated by Indignation at the daring Designs of an Enemy, whose Fleet has hitherto shunned in port the Terror of his Majesty's Navy, will cheerfully exert the utmost Efforts to repel all Insults, and effectually enable his Majesty, not only to disappoint the Attempts of France, but, by the Blessing of God, turn them to their own Confusion.[1]

The commentary of the editor of the *Annual Register* was that 'the threats of invasion increased our internal strength, without raising any apprehensions'.[2] With the advantage of hindsight, it was eloquent about the resolution with which the threat was met:

> Among the great men there was no difference that could in the least affect the conduct of the war. The dispute concerning the preference of the continental and the marine system, was entirely silenced ... Never did England keep a greater number of land forces of foot ... Never did she cover the seas with such formidable fleets, when her navy alone engaged her attention. Such is the effect when power and patriotism unite; when *liberty and order kiss*; and when a nation sits with a happy security under the shade of abilities which she has tried, and virtues in which she dares to confide.

But at the time there was great uneasiness, and some dispute about how the threat should be met. Newcastle was worried enough that he wished to recall Saunders's fleet from its assault on Quebec so that it could reinforce Hawke in the Channel. Had this been done, Choiseul's strategy would have proved highly successful even if the invasion force never left France, but Pitt successfully resisted.[3] In July Charles Wesley published a collection of *Hymns on the Expected Invasion*, pleading for God's mercy: 'Is this the guilty nation, Lord ... Now to be visited by sword, And purified by fire?'[4] Later in the year, when the weather turned decidedly bad, there were additional fears that the Channel Fleet would be destroyed by the elements, leaving the way open for a French invasion. Newcastle was to be one fearful of this possibility, but there were others. Not a few questioned the competence of the fleet, and were alarmed whenever it left its station off Brest.

The landward defence of England was the responsibility of John Legonier, who had succeeded the Duke of Cumberland. During the invasion scare of 1756 the Newcastle administration had brought 8,600 Hanoverian and 6,500 Hessian soldiers to bolster the defences of England, but three years later the use of German soldiers was not an option.[5] The *Annual Register* reported that in June 1759 there were in England 'two troops of horse Grenadier Guards; seven regiments of dragoons; three regiments of foot guards; thirty-four regiments of foot; and thirty-two independent companies. In Ireland, four regiments of horse; six of dragoons; and twelve of foot.' There were also the county militias. Newcastle had successfully opposed their creation by Pitt in 1756, but had relented in 1757 during the Pitt–Devonshire coalition, and did not resist their embodiment to meet the threatened invasion, despite his continuing concern that popular militias endangered the aristocratic leadership of England.[6] With Newcastle's support, parliament agreed that the militias might be called out for active service so that the regulars would be released from garrison duties.[7] Pitt had set the pace by demanding on 17 April that shipping be contracted for the transport of 5,000 men. He had not thought it necessary to indicate even to the king that they were intended as a feint to confuse the French. Newcastle complained about this 'abominable act & most unheard of measure, to send to the Admiralty for such an expence, without condescending to tell either King or Ministry, what that service should be'.[8] It was decided by the cabinet on 9 May that the regulars should be concentrated on the Isle of Wight, which was an attractive beachhead for an invasion force but valued by Pitt mostly as a *place des armées* for possible offensive operations. It was also decided that a fleet of transports should be stationed at the Nore buoy in the Thames estuary so the soldiers could be moved to any point in the British Isles.[9]

But the main reliance was naturally upon the Channel Fleet, and the smaller squadrons blockading Ostend and Nieuport where the invasion army was concentrated, the privateer port of Dunkirk, and Le Havre-de-Grâce at the mouth of the Seine where the landing barges were being built. Commodore Sir Peircy Brett, who had sailed to the Pacific with Anson and returned in command of Anson's ship, *Centurion*, was stationed in the Downs in *Norfolk*, a new third rate of seventy-four guns. He was employed on a commission for examining the defences of the Essex, Kent and Sussex coasts, completing his report on 15 June. Commodore William Boys, flying his broad pendant in *Preston* of fifty guns, commanded a squadron stationed watching Dunkirk.[10] One of the provisions of the Peace of Aix-la-Chapelle had been that Dunkirk should be dismantled, because it was a notorious base for privateers. But work had commenced on restoring the harbour as soon as war with Britain had become probable, Wolters's intelligence indicated that a squadron was fitting out there.

A larger effort was made against Le Havre where the invasion barges and escort praams were being built. In the *London Magazine*, it was noted that 'the harbour of Le Havre is within the walls of the town, and can contain more than 300 vessels at once'. Because of the pressure into the harbour from the Seine flowing past the stone fortified jetties, the ebb was delayed for up to three hours, with the result that 'fleets of 120 sail have often been observed to get out of it on one tide, even with the wind against them'.[11] The ability to surge an invasion fleet out to sea on one tide was really important, even if the boats would then have to make a long passage to the Flanders ports to collect the army. Rear Admiral George Bridges Rodney, who had served as a captain under Hawke in the second Battle of Finisterre and under Boscawen in the 1758 Louisbourg campaign, was ordered to hoist his flag on *Achilles* of sixty guns on 19 May, and take command of a squadron of five ships of the line escorting a flotilla of bomb ketches. A deception plan was employed indicating that his squadron was under orders for Gibraltar, but instead it bombarded Le Havre on 4 and 5 July.

Closely following Rodney's official dispatch, Tobias Smollett, the Irish physician and author, wrote in his contemporary *History of England* that

> the bomb vessels, being placed in the narrow channel of the river leading to Honfleur, began to throw their shells, and continued the bombardment for two and fifty hours, without intermission, during which a numerous body of French troops were employed in throwing up entrenchments, erecting new batteries, and firing both with shot and shells upon the assailants. The town was set on fire in several places, and burned with great fury: some of the boats were overturned, and a few of them reduced to ashes, while the inhabitants forsook the place in the greatest consternation.

Smollett's conclusion, however, was much less enthusiastic than was Rodney's:

> The damage done to the enemy was too inconsiderable to make amends for the expense of the armament, and the loss of nineteen hundred shells and eleven hundred carcasses, which were expended in this expedition ... Bombardments of this kind are at best

but expensive and unproductive operations, and may be deemed a barbarous method of prosecuting war, inasmuch as the damage falls upon the wretched inhabitants, who have given no cause of offence.

Clevland thought that in the circumstances 'more could not be expected, and that we have been in good luck not to receive any damage in our shipping'.[12] Corbett's later judgement differed from Smollett's only to the extent that the bombardment 'had demonstrated to the most nervous and sceptical' that the light forces were more than capable of dealing with the Le Havre invasion flotilla should it attempt to put to sea without the support of the Brest fleet.[13] Wolters's agent at Le Havre simply wrote of '*les Horreurs de la Guerre ... il est impossible de vous depeindre la Consternation: on a fait sortir les Femmes, les Enfants et les Vieillards; les Chemins sont remplis de gens qui fugent avec leurs Effets.*'[14]

The Admiralty was not deterred from making preparations for a second bombardment, but the French so strengthened their defences that it proved impossible to bring bomb vessels within range, and when a second raid was attempted two months later Rodney only just managed to avoid disaster:

> the squadron under my command, was in imminent danger of being drove on the enemy's coast, in a hard gale of wind at W.N.W., the ebb tyde coming on with the gale was the preservation of the fleet. Had it blown hard with the tyde on flood, the bombs, their tenders, and the small craft, could not possibly have rode it out, this has obliged me to get under sail, and keep an offing, with the three large ships, and the small craft, leaving the *Brilliant*, *Unicorn*, *Eolus*, *Boreas* and the two sloops in shore, to watch the motions of the enemy, as those frigates, can much easier claw off a lee shore than the three fifty-gun ships who are very foul, and go very ill.[15]

No further attempt to destroy the invasion flotilla was made before Hawke's victory in Quiberon Bay caused the French to strike their camp and move the completed barges to safety up the River Seine. Rodney was able to report, however, that the French flat boats appeared to be 'very unwieldy vessels, and calculated only for smooth water and a fair wind'.

It was agreed at the meeting on 9 May that the number of seamen available in home waters should be increased from 18,000 to 25,000 men, and on the same day Hawke was ordered to take command of fourteen ships and frigates at Portsmouth, and another eleven at Plymouth; he was to proceed with the former to Torbay where Rear Admiral Sir Charles Hardy, his second in command, would meet him with the ships from Plymouth. Hardy had been made Governor of New York in 1755 when that city was being developed as the main base for military operations, and had served as second in command during the 1757 and 1758 Louisbourg campaigns. Apparently no rear admiral was appointed because there had been some thought that Anson would resume his place in command over Hawke.[16] A few days later orders were given to the Victualling Board to supply the fleet at Torbay, for which purpose 300 tons of shipping should be made ready, and specifying that a portion of the usual beer allowance should be replaced with wine to be sent from Guernsey.[17] Hawke found Hardy already in Torbay when he arrived there on 13 May with the ships from Spithead, and there he received his secret instructions on 18 May:

> Whereas we have received undoubted intelligence that the French are pressing their armament at Brest, L'Orient, Rochefort, and the other ports on the coast of France; that on the 7th instant there were nine sail of ship of war in the inner road of Brest, five of them of the line; that others were ready to proceed out of the harbour and that four of the line were expected there from L'Orient; that provisions and stores are collecting to Brest from several parts of the Bay; and it's given out that the enemy propose to attempt an invasion either upon Great Britain or Ireland; and whereas it is of the greatest consequence to prevent any such design of the enemy taking effect, you are hereby required and directed, so soon as you shall be joined by Sir Charles Hardy with the ships from Plymouth, to proceed with the squadron under your command off Ushant and cause as accurate an observation as possible to be immediately made of the enemy's force in Brest Road and forthwith send us an account thereof ...[18]

A 'List of the French Navy at Brest, Rochefort, and Port Louis to rendezvous at Brest' among the Hawke papers in the National

Maritime Museum at Greenwich showed twenty-six ships, with notes about their readiness for sea. The largest was the *Royal Louis*, but she was still under construction, being only completed to the middle deck. Two 64s were shown as repairing at Rochefort, and an 84 and a 70 were shown as needing repair. That left four 80-gun ships, of which the *Soleil Royal* was the flagship of Maréchal Conflans, seven 74s, two 70s, and ten 64s.

In 1756 Conflans had been designated Vice Admiral of the Ponant, the Atlantic fleet, and on 18 March 1758 Louis XV made him Marshal of France in reward for his service. He had refused the post of Naval Minister during the crisis of 1758 as beneath his dignity. As with many French admirals, his career had included periods serving ashore, and he had been captured in 1747 en route to Saint-Domingue, where he was to have been Governor General. He had been responsible for preparing a fleet at Brest for service at sea in 1756 and in 1757, but had not been able to take it to sea either year. In 1758 the Brest fleet had not been brought forward for service. In 1759 he succeeded in preparing for service a total of twenty-one ships of the line, the first of which began to move out of Brest dockyard and into the Roads on 30 May. His personal incentive to carry out his orders at all hazzard was very great, and he believed the honour of France was at stake.[19] Wolters's correspondent in Brest reported on 6 July that '*tout se dispose de plus en plus pour le prochain Départ de la Flotte*'.[20]

Hawke's orders stressed the importance of interdicting the flow of naval stores and provisions to the French dockyards at Brest and Rochefort. The French navy had come to depend nearly as heavily on timber, masts, tar and hemp from the Baltic countries as had the British navy, although masts were available from the Pyrenees, and because of their weight and bulk these materials could only be moved a few miles by land. Rochefort was near productive agricultural areas, and could be supplied with fresh provisions by river, but Brest had an unproductive hinterland, and was dependent on sea communications for almost all requirements. Interdiction of coastal supply convoys could destroy fleets in harbour, and certainly prevent them escaping to sea. The possibility that what appeared to be a coastal supply convoy might actually be intended to supply French posts overseas, or to transport an

View of Brest, Admiralty Hydrographic Department, 1798 (National Archives, United Kingdom, ADM 344/505)

invasion force to Ireland, added to the importance of the their interception.

To deal with these issues, Hawke was given detailed instructions:

> you are to appoint such of the smaller ships of the line and frigates as you shall think sufficient to cruise on the most likely stations for intercepting the said convoys, ordering their commanders, in case they shall observe any number of ships of war and transports of sail from the French ports and they shall be too weak to attack them, to send one of the frigates immediately to give notice of it, either off Ushant or in Torbay, and another frigate to follow and observe their course till her commander shall be able to form a judgement whether they shall be bound to Ireland or not, and then to return and acquaint you therewith that you may detach such force after them as you shall judge necessary ...

Hawke was optimistic as he set out, noting that when his ships were all assembled he would command 'a very strong squadron, not ill manned as times are, and full sufficient, I hope to frustrate any designs the enemy may have on this country'. He commanded a force of twenty-five ships of the line, including the 100-gun *Royal George*, which was a private ship, and two 90-gun ships which flew the flags of Admiral Hawke and Rear Admiral Hardy, the *Ramillies* and the *Union*. He divided his force into three divisions, 'for the better carrying on the King's service', and put the rear division under the command of Francis Geary. The three-division organization had become standard, but in any case it ensured better control over a fleet of that size, and also increased tactical flexibility.[21] Geary was still only a captain, but he flew a commodore's broad pendant, and in June he was to be promoted to rear admiral.[22]

When drafting Hawke's Secret Instructions the Admiralty were apparently not thinking of an extended blockade of Brest. Hawke was 'to continue cruising with the squadron near Ushant and Brest (taking all possible care not to be drove to the westward) and to defeat any designs the enemy may have conceived of invading these kingdoms, and to protect the trade of His Majesty's subjects, and also to annoy and distress the enemy by every means in your power; and you are to return with the squadron to Torbay, so as to be there by the expiration of fourteen days from the time of your sailing from thence.' But he was again given latitude to extend the patrol if 'the attempts or operations of the enemy against this kingdom should make it necessary for the defence and security thereof'. When he reached his station off Brest, and sized up the situation, including the advanced state of four ships building at Port Louis near L'Orient, he came to the decision that was to establish the close blockade. 'Upon the whole I do not think it prudent, as they may soon be joined by more from Brest Harbour, to leave them at liberty to come out by returning to Torbay till I shall receive farther instructions from their Lordships or the wind shall appear to be set in strong westerly.'[23] An open blockade based on Torbay would have been preferable were the objective only to guard against the invasion of England, but Hawke also needed to prevent the French sailing to the westward, to invade Ireland, or to take the offensive in Canadian or West Indian waters.

Hawke had sent *Minerva* under the command of Captain Alexander Hood, supported by the *Nottingham* under Captain Marshall, to look into Brest. They reported that they had seen 'very distinctly eleven sail in the Road, all of which they judged to be large ships of war, with their colours hoisted, yards and top-masts up, and topgallant yards across. One of them carried a flag on her mizen topmast head and another a broad pendant on her main topmast head. They all seemed ready for sailing. There were only two or three small vessels within the great ships in the Road.' The fact that yards and topmasts were in place indicated the ships were able to sail, as they would probably have been struck down to reduce wear and tear until the ships were stored and manned for sea; it could be concluded they were ready in all respects. However, Hawke did not think the appearances were consistent with plans to invade England. 'Having maturely considered the

95

View of Camaret Bay, Admiralty Hydrographic Department, 1798 (National Archive, United Kingdom, ADM 344/505)

intelligence, I will venture to give my opinion that the enemy's intentions are not against Great Britain or Ireland but aimed at the relief of their islands. If their carpenters are sent to the eastward [to Rochefort?], I apprehend it is to repair the great loss of frigates they have lately sustained, as they have been for the most part built in these ports, where they have the timber and other materials for that purpose more at hand.'

When his dispatch was received in London, their Lordships approved of Hawke's decision to remain off Brest and L'Orient 'with a sufficient force ... to prevent the French putting to sea, taking care to send from time to time such of your squadron as you shall find necessary to Plymouth or Torbay to recruit their provisions and water, and to refresh their companies.' He was also to send cruisers south to Cape Ortegal at the north-western corner of Spain, and thence into the Bay of Biscay to encounter any ships that might have eluded the blockade force.[24] Before Hawke received the dispatch, his decision to remain before Brest had been confirmed by further intelligence: 'On the 29th of May', he reported, 'the *Rochester* and *Melampe* looked into Brest Road. Captain Duff acquainted me next day by letter that he saw there seventeen ships, sixteen of which were rigged and had their sails bent. Only one of them had topgallant yards aloft ... Thirteen of the number appeared to be large, the other four frigates.' No ships were seen in Bertheaume or Camaret Roads.

The *Venus* and *Chatham* had looked into Port Louis at the mouth of Port de L'Orient on 11 and 12 May, and reported there were four ships of the line fitting out, possibly to join the fleet at Brest. This intelligence had been passed to Hawke, who thought they were more likely intended to sail for America, but on 25 May he sent a detachment into Audierne Bay south of the Bec du Raz, to watch Point Penmarch, around which they would have to pass. Command of this squadron was given to Augustus Keppel, captain of *Torbay* of seventy-four guns. Keppel had been one of Anson's

midshipmen during his circumnavigation, being promoted during the extended mission first to master's mate, and later to master after the capture of the Manila galleon in 1743. Another ship in the group was *Monmouth* of seventy-four guns, commanded by Augustus Hervey. During the patrol Hervey discovered that *Monmouth* was the fastest ship of the squadron, and rejoiced that 'if we met the enemy I should at least have had the satisfaction of leading these noble companions into action'.[25]

Following a shift in the wind on 2 May that reduced the chance of any ship sailing from Port Louis, Keppel's detachment had been recalled and added to the battle force outside Brest. The frigate *Southampton* commanded by Captain Fraine was sent on her own to look into Port Louis, and on 27 May she was able to close the harbour within two cannon shot, when she discovered that the only ship there appeared to be a frigate. The ships of the line might have gone into L'Orient, but Hawke thought that unlikely: 'By the best information I have ever received, their ships of war are generally fitted up at L'Orient and seldom drop down to Port Louis till they are on the point of sailing.' It was probable that the four ships had sailed before Hawke arrived on station 'and may be numbered with those in Brest Road'. Hawke left *Colchester* and two frigates off Port Louis, and two frigates, the *Melampe* and the *Minerva*, to watch the Passage du Raz.

On 31 May Captain Duff was able to bring *Rochester* where he could look into Brest Road and this time the count was twenty French ships; fifteen were ships of the line of which all now had their topgallant yards aloft, although only ten of them had their sails bent on to their yards. There were also three frigates and a snow in the anchorage. Five days later Hawke included these reports in his dispatch to the Admiralty, but had to add that thick weather prevented any further observation. He also had to add that a Danish provision ship that had been stopped, but had been allowed to proceed when its papers appeared to be in order for a

Appearance of Brest, Admiratly Hydrographic Department, 1798 (National Archives, United Kingdom, ADM 344/505)

voyage to the island of St Thomas, had run into Brest as soon as it was able.[26]

The weather continued to worsen, and, despite his intentions, Hawke's next letter to the Admiralty was written from Torbay on 6 June:

> For several days preceding my last, by express of the 4th instant, we had had very fresh gales with a great sea. Yesterday it increased so much at south-west, with a thick fog, as to make several of the ships complain, more particularly the new ships. As in this weather it was impossible for the enemy to stir and our own ships stood in need of a day or two to get themselves to rights, in the evening I bore away for this place. I shall use the utmost dispatch in getting them ready for sea, which I hope will be by the time, or before, I can receive an answer to this. In that case, I shall sail again with any moderate wind, as, from the last accounts of the enemy, it appears to me to be of the greatest consequence that we should be on our station again before they can get a fair wind to bring them out.[27]

It was then that he ordered for immediate delivery 46,926 pounds of fresh beef from the Exeter contractor, who defaulted. He also wrote to the dockyard Commissioner at Plymouth, Rogers, and asked him to dispatch 'all the vessels you can procure' loaded with beer – 'no time must be lost in this, as I purpose going to sea on Saturday', only three days away. Five victualling sloops arrived on the Friday with 260 tons of beer, and once they had been unloaded Hawke ordered them back to Plymouth to be loaded again 'in case their Lordships shall think proper to send them under convoy to my rendezvous. At present we have as much as will enable me to keep the squadron out a month or five weeks, if the wine should not come through from Guernsey.' If the wine were to arrive in time to be taken on board, so that the fleet could

Cornevail

stay longer on station, Hawke wrote that it would need more water.[28] The measure of the success of the navy's provision of supplies, and Hawke's sensitivity to the need to rotate exhausted crews into port, was that James Lind, who had been made Chief Physician at Haslar Naval Hospital in 1758, was to report that Hawke's command enjoyed 'a most perfect and unparalleled state of health'.[29] When finally Hawke was able to bring the French to battle his crews were strong.

The fleet was scarcely back at sea, and making its way to Ushant, when it was struck by a 'violent storm' eight leagues south-east by east of the Lizard in southern Cornwall, and suffered storm damage to spars, sails and *Bienfaisant*'s rudder. *Hero* lost all her masts and was taken in tow by *Nottingham*, but the hawsers broke, and she was finally towed into Torbay by *Montagu*. *Hero*'s carpenter was killed while trying to clear away the wreckage. Fortunately a sloop, *Albany*, loaded with spare top-masts had stood up to the storm under the command of Andrew Snape Hamond, who only held a rank of acting lieutenant. For his exemplary service, Hamond was appointed Fifth Lieutenant of *Magnanime*, Captain Howe's command, and a very successful career was launched. On 15 June Hawke wrote to the Admiralty from Torbay that he had never seen such bad weather in the summer. 'We got in here very luckily, for it now blows extremely hard without and, had we laid to some hours longer, we should have drove past this bay.'[30]

Hervey breakfasted with Hawke on 16 June, and was informed that he was to take responsibility for the inshore squadron off Brest as soon as the fleet could get to sea. Hawke's judgement in this is interesting, as Hervey's observations in his journal had continued to be contemptuous, although it must be remembered that he did not write it until many years later. Hervey would recall that in February Hawke had expressed his dismay at Byng's condemnation, saying that 'he would go live in a cottage rather than serve to meet such treatment ... Sir Edward was as double in all his boastings.' Hervey entered into that same journal that Hawke, in Torbay, 'expressed great concern at being drove in, and told me that he had destined me for a very honourable employment, for I should command his vangard [sic] in at Brest water to watch the fleet's motions, and that on my diligence and skill much must depend, but he was pleased to say he did not doubt of success in my hands.'[31] Was Hawke blind to Hervey's duplicity, or dismiss it as unimportant, or were Hervey's fulminations only a result of his later political and social associations?

While dealing with the problems of repairing the fleet, including questions asked about the work done at Plymouth yard, Hawke also had to deal with the realities of eighteenth-century society. Prince Edward, younger brother of the future George III and later styled the Duke of York and Albany, had joined the navy as a volunteer on 24 July 1758, and had taken part in the raid on Cherbourg and the unsuccessful attack on St Malo. Hawke had to find the time to thank Admiral Anson for sending the Prince some comfort foods:

> Lord Anson is extremely kind in thinking of the situation I am in with regard to my providing for Prince Edward, for I came away in so great a hurry that I had scarce time to get even common necessaries on board therefore only gave directions for sending me the plainest things I had, with the utmost dispatch. Though this is the case, I am in hopes I shall do pretty well with Lord Anson's assistance, as I shall take particular care that his Highness wants for nothing that lies in my power to provide for him. To be sure, he will not be so happy with me as if he was with his Lordship, but I shall do my best to make everything as agreeable as possible to him, from a just sense of the duty and gratitude I owe to the King.'

Edward was thus able to support the exigencies of the service until October, and established a glamorous and valiant public image, but he was to miss the action at Quiberon Bay in November.

Hawke also looked after the interest of the Admiralty Secretary, John Clevland, by ensuring that his son Archibald, who was a post captain and commanded the frigate *Pallas*, returned to Portsmouth for the ship to be cleaned. His father preferred him to be employed out of Portsmouth, apparently so he could get home more often. It was *Pallas* under a new captain, Michael Clements, that a few days later brought to Hawke the formal order 'for receiving and entering His Royal Highness Prince Edward and retinue', and a letter 'relating to the furniture and necessaries lodged with the storekeeper at Plymouth for His Royal Highness'. Archibald Clevland was transferred into the *Windsor* of sixty guns. The King, the First Lord and the Admiralty Secretary – their family and political interests could not be forgotten in the midst of fighting a war.[32]

Finally, on 17 June, the weather turned moderate, the gale being followed by a flat calm. On the morning of 19 June the fleet boats towed the ships to seaward, and all sail was set. The victuallers from Plymouth were met at sea before the fleet was clear of the coast, and Hawke ordered them to accompany him to the rendezvous off Ushant. He arrived there early on 20 June, but the victuallers escaped from their escort and fled west, away from danger. Hawke had to send the *Swallow* to look for them in Falmouth, Plymouth and Torbay, with orders that 'if their masters should refuse to accompany him, to put careful persons from the sloop on board them and bring them to my rendezvous'.

On 27 June the *Annual Register* reported, wildly, that 'the lieutenant of a cutter from Admiral Hawke, arrived at the Admiralty, with advice that when the cutter left the squadron, the men of war in Brest water were under weight, and that a great number of troops were embarking all that day onboard the French fleet.'[33] The diarist Thomas Turner heard by post on 7 July the news 'of the French being landed in Dover'.[34] In fact, Conflans had not stirred.

Duff had been left on station outside Brest, to watch the French and find what shelter he could. He reported to Hawke that the French had not sailed. However, they appeared to be ready for sea, and this assessment was confirmed when two French fishing boats were detained off the Passage du Raz. 'The prisoners were all kept separate and, on examination, agreed to the ships named in the accompanying list being ready in all respects, excepting a few men, and victualled for five months. They added that there were no troops more than usual at Brest.' That was brought into question, however, when a Spanish ship was detained on its departure from Brest, its captain 'affirming' that troops were collecting. Captain Duff also reported that he was able to count seventeen French ships still in Brest Roads, and was 'of opinion' all the twenty ships previously counted might be there, but most of the ships had struck their yards and topmasts, presumably to reduce windage during the storm. 'I am very happy,' Hawke concluded, 'after all the bad weather, in having got safe on my station again before they stirred.' He had to be ready for anything, and advised on 3 July that 'the operations of the enemy indicate a long cruise for the squadron. In order to preserve it in a condition to keep the sea, I purpose to send in two ships of the line to clean at Plymouth every spring' tide.[35]

On 4 July Hervey, accompanied by *Pallas*, had a good look into Brest Roads, and decided that the French were not really ready for sea: 'I think the ships in Brest in general seem but light and are certainly not yet ready for the sea; and though I could discern men in boats alongside of them, I could not see any number about the ships sufficient to think them anything like manned, as they would have appeared on the decks on our standing in, as they did everywhere on shore.' For a moment there was thought of cutting out some Dutch doggers Hervey had sighted sheltering under a French battery, but it was decided the guns were too well sited for the attempt. Instead, Hervey was able to take advantage of a fresh east-north-east wind to come within three or four miles of the citadel at Brest, when he found that the anchorage was empty of anything but the Danish ship. The French did not attempt to fire. Hervey ordered that nobody was to write letters home so that Hawke would be certain the intelligence he received was not shared with the enemy.[36]

Not wanting any repetition of the experience with the Danish blockade runner, Hawke ordered that all neutral ships should be denied entrance to Brest. To do so, legally, he had to establish what is known as a 'close blockade' that made it possible to ensure no ship entered undetected, and without it being possible to intercept it. 'As I have cruisers off Brest Road [and] the Passages du Raz and du Four', he wrote to the Admiralty on 16 July, 'I considered Brest as blocked up in the strictest sense.' In consequence, Captain

Hervey seized an opportunity to cut out from under the guns of the Conquet forts four Swedish ships laided with 'cargoes, according to their own account, which appear to be but too necessary to the enemy in their present equipment'. It was one of those daring exploits that punctuate the naval history of the time. 'Yesterday, seeing four sail coming through the Passage du Fore,' Hervey advised Hawke,

> to which the castle of Conquet hoisted a red flag – and they immediately hauled in for that road and anchored, the tide not letting them go into the harbour – I consulted the pilot and, finding that the wind, tide and weather assured the safety of the ship and that he could place me, without anchoring, to cover the boats, I went immediately within the rocks up abreast of Conquet forts with the *Pallas* and all the boats, leaving the *Montagu* [Captain Lendrick], off St. Matthew, convent to observe the motions of the French fleet, and in about two hours and a half the boats (being covered by the fire of our two ships) brought those four vessels out (who hoisted Sweden's colours) from the fire of four forts and a battery and other detached pieces of cannon on points of rocks. I cannot help, Sir, commending to you the bravery of the officers and seamen on this occasion.

In describing the action in a letter published in the *London Evening Post*, one of the fleet officers reported that the hills behind the fort were covered with spectators.[37]

Hervey then stood into Brest Road and found the French battle fleet lying as it had previously been, and 'exercising their people at loosing and working their sail – which they do surprisingly bad indeed, and convinces me of the truth of that part of the intelligence in which we have agreed with regard to their want of men.' The following morning he sent the masters and mates of the three ships under his command to sound in Fontenoy passage and around the tide race. Apart from the naval stores listed in the Swedish cargo manifests, Hawke advised the Admiralty that 'from their manner of stowage and some other circumstances, there is ground to suspect they have guns and other contraband goods underneath all.' He sent them into Plymouth, where the Admiralty ordered they should be 'thoroughly rummaged in the presence of the Customs House officers and some person on behalf of the

A sandy Bay with an Intrenchment

View of Conquet Creek, Admiralty Hydrographic Department, 1798 (National Archives, United Kingdom, ADM 344/505)

captors'. Hawke's dispatch was minuted: 'Let Sir Edward Hawke know the Lords extremely approve of what he has done.'[38]

The plan to maintain the blockade without any breaks except for those imposed by really dangerous weather conditions was innovative, and very demanding. The Admiralty paper published following Byng's condemnation, probably written by Anson, remarked that the benefits of a strong Western Squadron 'are not cheaply gained. A fleet superior to what the enemy can send out must be always employed, otherwise the moment of weakness or absence may be seized; our ships must always be clean, otherwise the enemy coming fresh out of port may outsail us. Cruising in all weathers and often with tempestuous and contrary winds wears out the ships, the masts and the rigging, and ruins the health and cost the lives of the seamen; it often disables a ship in a week which has been three months in preparing, and it demands a great part of our naval force. Less than thirty ships of the line completed [and] manned will not keep twenty constantly at sea, even in the summer.'[39] But the navy was sufficiently experienced that it knew how to make it work, and had the resources for it. On 19 June the Admiralty instructed the Victualling Board to station two vessels at Plymouth, so that one could make the passage each week to Hawke's rendezvous with a cargo of live oxen and sheep. The Admiralty order to impress seamen on 21 June provided against the all-too-possible outbreak of disease among Hawke's crews, but also risked introducing into the fleet men infected with disease-carrying lice. Fortunately, the efforts to provide a nutritious diet proved effective.

Hervey took advantage of an intelligence-gathering raid on the island of Benequet to obtain twenty head of cattle. An inhabitant of Conquet was brought on board, and confirmed Hervey's opinion that the French were short of men, and very short of skilled ones.

104

A rumour that the Brest fleet would sail on 25 August was dismissed as unlikely.[40]

On 21 July Hervey was again engaged against the guns of Conquet, intending to capture or destroy a convoy that had arrived from Biscay and passed through the Passage du Four between Ushant and the Breton coast. This time conditions were less favourable, however, as the French had anchored at the top of the tide and the wind was light. It would have been foolhardy to have attempted to approach them among the rocks on a falling tide.

> About 11, tide of flood beginning to slacken and the wind rather freshening, I persuaded the pilot to take charge of us to run up and let us at least see if it were possible to cut those ships away or destroy them. The *Montagu* I ordered to follow as close as possible. About noon we got abreast of the ships which were warping in the little harbour of Conquet. Finding there was no possibility of cutting them out where they lay, and the forts firing constantly at us, we began to fire at the frigate and two ships, as well as the forts, which we continued about half an hour, throwing several shot into them and the forts, when the wind dying away and veering to the southward of east obliged us to get out as fast as we could, this place being very narrow, tides very rapid, surrounded with rocks and shoals, and not above one mile and a half to work in.

The next day Hervey sighted four ships coming from Brest Road with the evident intent of escorting in the convoy sheltering at Conquet. After hastily sending the cutter to Hawke with a report, he stood his ground, with *Colchester* (50 guns) and a frigate in sight to support him: 'we will not', he wrote, 'be drove off easily.' The French ships soon withdrew, and the convoy put back into harbour. 'I never imagined', Hervey added, that 'they would make more than a show of coming out with the whole, as I am certain it took most of their people to man these. They worked very badly, and had we had but three leagues further, we should have worked alongside of the one we fired at ... I was in great hopes I had drawn their fleet out – at best, some of their ships into your hands; but their situation is every way too favourable in this dangerous part of their coast.'[41] When this action became known to the public, Hervey's mother was deluged by compliments: it was, she wrote, 'indeed nobly done and must gain you immortal honour'.[42]

Hawke reported that

> the whole squadron of the enemy had loosed their topsails at daybreak. About 11 a.m. they made a show of coming out. I had, full in their view and close to the entrance of the road, the squadron formed and lying to for their reception. On the enemy's furling their topsails, I came to an anchor a few miles without, where I purpose staying while the winds and weather will permit ... Your Lordships will perceive how difficult it is to guard the Passage du Four without cutters, of which I have only one. Though I have hitherto, to my utmost, prevented vessels getting into Brest, yet what get through du Four are sure of a sanctuary in Conquet harbour, which is daily more strongly fortified.

When Brest was again being blockaded in 1800 the then First Lord was a civilian, Lord Spencer, and he arranged for a marine artist, John Thomas Serres, to prepare a series of pictures of the coast to help the Admiralty. But in 1759 Hawke could count on Admiral Anson knowing the Brittany Coast as well as he did, and to understand the problems. Hawke was quick to congratulate Hervey for his 'conduct and bravery' and to ask him to 'thank your officers and company for their gallantly seconding your endeavour to destroy the enemy'. But he also warned that the stakes were very high, and ships should not be risked without effect. 'I have too just an opinion of your discretion, conduct and resolution to doubt the utmost's being performed in every service on which you shall be employed. But I cannot think of running the risk of disabling three ships of the line for an object so inconsiderable as a privateer and four or five empty transports –

for such they are.' He ordered that three of the five ships of the line close into Brest should rejoin the fleet, leaving only *Achilles* and *Colchester*.[43]

The need to ensure that his battle fleet was kept up to strength also necessitated taking action about deficiencies in dockyard and victualling arrangements. Hawke decided to suspend sending ships in to clean, having been disappointed when the first two he sent failed to catch the spring tide. It was unfortunate, but, 'if the enemy should slip out and run, we must follow as fast as we can'. Should the enemy sortie, every ship would be needed. 'I never desired or intended to keep more line of battle ships than equalled the number of the enemy, which is now augmented to twenty-two. I have at present twenty-three and seldom have had more than twenty-four, and that only during a day. If ships take up a month by cleaning from the time they leave me to their return, it will be impossible for me to keep up the squadron.'

He was concerned not only about the number of ships available for action. No fleet can be better than its crews. He suggested that if the spring tide needed to take ships into dock were missed, they should be heeled only enough to clean the boot topping. Later he explained that 'the relief of the squadron depends more on the refreshment of the ships' companies than in cleaning the ships. By the hurry the latter must be performed in (unless the ship continues a month or five weeks in port, which the present exigency will by no means admit of) the men would be so harassed and fatigued that they would return to me in a worse condition than they left me. This made me prefer ordering some of them to heel and boot-hosetop only, remaining at rest for ten days in port.'

Even the refreshment of the men, however, had to be undertaken quickly. Hawke ordered the senior captain at Plymouth, Captain James Young, to ensure that the captains of ships sent there expedited any refitting, hurried ships and cutters back out to the rendezvous, and ensured that the supply convoys were made up without loss of time.[44] Young had fought under Byng in the Battle of Minorca in 1756, and had taken part in Hawke's Rochefort expedition. He was to command the rear squadron on 20 November in Quiberon Bay.

Victualling was Hawke's biggest concern, and not only Hawke's. In July an officer of the *Bellerophon* had written the editor of the

London Evening Post complaining that the Victualling Board did not send the fleet 'fresh provisions nor Greens for our People. If the French don't chuse to come out,' he continued, 'we shall have a Four-month Cruize, and consequently the Scurvy will prevail amongst the Seamen, whom I look upon as the strength of the Nation. I wonder how a Parcel of Land-drones', he added, referring to the Members of Parliament, 'can see poor Jacks suffer so.'[45]

Another to voice the perennial seaman's complaint about his rations was Lieutenant Edward Thompson of the *Dorsetshire*, which had been one of the ships Hawke ordered to support Hervey when it appeared the French might sortie. After the skirmish he had written gloatingly to a friend: 'We are now anchored in the Road of Brest, with all the ease and composure you can conceive men to have, whose most ardent wishes are to try their strength with their foe: – we ride in sight of four French flags, and 13 sail of line of battle ships, – and offer such daily insults on their own dunghil [*sic*], that, were they men of courage, – they would fight though sure of losing the victory.' But he felt the British public did not truly appreciate their navy.

> Every news-paper which is brought out here, – is filled with sarcasms and abuse of us – for bad conduct &ca., ... Every time you hear that we are to northward of *Ushant*, – the cry goes out, 'What can they be doing, to give the French such an opportunity to come out?' – not considering or knowing at this time it blew a storm from the west. These gentlemen should be a little more acquainted with geography and navigation, before they commit their opinions to the press: they should consider with a westerly wind, it is necessary to keep the English Channel open, for fear of wrecking this fleet on the coast of France; – and likewise, that that very wind, prevents the stirring of any ship in Brest water.

And taking the bit between his teeth, he continued:

> Tho' you truly think upon this fleet your lives and fortunes depend, yet to support the people in it, you have at last considered fresh provisions are necessary: – it is a pity this charitable thought did not occur sooner, – for alas! we are very sickly; besides, there is such an abuse of the provisions sent out, – that immediately on their arrival, a third part have been condemned not fit to eat. This

arises from venal contracts and bribery, which make it absolutely necessary for the government to appoint men of sworn integrity, to inspect into everything, before shipped by agents and contractors.[46]

Thompson was a minor poet, amongst other attainments. Following the war he was to write, we are told by Thomas Campbell, 'some light pieces for the stage, and some licentious poems; the titles of which need not be revived'. In his introduction in a book of *Specimens of the British Poets*, Campbell noted that Thompson edited the works, among others, of Andrew Marvell, for which work 'he was grossly unqualified'. Nevertheless, 'though a dissolute man, he had the character of an able and humane commander'.

To John Ommanney, the victualling agent at Plymouth, Hawke complained that there had been reports of 'great delays and neglect from the office under your direction, which have greatly obstructed the service and, if continued, will oblige me to break up the squadron watching the motions of the enemy'. He urged Ommanney to 'use your best endeavours immediately on any ship's arrival in the Sound to get her empty casks on shore, and her water and provisions shipped,' and complained that the bills of lading for the overdue victualling convoy showed that the cheese being sent the fleet was nearly past its warranty date, by which the ships' companies 'must suffer greatly, as they do already by the beer brewed at your port, which is daily condemning'. The next day, when the convoy arrived, he wrote again to Ommanney.

The beer brewed at your port is so excessively bad that it employs the whole time of the squadron surveying it and throwing it overboard, so it is my direction that no more of it be sent, as I have dispatched an express to the Lords of Admiralty to supply the squadron from the eastward. I likewise desire that the utmost dispatch may be used in sending out all the live bullocks and sheep ordered by the Board. A quantity of bread from the *Ramillies* will be returned you by the *Elizabeth*. Though not altogether unfit for use, yet so full of weavils and maggots, it would have infected all the bread come on board this day. We had not time to pick it. It is my direction that you receive it into store for port expense.

109

Ommanney, of course, saw the other side of the story. 'Sir, if you knew the duty that have been done here, loading out twenty-two sail of victuallers, unlading them of their empty casks, staves, hoops, etc., and the unlading a number of victuallers here with stores and provisions for the Office, and victualling the sundry men of war that have been lately here, and with the interruption of winds and weather sometimes, you would think the complaint groundless.' For their part, the Lords of Admiralty were 'concerned' at the quantity of beer 'brewed in the King's own brew-houses' that had been condemned, and wanted a flag officer to look into the situation. Nonetheless, they did order that beer should be sent directly to the fleet from the eastward', and that wine should similarly be sent directly from Guernsey. On the back of Hawke's dispatch of 12 August, which was read at the Admiralty on 22 August, it was minuted that the problem with the beer was occasioned by the summer heat. The wine from Guernsey, it was noted, was 'extremely good', but their Lordships acknowledged the truth of Hawke's observation that 'as stinking water must be drunk with it, it will not support a squadron for continuance'. Clevland was instructed to write to enquire 'if the water in the ships under his command is worse than the water generally is'.

The Admiralty suggested to the Victualling Board that a quantity of beer should be racked from the casks into clean ones before it was moved, so as to avoid stirring up the lees. By then, the Victualling Board had already reacted to the crisis, first dispatching from the Thames, Dover and Portsmouth twelve to thirteen hundred tons of beer to meet Hawke at his rendezvous, and then sending Captain Robert Pett to take charge in Plymouth. Pett was a member of the Victualling Board, but he was also the man against whom Hawke had testified following the Battle of Toulon. He had been acquitted by the court martial, but there may have been some resentment dating from that incident. A somewhat acrimonious correspondence took place in which Hawke revealed that he did not know much about brewing. He suggested to Pett that perhaps the brewers at Plymouth were 'reboiling' bad beer and sending it out, but Pett dismissed that fantasy. By 8 September Hawke was prepared to risk getting more beer from Plymouth, 'if the Commissioner and Agent Victualler will answer for its keeping but six weeks or one month'. He also requested that a large supply be sent all at once so that fleet movements would be the least affected by ships being brought to alongside the victuallers.[47]

Hero joined the fleet off Ushant on 2 August, with Prince Edward serving on board. Although only rated a midshipman, he had to be treated with fawning respect. When he called on his admiral the royal standard flew from his barge, and he was accompanied by the three subordinate admirals with their flags flying, and all the captains of the fleet following in order of seniority. A twenty-one-gun salute was fired, and as he was rowed past the ships of the force, the sides were manned, three cheers called for, and a march beat on the drums. Thompson was impressed:

> We received him yesterday, with all those military honours due to his illustrious birth and rank, – and with that peculiar pleasure which the subject must feel for a prince, whose qualities render him the admiration of all the world. – We are not a little proud of a king's brother being a midshipman; his *Royal Highness* going thro' the different degrees of the service, gives spirits to the whole corps, – and the attention he pays to the various duties of the fleet, will one day, be the happy means of making him a glory to his country.

Edward was not literally the king's brother until George III succeeded in October 1760, and any illusion about the monarchy being willing to compete with lesser mortals on an equal footing was to be dispelled the next year when, despite his going ashore before the Battle of Quiberon Bay, Prince Edward was promoted Captain on 14 June, and in 1761 promoted again to Rear Admiral.[48]

At the end of July a Dutch master had informed Hawke that 5,000 soldiers had been seen marching through Morlaix, where were also four 'transports' waiting to slip into Brest. Subsequently two other Dutchmen departing Brest reported that the French fleet was manned, with the soldiers embarked. And in early August Hawke received intelligence that there was an enemy convoy with two frigate escorts sheltering in Quiberon Bay, and a hundred sail laded with stores and provisions for Brest sheltering at Port Louis.

How much importance should be attached to these reports, however, was uncertain. ''Tis true', Hawke wrote to Clevland on

4 August, that 'in obedience to my instructions I send their Lordships from time to time such intelligence as I can procure, which has in general hitherto been from men intercepted in French boats. But I depend not on it. What I see, I believe, and regulate my conduct accordingly.' Hawke continued to send ships away as they were needed to convoy returning victuallers, and so that they could be cleaned. 'As to myself,' he wrote, 'it is a matter of indifference whether I fight the enemy, if they should come out, with an equal number, one ship more or one less.' All the same, he was concerned at not having a second fifty-gun ship that he could attach to the force consisting of *Colchester* (50 guns), *Windsor* (60 guns), *Sapphire* (32 guns) and *Melampe* (36 guns) cruising to intercept the convoy expected from Rochefort, 'the stopping of which is very material'.[49]

Hervey continued actively to harass the enemy and collect intelligence. On 15 August he landed marines on Molène Island for the not very creditable purpose of stealing cattle and vegetables from the impoverished peasants, justifying his seizure by the propaganda value of showing that the French navy could not even defend its own coasts, let alone support the invasion of England. His attention was then taken by the movement of three ships out of Brest and anchored in Cameret Bay, which he watched carefully until they returned to Brest. On 28 September he organized a boat raid into the entrance of Brest harbour to seize a small yacht belonging, apparently, to Conflans himself. An officer from *Achilles* published an account in the *Annual Register*:

> As soon as Commodore Hervey, who led us, got sight of the fort, under which the vessel lay, the yacht hailed the *Monmouth*'s boat, and fired; we immediately all fired our small arms, and pulled on board as fast as possible. The commodore himself and his people were first on board, and carried through all their fire. We boarded next, to follow their brave example. We found them with swords and pistols in hand; the French running under deck, begging their lives. Our people cut her cable, and our boats brought her out in the midst of incessant firing from the shore.[50]

On 4 August Duff forwarded to Hawke further news of the ships in Quiberon Bay, which he chased into the Morbihan estuary of

Above: The *Royal George*, Hawke's flagship at Quiberon Bay,
depicted at Deptford by John Cleveley the Elder.
Left: Admiral of the Fleet the Right Honourable George Lord
Anson, engraved by Ridley after a painting by Sir Joshua
Reynolds. (*Naval Chronicle*)

Top left: Vice-Admiral Charles Saunders, engraving by J. McArdell after Sir Joshua Reynolds. (*London Magazine*, 1759)
Top right: Plan of Louisburg. (*London Magazine*, 1758)
Middle: *Halifax*, engraving by Welles after Dominic Serres. (*Naval Chronicle*) Left: The St Lawrence showing the track of the British Fleet, by T. Kitchin. Bottom right: William Pitt, stipple engraving by E. Bocquet after Richard Brompton.

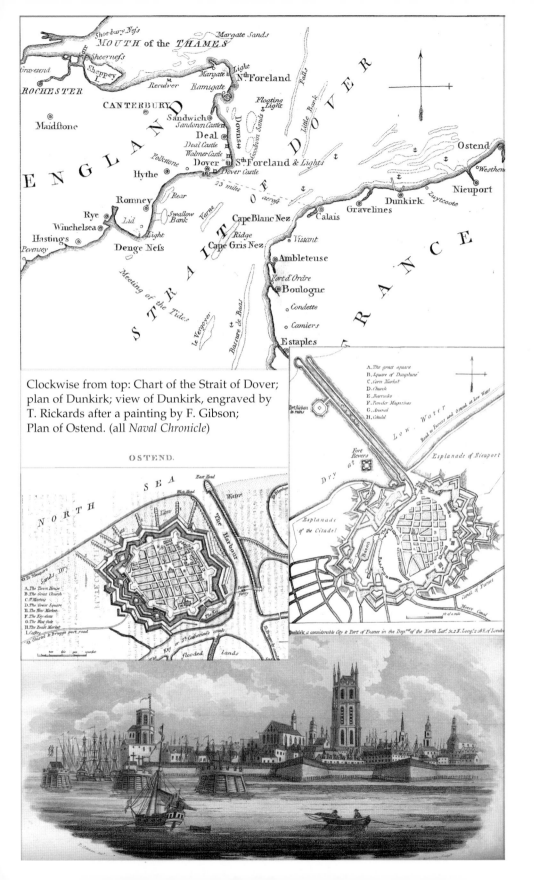

Clockwise from top: Chart of the Strait of Dover; plan of Dunkirk; view of Dunkirk, engraved by T. Rickards after a painting by F. Gibson; Plan of Ostend. (all *Naval Chronicle*)

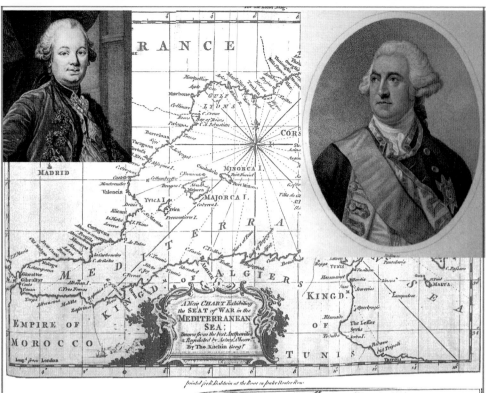

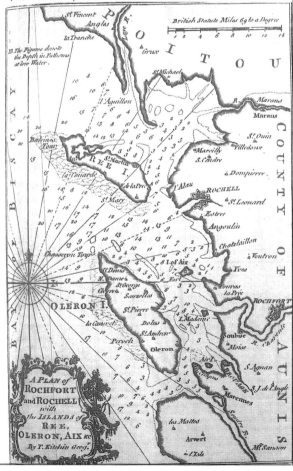

Top left: Duc de Choiseul-Amboise, engraving by Fechard (*Naval Chronicle*); top right: Edward Lord Hawke, engraved by Ridley after Francis Cotes (*Naval Chronicle*); above: A *New Chart Exhibiting the Seat of War in the Mediterranean Sea* by T. Kitchin (*London Magazine,* 1756); right: *A Plan of Rochefort and Rochelle* by T. Kitchin (*London Magazine,* 1757); below: Earl Howe, engraving by Ridley. (*Naval Chronicle*)

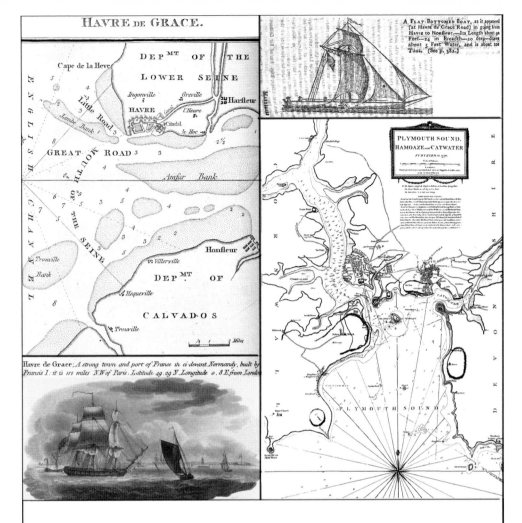

Clockwise from top left: Le Havre-de-Grâce (*Naval Chronicle*); a flat-bottomed boat (*London Magazine*, 1759); detail of Plymouth Sound by Thomas Jeffreys; *View of Berry Head, Torbay*, engraving by Wells, and *Marine View From Spithead*, engraving by F. Cheshance, both after Nicholas Pocock (*Naval Chronicle*).

COAST of FRANCE from L'ORIENT to the ISLE of RÉ.

Contemporary chart showing the coast of France from L'Orient to the Isle of Re.

Published 1 May 1813. by Joyce Gold. Naval Chronicle Office, 103, Shoe Lane, London.

Top: *Distant View of Brest Harbour,* engraved by Robert Pollard after Nicholas Pocock and Francis Mason.
Below: Chart of the road and port of Brest. (all *Naval Chronicle*)

Brest Harbour, engraving by T. Melland. (*Naval Chronicle*)

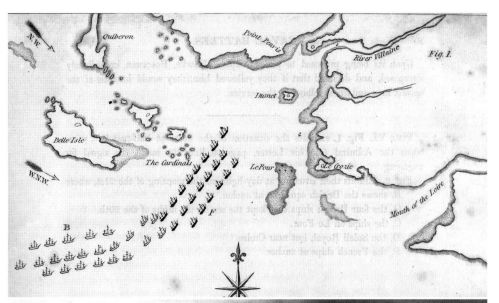

Top: Charles Ekins' chart showing the fleets at 2.30pm, when Admiral Hawke gave the signal to engage. (*Naval Battles*)
Middle: Detail from *The Battle of Quiberon Bay, 21 November 1759: The Day After* by Richard Wright.
Bottom left and right: portraits of Captain Augustus, later Admiral Viscount Keppel, and Vice-Admiral, later Admiral, Sir Charles Hardy. (*Naval Chronicle*)

the Vannes River, and of a convoy from La Rochelle bound for Port Louis and Brest, of which fishermen said thirty of the ships were troop transports. They went on to add that there were twenty-five transports at Nantes ready to sail to Port Louis to take on troops. The presence of troops at Port Louis to be embarked in ships from Nantes was confirmed by the master of a French barque from Port Louis who was captured by a Guernsey privateer.[51] On 18 August Clevland warned Hawke that the Admiralty had intelligence that four of the Brest fleet were intended to provide an escort for the ships sheltering at Vannes, and at Paimboeuf near the mouth of the Loire. Then on 22 August Clevland sent Hawke the Admiralty orders that were eventually to lead to the Battle in Quiberon Bay in November.

> My Lords Commissioners of the Admiralty having received inform-ation of the preparations of the enemy at Port Louis, Vannes, [and?] Auray [also on the River Vannes], where a considerable number of transports are collected together under convoy of several frigates of war, and that a large body of troops are actually embarked on board the said transports to be employed on a particular service against some part of His Majesty's dominions; their Lordships recommend it most earnestly to you to do everything in your power to defeat their designs by taking or destroying these ships. And it appearing by Captain Duff's letter you have enclosed to their Lordships that he has been very active on this station, they wish to have him continued thereon as long as possible, and that you will cause him to be supplied with provisions and water for that purpose, and that you consult him to see if it will not be practicable, with bombs or fireships or both, to destroy the enemy's ships and vessels in the before-mentioned harbours, or wherever they may be, and to give their Lordships your opinion thereon.[52]

By the time this was received on board Hawke's flagship, Duff had already been detached in *Rochester* to Spithead, and Hawke said that even had his orders reached him in time he still would have had to send her in because her crew needed refreshment in port. 'I have nothing at heart', he wrote, 'but the good of the service.' He explained that his principal consideration in reducing the number of times ships were taken into dry dock to clean was that the ships' companies, 'which were raw unseasoned men,

[were] so harassed by preparing for dock and fitting after it that they returned to me in a worse condition than that in which they went, I was thereby induced to alter my plan with regard to some of them, and in particular the large ships ... With regard to Port Louis and Vannes,' he continued, 'I was pretty easy, as I had directed Captain [Robert] Roddam in the *Colchester*, with the *Windsor*, *Sapphire*, *Melampe*, *Pallas* and *Actaeon*, to guard them. And as to Nantes, I imagined their Lordships had been satisfied from the *Brilliant*, *Deptford* and *Aeolus* which I found had been cruising there.'

Nevertheless, he detached Captain John Reynolds in *Firm*, a new third-rate ship, to assume command of all the ships in the Quiberon area, with orders to look into Port Louis, Vannes and Nantes, and if he found any had sailed, to 'make the best of his way to the coast of Ireland in quest of them and, whenever he should meet with them, to make the destruction of the transports his principal object'. *Windsor* was a sixty-gun ship, but her commander being the same Archibald Clevland who owed his promotion to his father being Secretary of the Admiralty, and only twenty-one years old, Hawke had sent her to serve with the frigates where she could do less harm.[53]

If the French had not sailed, Reynolds was to look into the possibility of destroying them in their harbours with bomb vessels or fireships, or both. Reynolds had combined a naval career with a less-than-successful period as Governor of Georgia. His assertive personality was more in its element on the stormy Brittany coast. Hawke passed on to him the information that was later to be of importance: that the French charts showed there were three and a half fathoms of water at low tide at the entrance to Port Louis, and three or four at the entrance to the Morbihan, although only room for two frigates to anchor before the river shoaled. The bar at Nantes had only five feet of water at low tide, and a rise of twelve feet. Finding that the transports at Nantes had not moved, Reynolds settled down to watch them and those in the Morbihan and at Port Louis with up to twelve frigates and fireships, backed up by *Firm*.

Supplying these vessels was more of a problem even than it was for the Channel Fleet off Brest, because being smaller they could store less, and they were more distant from Portsmouth and

Plymouth. Hawke gave orders that before any of them returned to England for cleaning, or other reason, they were to discharge all the remaining stores into the other frigates.[54]

While these operations were going forward, Hawke had also had to find an opportunity to carry out instructions he received from the Admiralty to stage a 'feu de joie' off the entrance to Brest harbour in honour of the victory of the Army of Observation at Minden. The triumphant broadsides Hawke fired in honour of the occasion amounted to psychological warfare, which certainly would have encouraged the British fleet more than it did that of their enemy. But news was soon to come that was more directly encouraging for the weary crews.

* * *

The Admiralty's planning had to allow for the possibility that the Toulon fleet would sail, and that it would get past the squadron under Boscawen at Gibraltar. The danger to Britain should that happen was evident, and the British ambassador at Madrid, the Earl of Bristol, was alert for news from Toulon. Bristol was Captain Hervey's elder brother. When he heard that Chef d'Escadre Jean-François Bertet de la Clue Sabran, who had commanded the French rear under la Galissonière in the Battle of Minorca and succeeded to command at Toulon, had sailed from thence with twelve ships of the line and three frigates, and successfully passed Gibraltar in the night of 16–17 August, he immediately sent a dispatch by the Corunna packet. Five of the ships and the frigates were reported put into Cadiz, but the remainder were unaccounted for. The packet was encountered at sea by the *Success* of twenty-four guns commanded by Captain Paul Henry Ourry, and reached Hawke off Brest on 7 September, shortly before the receipt of news via London of la Clue's departure from Toulon.[55] The sense of urgency in London was increased when a report was received from Wolters's agent at Vannes, dated 12 September, that orders had been received there to hurry the embarkation of the army.[56]

By the time the news from Spain reached Hawke, la Clue's squadron, which was in fact under orders for Martinique, had been brought to action.[57] Boscawen's force of fourteen ships of the line had failed to intercept the Toulon fleet because they had been obliged to go into Gibraltar to take on stores and water, and to effect repairs on some ships that had been damaged by a French battery. The fleet were inside the mole a day before la Clue left Toulon on 5 August, and were still there when he passed the straits of Gibraltar in the night on 17 August. Indeed, Boscawen was several miles away having dinner with the Spanish Governor of San Roque. The French ships were sighted as they passed in the dark, however, and someone on board Boscawen's flagship made the signal to unmoor, bringing the admiral back in haste. Some of the ships had unbent their sails, some had freshly tarred their spars, others had struck them and sent down their topmasts, and some were overhauling their rigging. Officers and men ashore had to be hastily recalled. Boscawen sailed in pursuit, and his second in command, Vice Admiral Thomas Brodrick, whose squadron was moored further up the harbour, followed. 'It was a splendid feat of seamanship,' Corbett wrote, 'such as only seamen who know the Rock can fully appreciate.'[58] Had la Clue's orders been to break the British hold on Gibraltar he might have been able to fight and win a battle against this disorganized force, but his orders were to evade the British. He might have got clear away, but in the confusion of the dark he lost control.

La Clue had his squadron in two divisions, and he and his captains had sealed orders that were to be opened only after passing the straits. These provided for a possible diversion into neutral Cadiz, and the senior captain of the Second Division acted on this option. Three frigates and five ships, three 64s and two 50s, succeeded in getting into Cadiz. Le Clue, however, was unaware that the Second Division had changed course in the dark, and used a night signal, probably number twenty-seven in his signal book, to tell the fleet to hold their course for Cape St Vincent, for which he had a favourable wind. This signal called for him to extinguish his poop lanterns and fire three guns, after which the rest of the fleet were to extinguish their lights, and follow in the dark. Boscawen's force continued to chase la Clue's now greatly outnumbered squadron.[59] The editor of the *Annual Register* was triumphant: 'the evil genius of France operating on the cowardice or incapacity of their commander, induced them to separate their fleet and fly. The English ships were newly refitted; they proved better sailors, and the men animated with the spirited example of their admiral, engaged the French ships as they could overtake them.'[60] More recent authors are more respectful. La Clue apparently mistook the approaching British as the missing part of his own fleet, and lost precious time waiting for them to catch up. The French also lost their wind, despite the good breeze that still favoured the British. About 2.00 am la Clue's ships began to come under fire from the British chasse guns, and the action became close in the afternoon of 18 August.

According to the account in Robert Beatson's nearly contemporary *Naval and Military Memoirs of Great Britain*, la Clue saw that Boscawen was going for his van and centre, and he

> made his fleet luff up as much as they possibly could, so as to form a sort of crescent, by which position, the whole of his ships in their van and centre were enabled by their fire not only to assist the rear, but each other, in their endeavours to repel the attack which they looked for every moment from the British Admiral. By this manoeuvre of M. De la Clue's, such of our ships as first got up with the enemy's rear, and to leeward of their line, were thrown out of action; while, for want of a sufficient breeze of wind, they could not get into it again.[61]

At about 2.30, Boscawen's flagship engaged la Clue's flag, *Océan*, continuing to fire on her for half an hour, but then lost her mizzen and both topsail yards, and fell astern. Boscawen had to transfer to *Newark*. But la Clue was outnumbered, and signalled a retreat, which was facilitated by the wind freshening again. Not all his command were able to follow. His rearmost ship, *Centaure* (74 guns), which sacrificed itself to delay Boscawen's attack, received heavy punishment and was partly dismasted. She was captured, and Boscawen pressed on after the remainder. He later claimed that he wanted his leading ships to execute a modification of the tactic Anson had devised and Hawke used in 1747, with his leading ship engaging the last ship of the French line, while the second passed it on the disengaged side and brought the next French ship into action, and so on, until the leading ship was in action. Boscawen needed to arrest the flight of the leading French ships. But he had not issued his fleet with a signal to that effect, and he could only signal for his leading ships to make more sail, which they misunderstood. He might have destroyed the entire

French force, because la Clue made a navigational error, and failed to weather Cape St Vincent. But in fact two of la Clue's ships managed to get away, *Souverain* and *Guerrier*, respectively finding shelter in Rochefort and the Canaries. The remaining four sought the protection of the neutral beach of Lagos Bay, under the guns of a Portuguese fortress. But Boscawen ignored the conventions, returned the fire from the fortress, drove *Océan* and *Redoutable* ashore where they were destroyed, and captured *Téméraire* and *Modeste*.[62] La Clue himself was mortally wounded.

The Admiralty forwarded to Hawke on 6 September Boscawen's account of his partial victory, and advised Hawke on 10 September that Boscawen was being sent orders to detach any of the ships under his command fit for duty to reinforce the fleet before Brest. The rest should go into Plymouth for a rapid refit, when they, and any Channel Fleet ships at Plymouth, would be sent back to the Ushant rendezvous. 'You are required and directed,' Hawke was instructed, 'so soon as you shall be joined by a sufficient number of the said ships, to keep a detachment of proper strength down in the Bay either for intercepting the abovementioned French ships [i.e. those in Cadiz and the two seventy-fours that had escaped the battle] or, if they should get in [to Port Louis], to prevent their sailing with any embarkation from thence.'[63] On 14 September, however, the Admiralty was able to advise Hawke that Boscawen's second in command, Vice Admiral Brodrick, had the ships in Cadiz under observation, so that only the two seventy-fours could be expected to appear in the Bay. In the circumstances, it was decided not to send Boscawen's ships into Portsmouth for cleaning and relieve their crews as the dry docks became available.[64] When Hawke passed the news of Boscawen's victory to the fleet, which reached Captain Reynolds in Quiberon Bay, he reported that it had given 'vast pleasure to all the squadron'.[65]

*   *   *

As he had been instructed, Reynolds called a council of war on 7 September of the captains who had been put under his command, to consider whether they could destroy the enemy ships in their harbours with bomb vessels or fireships. They were unanimously of the opinion that they could, were adequate pilots provided, and Captain John Strachan of *Sapphire* also suggested that it would be useful to seize the Island of Yeu between Belle Île and the Île de Ré, which Reynolds thought 'would certainly be a place of great use to us, as it is now to the enemy'. Reynolds' only concern was that if it were intended that he should prevent neutral vessels joining the growing number of merchantmen in French harbours he would have to be provided with more men for prize crews.[66] Until the appropriate resources could be assembled to launch raids into the enemy harbours, Hawke concentrated on containing the threat posed by the fleets of transports, and on 11 September he instructed Reynolds to

> station one of the 50-gun ships and at least three or four frigates to cruise N. and S. off the west end of the Isle of Groix to cover Port Louis, which is now become the principal object; two frigates off Nantes, which in bad weather may come to an anchor just within the Cardinals [rocks] in the entrance of Quiberon Bay; whilst you in the *Firm*, with the *Pluto* and the other 50-gun ship [*Colchester* or *Falkland*], shall cruise off the north end of Belle Île at the distance of four or five leagues, so as best to support your cruisers of [on?] each side, keeping frigates constantly running between you and them with proper signals to make on discovery of an enemy and [of] the course they shall steer.

He did not adopt the idea of occupying Yeu, which would have taken too great a part of Reynolds' resources. As for the problem of prize crews, he told Reynolds that while he wanted the neutrals denied entrance to French harbours, they were not to be detained.[67]

The Admiralty attached enough importance to destroying the transports that on 14 September Hawke was instructed to undertake a raid on those in Pierre Percée Road below Nantes, and told that pilots familiar with the water would be sent out to him from Portsmouth and Plymouth. If enough of them could be located, or if there were enough pilots for those waters already in the fleet, they were to be sent out to lead the attack. On 17 September Captain Duff returned from Portsmouth in *Rochester*, and was immediately dispatched to take command of the ships off L'Orient, followed by three pilots for the French coast. Hawke, however, was sceptical the plan would come to anything, writing to Clevland on 23 September that, in his opinion, 'if it was practicable to

119

destroy the enemy's ships and vessels at Pierre Percée, I cannot doubt of Captain Reynolds having attempted it long before now'. Duff told him on 22 September that only two of the pilots with him had any knowledge of the Morbihan, and they had only been as far as the entrance, which in fact was the only place ships could lie afloat.[68]

Meanwhile, the work of the cruisers off Brest was continued. Hervey pounced on three French ships, which he identified as *Bizarre* (64 guns), *Sphynx* (64 guns) and *Grette* (32 guns), attempting to exit Brest 'to join the transports and ships at Nantes and Port Louis', but they got back into harbour.[69] Captain Alexander Hood guarding the Passage du Four chased five sail into a bay by the Isle Gaspis, burned one and drove two ashore, but his First Lieutenant, Swinton, accused him of not having done his utmost against the enemy, and it was necessary to arrange a court martial, which exonerated him. Lieutenant Swinton, having made himself dreadfully unpopular, then asked to be relieved of his duty for reasons of health. Hawke was under orders not to conduct courts martial, but the Admiralty approved his acting on his judgement as circumstances should require. The reason for the ban had been to protect him from the need to take officers away from their duty.[70]

The limited ability of cruiser forces to prevent naval movement, even on a large scale, when weather conditions favoured the enemy was shown when a large convoy, reported by a privateer to number sixty ships under the escort of three or four warships, managed to slip out of Nantes and join those in the Morbihan. Reynolds again summoned his captains to discuss the practicability of raiding the harbour, and they landed on Méaban Island where they could see into the estuary. Captain Duff was with them. This time voices were definitely against. The entrance is only two or three cables length in width, with a rock in the middle. The tide was believed to run at six knots and to rise and fall four fathoms or twenty-four feet, making an attack by the frigates exceedingly hazardous. The logical alternative was to use the fireship, but the ships sheltering in the harbour were dispersed up the rivers and separated so that there was little prospect of destroying them. The French had fortified the entrance to the estuary, and were an attack to be attempted, it would have to be on a flood tide that would also permit the French to move their ships further up the branches of the river. It was generally agreed that losses would outweigh any advantage from a raid, but that a close blockade would be effective. Hawke's view that councils of war could not exonerate an officer from doing his duty was expressed long ago, and certainly burning the enemy transports would have had a definitive effect, but only if it could be done with the forces available. Hawke never suggested that Reynolds should have chanced his arm, and Duff decided to leave most of the squadron to watch the Moriban, while he took *Rochester* 'and some of the best sailing frigates' to watch Port Louis.[71]

John Thomas Serres's drawings of the French coast were not to be commissioned for another forty years, but the Admiralty under Anson was aware of the need to improve the charts of the French coast. The uncertainty about the estuaries into which French convoys were taken to shelter was matched by the uncertainties about offshore hazards. Skilled seamen could tell much by looking at the disturbances made by submerged rocks to the ocean swell, and it was that skill that was to make it possible for Hawke to chase the French fleet into Quiberon Bay two months later. And the fact that the battle was fought in a gale of wind actually helped the pilots avoid the rocks, because they could con their ships to avoid breaking water. But at best, this was not as good as having accurate charts of the coast, and was no help at all at the Admiralty in assessing possibilities. Accordingly, on 3 October, Hawke was informed that

> their Lordships are desirous of having, as well for their own information as for that of their successors, as accurate draughts and surveys of the French coast as may be, they desire you will please to send them such as you may have collected and that you will order the commanders of all the ships and vessels of your squadron, whom you shall hereafter detach to cruise upon the coast, to make the best remark they can of the soundings, dangers, anchoring ground, and batteries within the limits of their cruise, with their bearings, the flowing of the tides, their setting and the heights they rise, and to make draughts thereof when they have artists on board to draw them, which their Lordships would be glad to have sent to them from time to time, as opportunity offers.[72]

At the time there was no Admiralty Hydrographic department, and the man who was to be in 1795 appointed its first chief Hydrographer, Alexander Dalrymple, was then only a junior writer in the East India Company. On 3 August Hervey had attempted to obtain soundings in Douarnenez Bay, south of Brest, but had been frustrated when the wind came west by south putting the ships in danger of being embayed. Duff was more successful when he ordered the Teignouse Passage between Quiberon Point and Houat Island sounded, and steering marks identified. This provided a shorter route for the force watching the Morbihan to stretch north-west to Port Louis, but it later proved a dangerous one, and cost the destruction of *Achilles*.[73]

* * *

As September drew to an end, Hawke began to have doubts that it would be possible to continue much longer the close blockade of Brest. On 29 September he wrote to Lord Anson that he had 'hitherto kept as close a lookout upon the enemy at Brest as was possible' and that he would use his 'utmost endeavour to do so' while he remained in command, but that he was 'much afraid' that as it grew late in the year 'the weather will grow bad and not permit us to watch them so narrowly as we have done'. To Clevland he wrote that 'the supplies of beer and water arrive so slow, and the continual disappointments I meet with from the Plymouth beer, with which the clean ships are supplied, not lasting in a condition to be drank above a week, I am afraid may occasion the breaking up of the squadron.'[74] So long as the weather permitted, Hawke had no intention of abandoning the watch on Brest, and the Admiralty were to express their wish clearly that the new supplies of beer and wine being sent him would enable him 'to continue on your station, where it is more necessary than ever for you to remain as long as possible at this very critical conjuncture'. But the deteriorating conditions did pose a challenge. Captain Hervey warned from his station near the Black Rocks off the entrance to Brest that, with the season changing, he feared that 'if the enemy is so intent on getting out two or three ships, they must at last find an opportunity of a shore wind and thick weather, when our ships have been obliged to stand off, by which means the greatest vigilance and boldest perseverance to keep this dangerous coast on board may be frustrated.'[75]

La Clue's squadron had been accounted for, but Hawke also had to provide for the possibility that the squadron the French had sent to the West Indies in January under the command of Chef d'Escadre Maximin Bompar, believed to consist of five 74s, two 64s a 50 and three frigates, might return and make it possible for the Brest fleet to fight its way out of harbour, or might appear off Port Louis or Rochefort and release the invasion force. In response to a warning sent by the Admiralty on 21 September Hawke had ordered Rear Admiral Geary to watch Rochefort in *Sandwich* with *Chichester* and *Anson*, cruising east and west of the Pertuis d'Antioche, the sound north of Île d'Oléron, and on 3 October he sent *Windsor* and *Fame*, both of sixty guns, to join him. The Admiralty, however, decided that Hawke had over-reacted, and advised him to recall some of the ships: 'Their Lordships command me', Clevland wrote, 'to observe that they think the number of ships stationed off Rochefort is too great, since the particular objects of attention at this time are the inter-cepting the embarkation of the enemy at Morbihan and keeping their ships of war from coming out of Brest, wherefore they recommend it to you to station the ships under your command accordingly.' They were able to share with Hawke intelligence from the Commander in Chief on the Jamaica station, Vice Admiral Thomas Cotes, that suggested Bompar was unlikely to sail home until the end of the hurricane season. Perhaps this might have suggested that Hawke's decision to reduce his fleet off Brest was in the best interest of the service, but the Admiralty did not think so.

This micro-management of operations might have led to mistakes being made, and it certainly irritated Hawke. 'On the intelligence sent me in your letter of the 21st September relating to M. Bompar, I thought the intercepting him a very material object. For if the alarm [in England] is great now, it must be much greater, should he get into Rochefort.' However, 'since their Lordships rely on the opinion of Vice-Admiral Cotes', he had recalled Rear Admiral Geary with *Sandwich*, *Hercules* and *Anson* and ordered him to send *Fame*, *Chichester*, *Windsor*, *Belliqueux* and *Vengeance* to join Duff in Quiberon Bay.

> Their Lordships will pardon my observing that, from the present disposition of the squadron, I think there is little room for alarm while the weather continues tolerable. As to Brest, I may safely affirm that, except the few ships that took shelter in Conquet, hardly a vessel of any kind has been able to enter or come out of that port these four months. We are as vigilant as ever, though we have not so much daylight. And if we can give credit to their own people, they have suffered greatly, having even been obliged to unload near forty victuallers at Quimperlé [a small river port eastward of Penmarch Point on the south-west corner of Brittany] and carry their cargo by land to Brest. It must be the fault of the weather, not ours, if any of them escape.

Eventually the Admiralty would back off, and agree that a force off Rochefort was a matter of importance.

> If, after providing sufficient force for those purposes and your being reinforced by the ships that come home with Admiral Boscawen, you shall find a number of ships can be spared to cruise off Rochefort, their Lordships recommend it to you then to detach them, especially as it is not improbable the five ships of Monsieur de la Clue's squadron which put into Cadiz may endeavour to get into that place.[76]

Hawke had ordered Duff on 7 October to leave only a small force at Port Louis and L'Orient, and take charge himself in Quiberon Bay, and the next day he sent instructions that Duff was to reconsider the possibility of an attack on the transports in the Morbihan estuary. Captain Samuel Barrington had found two Frenchmen whom he trusted and who said they could pilot an attack force. Accordingly Barrington was ordered to join Duff in *Achilles* with the two pilots. Intelligence had been obtained that indicated the fortifications on the Morbihan were a limited threat, a battery of twelve twenty-four-pounders at Locmariaquer peninsula that closed the estuary from the west. But Hawke clearly did not approve of the operation, writing to Clevland 'to observe that, in my opinion, the enemy cannot stir from thence and that, should they attempt it, Captain Duff has sufficient force to destroy them in the entrance of the river, from whence such a number of ships cannot pass with safety in face of an enemy determined to attack them.' Duff made another assessment of the prospect from Méaban Island, and his enthusiasm for a raid did not increase.[77] The danger of mounting a raid into the river had to be seen in perspective: the anchorage off the entrance to the Morbihan, sheltered by the mainland from the north to south-east, Quiberon point from the west, and more distantly by Belle Île, Houat and Hedic islands from the south through south-east, was ideal for a blockading force, and the narrow opening to the river ensured that enemy ships trying to exit would be exposed to overwhelming force.[78]

Before anything could be attempted, the weather broke. On the evening of 11 October the fleet outside Brest was subjected to a hard gale blowing west-south-west, transforming the scene. By 6.00 am the *Royal George* had got down her topgallant yards, struck her topgallant masts, and was lying to. The *Royal Ann*'s caulking had shifted and by 3.00 am she was making six feet of water in an hour. At 10.30 she fired two guns as the distress signal and bore away for Spithead, where she arrived on 14 October. Other ships began to suffer lesser amounts of damage.[79] On 10 October the Admiralty had written to Hawke instructing him 'in case the enemy should escape' not to bring his fleet eastward of Plymouth and Torbay, unless in chase of the enemy 'upon well grounded intelligence of their having passed by those places'. Hawke had not received that dispatch, of course, but in any case he had no intention of running for Portsmouth, and being trapped there until the wind came easterly or northerly. There was no danger of the enemy getting out so long as the wind blew strongly in that quarter. Instead Hawke set the fleet's course for Plymouth, reaching the sound on 13 October, when he wrote to the Admiralty that he intended to 'keep the ships employed night and day in completing their water and provisions to three months'. In the days before the gale it had been getting increasingly difficult to transfer water and beer casks from the victuallers, so the run into Plymouth had its advantages. 'I shall not stir out of the *Ramillies* myself,' he added the next day, 'and hope to be at sea again in a few days in a condition to keep there without depending on victuallers ... While the wind is fair for the enemy's coming out, it is also favourable for our keeping in; and while we are obliged to keep off, they cannot stir.'

Still smarting from the Admiralty's meddling with his dispositions, he lamented having recalled Rear Admiral Geary. 'But as there are many ships now in England, I hope their Lordships will soon put it in my power to block up Rochefort, which will effectually distress the enemy everywhere.'[80] This had already been conceded, although Hawke had not yet received the order. It came too late to prevent the *Souverain* (74 guns) getting into Rochefort on 10 October, after her escape from Lagos Bay. Captain Jervis Porter, in *Herculese*, had alone been on station to intercept the *Souverain*, and had managed to engage her in a running action of which he later wrote a spirited account:

> About 3/4 after 9, being pretty near up with her though not near enough to engage, she put her helm hard a-starboard and gave us her larboard broadside, and then kept on as before and gave us her starboard broadside. We then immediately starboarded our helm and ran right down upon her whilst she was loading her guns and, getting close to her ported our helm and began to engage as the guns bore upon her. At 1/2 past 10, we was so unlucky as to have our main topmast head shot away, which she took the advantage of and made all the sail she could from us.

Herculese had to abandon the chase when the Île d'Oléron was five leagues to leeward, because she had suffered too much damage to her spars to risk approaching a lee shore. Porter himself had received a shot in the head and the wind from a shot had disabled his right leg.[81]

The Admiralty approved Hawke's decision to reach across to Plymouth, and the process of getting the fleet ready to return to its war station went forward rapidly. Attrition had already reduced its numbers as ships had had to be sent in for essential repairs, or because of sickness, but there were the ships from Boscawen's squadron that were now available to provide reinforcements. On 14 October Commissioner Hanway advised the Admiralty that to speed the provisioning and equipping of the fleet he had ordered that everything needed be taken by barges into the sound where the ships could be supplied at anchor; the surge of the sea kicked up by the west-north-west wind must have made the transfer difficult. 'I have proposed to Sir Edward Hawke, to send the ships' long-boats with anchors and hawsers to endeavour to warp the victuallers out of the Catwater, and have ordered the masters attendant to send two launches to assist in that service. The cutters are employed in removing thirty-two sick men from the *Foudroyant*.'[82] Later, Hawke was to comment to Hanway: 'I have had tolerable experience of the duty of a commanding officer in port, & always did, and still do, look upon his attention to the victualling office, as the principal part of it: as without being properly and seasonably supply'd with provisions, the rest of the ships fitting will avail little.'[83] On 17 October Hawke reported that 'the weather continues to grow worse or I should have been at sea again'. He warned that he was likely to have to shelter in Plymouth or Torbay frequently in the future because his rendezvous off Brest was exposed, but he could not change it without losing his ability to see into the entrance to Brest harbour. This was minuted at the Admiralty: 'The Lords conclude he will not put oftener into port than is necessary and leave it to his discretion.' While the fleet waited the end of the gale, Prince Edward obtained permission to come ashore. Had he had enough of blockade? Unfortunately for his heroic image, he was to miss the battle a month later.[84]

Hawke had a report that the frigate *Arethusa* had arrived at Spithead 'greatly shattered', and was concerned about six of his ships that were missing from Plymouth Sound. The Admiralty, however, was able to assure Hawke that none had been driven to the eastward, so that those missing could be expected to find their way back to the rendezvous. The safety of the ships and frigates under Duff's command was also a matter of concern, although Hawke hoped that there was enough shelter in Quiberon Bay that 'the ships under Captain Duff's orders have rode in safety'. This proved to be the case, except for *Achilles* that ran on Goué Vas rock in the Teignouse passage south of Quiberon peninsula – despite having on board the two French pilots, whose credibility suffered a total eclipse as a result, and despite the survey that had been made.[85] Captain Hervey was able to bring *Monmouth* back to his station by the Black Rocks on 18 October, and when the weather cleared two days later saw no sign that the Brest ships had moved, or that any other ships had been able to get in. Hawke was himself back at the rendezvous off Ushant on 21 October, having found most of the missing ships waiting him off the Lizard, and *Dunkirk* and *Bienfaisant* anchored with *Monmouth* off the Black Rocks.[86] Hervey, suffering from the gout and needing a spell of leave, on his own authority ordered *Bienfaisant* into port to deal with its sick list and shortage of stores. This Hawke could not approve, as he only had with him at the time seventeen of the line, and he ordered Hervey for the future always to check with him before detaching any units. *Monmouth* had been badly strained in the heavy weather, and reluctantly Hawke decided that both ship and its captain needed to be sent into port. 'I part with him with the greatest regret.'[87] *Achilles* had to be sent back to England, and *Actaeon* and *Gibraltar* were sent with her as escorts, but the arrival of five of Boscawen's squadron more than balanced the score.

* * *

Anson had advised that the French could expect better conditions for an invasion attempt in October, following the period of gales often experienced during the autumn equinox, but a gale that could force Hawke to seek shelter, and open a window for Conflans to sail from Brest, could easily destroy a transport convoy attempting to reach Scotland, or even the south of England. Nevertheless, the watch had to continue, and there was the important matter of the overseas campaigns. On 23 October Hawke received news from the Admiralty of General Wolfe's successful capture of Quebec, at the cost of his own life. But the British hold on Quebec was tenuous, and everything would depend on who would first manage to penetrate the ice of the St Lawrence in the spring of 1760 with reinforcements. Amherst had found he could not reach Montreal, or Quebec, in 1759 against Canadian resistance, which Wolfe's savage pacification campaign had stimulated. The blockade, and the battle in November, would be critical in determining the future of Canada.[88]

And that battle was to take place despite the lateness of the season. Wolters's agent at Paris reported on 19 October that word of the dispersal of Hawke's force due to the gales led to the Minister of the Marine, Berryer, following a meeting of the

Council of State, dispatching a courier to Brest with orders for Conflans to sail, and seek action.[89] On 29 October the Admiralty informed Hawke it had intelligence 'that positive orders are sent to M. Conflans to put to sea directly and at all events to engage His Majesty's ships under your command'. Urgent orders were issued to bring together all available ships under Hawke's direct command, and he was urged 'not to make the detachment you mention to cruise off Rochefort'. On the same day, Hawke advised that three bomb vessels, *Firedrake*, *Furnace* and *Thunder*, had joined, and been sent on to Quiberon Bay. 'By the *Melampe*, Captain Duff acquaints me that the master of a Spanish vessel, which came out of Auray the 20th instant, informed him that there were five regiments at Auray and eight at Vannes and about sixty vessels lying near Auray with their sails unbent.' Clearly, the French would react to a threat to their transports if they could, and the reality of winter weather would provide them with opportunity. On 30 October the Admiralty Secretary informed Hawke that

> My Lords Commissioners of the Admiralty considering it is very probable you may at this season be drove from your station off Ushant up the Channel and that the enemy may take such opportunity of coming out of Brest, their Lordships therefore command me to recommend it to you, whenever that happens, to endeavour to leave some of your frigates to the westward of Ushant to observe the motions of the French ships in Brest and, in case of their coming out, to see which way they stand and then repair to such rendezvous as you may appoint with the intelligence; and that you may receive it as early as possible, and to enable you to follow them with the greater dispatch, you should give them a signal to make if the ships are sailed.
>
> And as it is possible, if the enemy come out, they may attempt to destroy His Majesty's ships in Quiberon Bay, their Lordships likewise recommend it to you to keep a cruiser off Belle Isle, that she may give the most early intelligence of the enemy's motion to the ships of His Majesty in Quiberon Bay and thereby prevent their being surprised.[90]

Hawke had not yet received that order when, on 5 November, he wrote that he had no intention of coming into port 'while there should be a possibility of keeping the sea'. But he warned that the fleet would have to take shelter sooner than might be the case for individual ships. 'Single ships may struggle with a hard gale of wind when a squadron cannot. It must always from wearing lose ground in working against a strong westerly wind in the [Iroise] channel where it cannot make very long stretches, but more especially if it should blow so as to put it past carrying sail.' Plymouth, however, was too exposed and he said he would not go there again. 'If for the future this should happen, I shall put into Torbay, as I cannot be induced to think there is sufficient room for so large a squadron, or water for the three-decked ships, in Plymouth Sound at this season of the year.'[91]

Hardly was the ink dry on the paper than another gale struck, from the north-north-west. Hawke found he was unable to weather Ushant and 'was obliged on the 7th to carry all the sail I could to the northward. The gale continued very hard between the N by W and NW by N, and at noon of the 8th the Start bore N by W distant nine leagues. Moderating a little in the evening, I worked under the Start by 8 in the morning of the 9th and, till afternoon, entertained some hopes of being able to keep the sea and get to westward.' He 'was obliged and lucky enough' to get into Torbay with fifteen of his fleet, a sixteenth joining the morning of 10 November. 'The *Essex* is at anchor about two leagues without and, in sight, the *Sandwich* and *Duke* working up under their courses. If the wind does not abate, I am in doubt whether the two latter will be able to fetch this place. I have found the *Anson* here, not having been able to get into Plymouth.'[92]

The decided change in the weather and the receipt of the Admiralty's warning, forwarded from Plymouth by cutter, that Conflans could be expected to sail caused Hawke to rethink his operational strategy. The fifty-gun *Portland* commanded by Marriott Arbuthnot had gone to Quiberon, and was to have been joined by *Intrepid* of sixty guns commanded by J Maplesden, but *Monmouth* and *Nottingham*'s deteriorating condition and Captain Hervey's poor health had led Hawke to order them to Plymouth to refit. Hawke had kept *Intrepid* on the inshore station, and on 5 November when fighting the gale to windward of Ushant he had sent an order to the senior officer, Robert Digby, commanding *Dunkirk*, by cutter: 'If the winds will not permit you to look in with the King's ships under your orders, it is my direction, that you put a careful intelligent officer on board this cutter and send her at all risques, to discover the state of the enemy in Brest water, and dispatch her immediately to me with the account.'[93] *Thames* of thirty-two guns had been sent to cruise off Cape Finisterre, and *Fame* and *Windsor* were under orders to proceed to Cape Ortegal and await Rear Admiral Geary, who was to be sent there with seven of the line. However, the weather reduced the certainty of containing Conflans in Brest and Hawke came to consider the presence of ships of the line in Quiberon as hostages to ill fortune. 'If, which is very improbable, the enemy should escape me and make their push there with their whole squadron, these two ships would be of little avail and, without them, the five 50-gun ships and nine frigates would be a much more manageable squadron and therefore better able to preserve itself until my arrival.' Hawke also came to the decision that the bomb vessels and fireships should be withdrawn from Quiberon Bay.

Hawke was more concerned that Bompar's squadron would be able to get into Brest than that Conflans would get out: 'no ship can stir from any port of the enemy in the Bay'. This reinforcement for Conflans did in fact occur on 7 November, within hours of Hawke being driven off station. It being evident that Hawke was indeed off station, and that even the inshore squadron was gone, Conflans seized the opportunity to sail offered by the easing of the gale.

Hawke later reported that Conflans had got out of Brest on 14 November with four ships of 80 guns, six 74s, three 70s, eight 64s, three frigates of 36, 34 and 16 guns, and one small lookout craft. He was flying his flag on the *Soleil Royal* (80 guns), with Chef d'Escadre Chevalier Budes de Guébriant commanding the First Division, the Centre or Division Blanche, with his flag in the eighty-gun ship *L'Orient*. Chef d'Escadre Prince Louis Charles d'Aubigne de Bauffremont, a prince of the Holy Roman Empire and styled as cousin du Roi, flew his on *Tonnant* (80 guns) in the Second Division, the Division Blanche et Bleue, which would be the van in the line of battle. The Third Division, the rear, Division Bleue, was commanded by Chef d'Escadre Saint-André du Verger flying his flag on *Formidable* (80 guns).[94] Among his captains were to be found such famous names as that of Bigot de Morogues,

131

who had been chosen as the first director of the Académie Marine when it was founded in 1752, and was now in command of *Magnifique* of seventy-four guns. *Thésée* of seventy-four guns was commanded by Guy Francois de Coëtnempren, Comte de Kersaint, a Breton who had distinguished himself in the East Indies in the War of the Austrian Succession. He was the father of Armand Guy Simon de Coëtnempren, who was to play a notable part in the French Revolution, as a moderate, for which he was eventually executed. Wolters's agent in Brest reported that the fleet only had stores for three months on board when it sailed, but that it had been reinforced with men from Bompard's squadron, and had taken on board Dunkirk pilots.[95]

According to an account by a French traveller, the Duke of Newcastle was worried about letting the fleet continue its operations before Brest in the worsening weather, and called on Pitt, who was in bed suffering from gout. But Pitt was 'positively determined the fleet shall sail'.[96] Hawke was able to depart from Torbay on 12 November but was driven back. *Dunkirk*, *Intrepid* and a cutter were driven into Torbay on 13 November, leaving Brest unwatched, but Hawke ordered *Actaeon* commanded by Captain Ourry, fresh out of Plymouth, to sail immediately for Brest. Hawke himself stood back out to sea on 14 November when the wind came fair. In a move he afterwards regretted, he left Geary to take his sick into the primitive medical services at Plymouth, and he shifted his flag to *Royal George* because *Ramillies* was leaking badly when working in heavy weather. She too was sent into Plymouth. Two days later, 16 November, when approaching Ushant, he dispatched *Fortune* with orders to Captain Duff to leave only four frigates, two fireships and the bombs in Quiberon Bay, with three frigates watching Port Louis, while he cruised with the rest of his ships off Belle Île. But that evening a victualler returning from Quiberon brought him the news that Conflans had sailed the Brest fleet, and that *Swallow* and *Juno* had run for Quiberon to warn Duff 'that the French fleet was in sight, consisting of eighteen sail of the line and three frigates'. 'I have carried a pressure of sail all night,' Hawke hastily advised the Admiralty, 'with a hard gale at SSE, in pursuit of the enemy and make no doubt of coming up with them either at sea or in Quiberon Bay.'

Juno had in fact been chased by Conflans, but had outrun his ships and encountered *Swallow* escorting the victualler convoy. *Swallow* carried a warning to *Firm* off Port Louis on 17 November, and Captain Reynolds ordered Captain Gamaliel Nightingale commanding *Vengeance* to proceed to Quiberon to warn Duff. Captain Ourry had brought *Actaeon* on to its station outside Brest just in time to see Conflans coming out, and he dispatched a cutter to warn Hawke.[97] *Juno* tried to find Hawke off Ushant, but speaking with *Actaeon*, she proceeded to Plymouth. Hawke sent orders to Geary to meet him at the Ushant rendezvous with all the ships he could collect, but Geary first heard that Conflans was at sea from *Juno*.[98]

Sailing again in the afternoon of 18 November, *Juno* encountered off the Lizard the next day Vice Admiral Saunders, who had departed the St Lawrence on 18 October after the fall of Quebec. On hearing the French were out, Saunders steered to join Hawke, sending a message to Pitt informing him.[99] This procedure was at the heart of Britain's naval defence: admirals and even captains were expected to, and did, act on their initiative with the highest priority given to defence of England. But before he could find the Channel Fleet, Saunders learned that the battle had been fought and won.

Chapter Six

The Battle of Quiberon Bay

La Clue's defeat at Lagos had no direct effect on French plans, because Conflans was not expecting the Toulon ships to be added to his fleet, but there was concern that Boscawen's squadron would join the British Channel Fleet. Even though in the end they were sent into harbour and put into dockyard hands, their arrival in home waters did reduce the already slender chance of Conflans being able to escort the landing craft from Le Havre to Ostend and then to Malden. With the advantage of retrospect, it is clear that the odds were so strongly against successfully carrying out the planned invasion that it should have been cancelled. Conflans was informed that the ships sheltering in Cadiz under the command of the senior captain, de Castillon, were given orders to head to an Atlantic port when they could, but in fact they were not to escape Brodrick's blockade until January 1760, when they successfully returned to Toulon.[1]

But cancellation of the operation would have been devastating to French credit, and have ended all hope of diverting British potential from America and India. Even an unsuccessful or incomplete invasion effort could provide relief for the French and Canadian army at Montreal. Consequently the Duc d'Aiguillon had been sent his final orders on 15 September, a modification of plan 'C' that put him at liberty to effect a landing on either side of Scotland, or if that proved impossible, to land in Ireland. He had wanted to limit the close escort of the Scottish invasion force to six ships under Morogues' command, while Conflans' reduced force, bulked out with merchantmen and as many frigates as could be found, trailed its coat off the Breton coast to draw off the British Channel Fleet. Louis XV's sailing orders prepared on 27 August made that arrangement, but Conflans later persuaded Berryer not to divide the already inadequate force under his command, tasked as it was with escorting the main invasion fleet from Flanders to Maldon. In the middle of October he received his orders to attempt to fight his way out of Brest, and then to proceed to Quiberon Bay to collect the transports, which he was to see safely on their way. If he then decided to return himself to Brest, he was to detach six ships to escort the invasion force. '*Je vous prescris seulement de ne point perdre de vue que le point principal de toutes nos opérations présentes doit être la plus grande sûreté de la flotte du Morbihan*':[2] his first duty was to ensure the safety of the invasion force. Before he actually put to sea, Conflans informed d'Aiguillon and Berryer that he intended to avoid combat with Hawke, and concentrate on dealing with the cruisers in Quiberon Bay.[3]

On 15 October the Franco-Irish smuggler Thurot managed to escape from Dunkirk in *Le Marechal Belleisle* of forty-eight guns with four privateer frigates and two smaller craft. Embarked were 1,370 volunteer drafts from regular regiments, commanded by Le Comte de Kersalls. Evading the pursuit of Commodore Boys, Thurot sailed north to Gothenburg and Bergen before rounding Scotland. With only three of his original five frigates he arrived on 21 February 1760 at Carrickfergus on the north side of Belfast Lough, and put the soldiers ashore, where they attacked and defeated the garrison at the cost of fifty men. 'The remonstrances of the English ministry had operated so little on the administration in Ireland', commented Horace Walpole in *Memoirs of King George II*, 'that Carrickfergus, though seated in the heart of the Protestant interest, where arms might securely have been trusted, was found by Thurot totally unguarded and unprovided.' Not quite, but again according to Walpole, the garrison was only seventy-two men commanded by Lieutenant Colonel Jennings, 'a man formed for a hero, for he had great bravery and a small portion of sense'.[4] Once out of ammunition, the garrison was reduced to throwing bricks worked out of the walls. Four months after the French defeat in Quiberon Bay, this effort was no longer a useful diversion. After getting provisions and fresh water on board, which Walpole says was Thurot's main objective, the troops were re-embarked on Tuesday 26 February. They were intercepted on their way back to France by a squadron of three frigates commanded by Captain Elliott in HMS *Aeolus*, and all were captured. The guns of the Royal Navy wreaked havoc in the privateers crammed with soldiers, and for a cost of four British dead and fifteen injured, the French lost three hundred, including Captain Thurot killed. Several dreadful songs, including one in Manx and another recorded by John Wesley, were written to commemorate the Battle of Ramsay.[5] This disappointing outcome, however, could not be anticipated at Versailles, and did not influence the French master plan.

The problems for Conflans were overwhelming. Due to the British sweep of French merchantmen before the declaration of war in 1755, the typhus epidemic, captures during the war and the failure to pay those sailors who were inscripted into naval service and who in consequence found ways to desert, in May 1759 complements at Brest were short of 3,507 petty officers and able seamen.[6] Compliments of Brest ships were necessarily filled with untrained sailors and the Brittany coastguard troops. Two days before the arrival of Bompar's squadron, on 5 November, a small squadron including the French *Achille* (64 guns) and two frigates that had been cruising in the south Atlantic under the command of Monsieur de la Marnière had managed to get into Brest. The seasoned sailors from the two weather-worn squadrons were offered a bonus to transfer into the ships of the Brest fleet.[7] Nevertheless, Chef d'Escadre Guébriant had so few seamen on board his flagship that he was only able to work *Orient* through the Goulet on leaving Brest by making his officers handle the sails.[8] The final muster of the Brest fleet was of 7,100 professional seamen, with 1,500 marines, 1,700 soldiers and 2,700 coastguards.[9] Lieutenant Thompson was to characterize the French officers as rendered incapable by seasickness, after their long wait safely in harbour.[10]

When writing about Captain Keppel's difficulties blockading Brest in 1761, Sir Julian Corbett was to express the view that they had 'proved, as was to be shown so often in the future, how weak a form of war is a prolonged close blockade; how the wear and tear of ships, and the consequent loss of speed and endurance ...

inevitably gives the enemy his chance sooner or later ... For permanent command it must always be doubtful whether it can compare with an open blockade conducted from a good interior position by a fleet that can retain its speed and fitness for action, without the demoralisation of absolute inactivity.'[11] But Corbett was at the time preoccupied with the question of the deployment of the Grand Fleet should war occur with Germany, and his mind was really on the limitations of steam-powered Dreadnaught and pre-Dreadnaught battleships. Hawke had managed to keep his ships reasonably clean by rotating them into harbour, and his crews, although worn by incessant labour, had become highly effective at sail handling, deck and gunnery drill, in all weather. Conflans' crews could not compete with them, and even if they had been able to, it is never satisfactory to work up ships with new crews while actually engaged in operations. Although Brest Roads is spacious, the training Conflans could give his crews without taking them out to sea was limited. And what was true before the mast was also true on the quarterdeck. Morogues was not alone in noting the pessimism amongst senior naval officers.[12]

When Conflans sailed on 14 November he was 200 miles ahead of Hawke, and had only 120 miles to go to bring Duff's command of frigates into a very unequal action, but Conflans was unlucky with his winds which now headed him, sometimes strongly, and his inexperienced crews were not skilful at beating. Because of their limitations, he did not risk the short route into the Bay through the Raz de Sein, and stood south and west until he cleared the shoals and islands extending from the Île de Saintes. On 15 November he was only about thirty miles from Belle Île, but it was to take until dawn on 20 November before he brought his enemy into sight, and by then he had to face the full power of the British Channel Fleet. He was to be censured by French historians for his slow progress, but Corbett was 'doubtful whether the accusation is just ... Hawke, with all his skill as a seaman and his highly trained and homogeneous fleet, had been able to do little better, but being well to northward of his destination the northerly winds had lost him nothing, and he had been able to gain a day on his adversary.'[13]

* * *

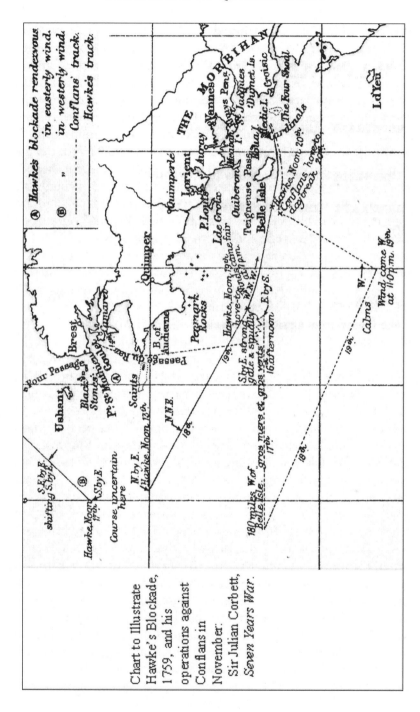

Chart to Illustrate
Hawke's Blockade,
1759, and his
operations against
Conflans in
November.
Sir Julian Corbett,
Seven Years War.

While working her way towards Belle Île to warn Commodore Duff of the French approach, *Vengeance* had several sightings of Conflans' fleet. In the dark hours early on 19 November Captain Nightingale was obliged to heave to so as not to endanger his ship in the approaches to Belle Île, but he came into sight of the blockade force in Quiberon Bay at 10.00 am and 'made the signal of seeing an enemy of superior force, and fired minute guns'. It was three more hours, however, before Duff 'saw a ship off the Teignouse Passage firing guns and making the signal of an enemy'. Hastily cutting their cables, Duff's squadron passed through the passage and then stood southward towards the sea. At 7.00 am *Vengeance* met Duff's *Rochester* north of Belle Île, and Nightingale went on board to report that the Brest fleet was out.[14] The squadron then proceeded to seaward of Belle Île, and at 7.00 am on 20 November sighted a fleet to windward. Uncertain whether it was the Channel Fleet, they bore up, but on discovering that it was the French, turned away and cracked on sail.

The wind being north-west, Conflans decided to attack them, signalling 'close on the general' (the usual dawn signal), 'clear for action', 'pay attention to battle signals', 'prepare for action' and 'general chase'. When Conflans saw Duff's force splitting up he sent his Second Division, or van, after one part, took his centre First Division after the other and left his rear close-hauled to observe some distant ships seen to be approaching. In his action report, Conflans said that *Tonnant* was within hailing distance and that he shouted his intention '*à poursuivre vivement les ennemis, à les faire attaquer sans ordre, puisqu'ils étaient en aussi petit nombre, et je m'abandonnai moi-même sur celui qui me parut le plus gros*' – to fight without attempting to form line of battle against the small number of the enemy, and to deal himself with the largest of the British ships.[15] One of the French seventy-fours was gaining on the *Rochester*, but when the fleet to windward was discovered to be Hawke's, Conflans at once signalled his whole fleet to 'abandon chase', 'close', 'order of sailing in a single line', 'pay attention to battle signals' and 'prepare for action'. He then took station at the head of his line and steered for the southern entrance to the bay, which lay roughly east-north-east of him. The wind was now west-north-west, but backing to west-south-west. This was an organized retreat, not a flight.

Hawke reported that Conflans governed his sails by those the least capable ship could carry, so that the French force could keep together.

In his orders of the day on leaving Brest, Conflans had informed his captains that he intended to fight from the windward side, at musket-shot range. If the enemy had the advantage of the wind, he intended to form line to leeward, and then employ the tactic Byng had attempted at Minorca, of an oblique approach that would enable all ships to engage the enemy line. He even indicated that, on the signal being given, he might want all his ships to attempt to board their opposite number. Corbett wondered whether Conflans issued this order simply to put heart into his captains, but at any rate, the circumstances now facing the French fleet made the matter moot. To starboard, between Conflans and Le Croisic lay the Four shoal, and to port between him and the Île Hoedic an irregular scattering of sharp-toothed rocky islets, known as Les Cardinaux. Conflans calculated that once inside the bay he could haul his wind and use the local knowledge of his pilots and masters to assume a strong defensive position protected by rocks and shoals. Should Hawke dare to follow, he wrote in his action report, he had only to shift his own position to the centre of the centre squadron to put his fleet in 'the natural order of battle'. '*Voici le plan que je me faisais, et vous en jugerez vous-même, monsieur, en l'appliquant sur une carte.*'[16]

Conflans had prepared for the campaign of 1759 by issuing a volume of signals that Brian Tunstall, who made a lifetime study of naval tactics under sail and whose collection of signal books is now part of the archive at the National Maritime Museum at Greenwich, characterized as amounting to a series of textbooks for a course of instruction rather than to a conveniently arranged guide for action.[17] In the first part of the book a standard format was employed with vertical columns for the intended order to the left of the page, the signal in the middle, and Conflans' additional explanations on the right. The signals are divided into groups, each headed by a general order, plan or advice. In the last part of the book were twenty-three tactical diagrams. The flags he used to convey his orders were of his own design – forty-four flags and three *flames*, six with saltire bands, six of plain colours with a border, six stripped, and eight with crosses. He reserved flags containing only red white and/or blue for signals directed to the entire fleet, and used flags with any of those colours with the addition of yellow for signals by private ships. As was still the universal practice at the time, the location in the rigging in which the flags were flown affected their meaning. For day signals, under sail, Conflans used the foretopmasthead for chasing signals, the mizzen topmasthead for navigational signals, and the ensign staff for non-navigational signals.

Tunstall believed that a great deal could be learned from this volume about Conflans' tactical system. Half a cable was his standard distance between ships in line of battle, weather permitting. No ship was permitted to quit or disorder the line unless disabled, in which case she was to be assisted by ships not in the line. Ships were not to open fire until at point-blank range. If the enemy tried to break the line from leeward, ships at the threatened point were to close up so that the enemy was obliged to run aboard and foul one or more. If the enemy were out-numbered, his van might be doubled from windward or leeward. If the fleet was to windward, and presumably if the attack were launched from windward, the overlapping ships of the French van were to pass to leeward of the enemy van, and then put about in succession so as to regain their original course, now parallel with the enemy van. The leading ships were to shorten sail until the whole detachment was properly formed in line. Meanwhile, these detached ships should not approach too close to the enemy because of the danger of being hit by gunfire from ships on the enemy's windward side, or of hitting them. The mere presence of the detachment was considered sufficient to worry the enemy and make it possible to cut off the retreat of any of his ships driven to leeward. In the meantime the detached ships were expected to attack the enemy frigates, fireships and storeships stationed on the unengaged side.

If the enemy were to windward, Conflans wanted the French van to crowd sail so as to be sure of weathering them, and then to put about together, thus coming on a parallel course with the enemy's van, and attack their frigates, fireships and storeships. To avoid the danger of the enemy doubling the French van from windward, the French van was to attack the enemy's as they came round, ship for ship. To double the enemy's rear from windward, the overlapping ships were required to pass as close as possible across the stern of the enemy's rearmost ship and crowd sail so as to draw up level with them on their leeward side. To double from leeward, the ships had to tack and pass the enemy's rear in bow and quarter line. Once to windward, they could tack again and crowd sail to draw up level.

He retained the system traditionally used in the French navy, but not in the British until much later, by which the order of sailing was the same as the line of battle, with the exception that the admiral's flagship led the fleet in order of sailing but commanded from the centre in battle. He provided for the fleet sailing in two or three columns, and then described carefully the by-then standard orders of sailing in line, line of bearing and wedge. He laid great emphasis on precise execution of evolutions and correct station-keeping, and in the traditions of the French Marine, emphasis is placed on mathematical models.

Tunstall commented that the mere recital of these recommendations raised the image of an accommodating and docile enemy. But, he continued, Conflans' combat signals 'show a great deal of tactical sophistication'. It was innovative, for instance, to include a signal for requesting advice from scouting frigates about the nature of the enemy fleet in sight, and among the night signals were those to prepare for and to commence night action against the enemy. Nevertheless, it is hard to imagine anything more different than the tactical ideas of the two enemy commanders: Hawke's emphasis on closing the French and engaging them closely depended on superiority in gunnery, morale and mutual support, while Conflans' depended on disciplined formations.

Conflans was not the only tactician in the French fleet. Bigot de Morogues would later publish a highly regarded book, *Tactique Navale ou Traité des Evolutions et des Signaux*, in 1763 with the imprimatur of the Académie Royale des Sciences. This provided a complete system of tactics and signals together with all the theoretical, explanatory and administrative guidance necessary to make the system effective, but Tunstall believed that Morogues's experience at Quiberon Bay reinforced a natural tendency to emphasize defensive tactics.[18]

* * *

'Concluding that their first rendezvous would be Quiberon,' Hawke reported, 'the instant I received the intelligence [of their sailing] I directed my course thither [towards Quiberon Bay] with a pressed sail. At first the wind, blowing hard at S by E and S, drove us considerably to the westward; but on the 18th and 19th, though variable, it proved more favourable.' Between 3.00 and 7.00 am the fleet was hove to in order to avoid closing Belle Île in the dark. Two frigates had joined, *Maidstone* (28 guns) under Captain Dudley Digges, and *Coventry* (28 guns) under Captain Francis Burslem, and Hawke now ordered them to scout ahead on the starboard and port bows. Sunrise that day was at 7.30, and 'at 1/2 past 8 o'clock in the morning of the 20th, Belle Île by our reckoning bearing E by N 1/4 N, the *Maidstone* made the signal for seeing a fleet'. Hawke signalled to form line abreast at two cables intervals in order to concentrate his force. He had earlier sent *Magnanime* under Captain Lord Howe ahead to find the land, and at 9.45 she too signalled she had sighted the enemy. With their bows plunging into the steep swell, ships beat to quarters, clearing away the bulkheads below decks that impeded the recoil of guns and would be turned to splinters by enemy shot. In the orlop decks, surgeons set up their tables and laid out their instruments.[19]

Seeing that the French were seeking to avoid action, he then signalled for 'general chase' and fired three guns, Anson's and his 1747 additional signal (Article 9): 'I threw out the signal for the seven ships nearest to them to chase and draw into a line of battle ahead of me and endeavour to stop them till the rest of the squadron should come up, who were also to form as they chased, that no time might be lost in the pursuit.' The chase signal also applied to the rest of the fleet, and Hawke was to keep it flying the entire day despite winds rising to forty nmph. While Conflans was ensuring that his fleet kept together, Hawke was prepared to risk the disintegration of this fleet if he could only get into action: 'Monsieur Conflans kept going off under such sail as all his squadron could carry and at the same time keep together, while we crowded after him with every sail our ships could bear.' At about 11.00 am Captain Duff was able to join the flag with *Rochester, Chatham, Portland, Falkland, Minerva, Vengeance* and *Venus.* At 2.30 pm Hawke heard firing ahead, and made the signal to engage the enemy. 'We were then to the southward of Belle Isle,' Hawke reported, 'and the French admiral, headmost, soon after led round the Cardinals while his rear was in action.'

Two letters that Hawke was to write in the last year of his life give a clear statement of his tactical thinking, although of course with the benefit of hindsight. On 6 June 1780 he wrote to his old friend Geary, who had succeeded to commander in chief in the Channel. Hawke urged him to take the fleet to the 'old station off Brest ... When you are there, watch those fellows as close as a cat watches a mouse; and if you once have the fortune to get up with them make much of them, and don't part with them easily.' Two and a half months later he wrote again: 'for God's sake, if you should be so lucky as to get sight of the enemy, get as close to them as possible. Do not let them shuffle with you by engaging at a distance, but get within musket-shot if you can; that will be the best way to gain great honour, and will be the means to make the action decisive. By doing this you will put it out of the power of any of the brawlers to find fault.'[20]

'Sir Edward Hawke gave the general signal for chase;' Lieutenant Thompson wrote, 'when all, with equal emulation seem'd to start for the lillies of France. At half an hour past noon, Sir John Bentley in the *Warspite* began the action, – but – at too great a distance – when Mr. Denis in the *Dorsetshire* passed on, reserving his fire tho' continually cannonaded by the whole fleet.'[21] Captain Sir Thomas Stanhope commanding *Swiftsure* of seventy guns believed that the French fleet was not 'formed into any regular order, and by their motions seemingly confused'.[22] However, Hawke's report that Conflans kept his fleet together indicates that any confusion was not more than might have been expected in the circumstances of wind and weather, and probably did not exceed the confusion in the British fleet.

Hawke's formal order of battle placed Captain Duff, in *Rochester*, in a position of great responsibility leading the frigates. The van division was commanded by Rear Admiral Hardy flying his flag in *Union* (90 guns) under the command of Captain Evans. Hawke's flagship, *Royal George* (100 guns), was commanded by Captain John Campbell, who had been pressed into the navy and had like Keppel been one of Anson's midshipmen during his circumnavigation. Campbell and Keppel's shared experience had established a close friendship. Campbell had served under Hawke in both the Rochefort and Basque Roads expeditions, and had been in command of *Essex* (64 guns) during Hawke's watch at Brest. He had found time during the blockade to engage in an experiment with the Astronomer Royal, James Bradley, that led to the development of the technique of navigation by lunar distances. He was also instrumental in the invention of the sextant. When the admiral was forced to move into the *Royal George* he appointed Campbell to be his flag captain. In the absence of Rear Admiral Geary, the rear division was commanded by James Young in *Mars* (74 guns), flying a commodore's broad pendant. Hawke had ordered the rear squadron fly the red ensign so there would be no confusion with the French white fleur-de-lys.[23]

Under their command there were twenty-three ships of the line, including Hawke's flagship of 100 guns, three of 90 guns, including the *Namur*, which was a private ship commanded by Captain Buckle, seven 74-gun ships, five 70s, two 64s and five 60s. *Dorsetshire* of seventy guns, the first ship into action, was commanded by Peter Denis, another who had served under Anson in the circumnavigation, as a lieutenant. He had later taken part in Anson's action off Finisterre with de la Jonquière, and was entrusted with Anson's battle report, which was always an indication of approval and could lead to a knighthood. He had commanded *Namur* during the 1757 Rochefort expedition. Captain Henry Speke, commanding *Resolution* of seventy-four guns, had been Vice Admiral Charles Watson's flag captain in the East Indies Squadron in 1756–57; Captain Austin Storr commanding *Revenge* of sixty-four guns had captured *Orphée* in 1758 when la Clue had been forced to take the French Toulon fleet into Spanish Cartagena; and Captain George Edgcumbe, commanding *Lancaster* of sixty-six guns, had taken part in the capture of Louisbourg the previous year, and been entrusted with Boscawen's dispatches reporting the victory.[24] As a chase action, in which the only tactical signals made by Hawke were the chase signal, with the gun signal to the leading seven ships, and that to engage, the order in which ships came into action depended entirely upon how recently they had been cleaned, their maximum speed when well handled, and the skill of their captains.[25]

In his action report, Conflans said that his intention was to get his fleet into the bay and there form a line of battle along the western shore.[26] He said that the reason he retained his position in the van, rather than use the firepower of *Soleil Royal* to cover the retreat of the smaller ships, was the need to lead the fleet to a defensible anchorage. In Corbett's opinion, 'seeing how the French ships were manned, and how great an advantage Hawke's seasoned fleet would have in an engagement in the open on a lee shore and in boisterous weather, it is difficult to say he was not right in assuming the defensive ... Nothing really could be more correct. If he had turned and, with everything against him, had fought Hawke, no good could have come of it, even if he had sacrificed his own fleet to put Hawke's out of action.'[27] From his listening post at The Hague, Yorke was to write to his sister, Anson's wife, that he could not 'help thinking the French if they have it in their power will avoid an action, tho' they will make a scandalous figure in the Eyes of Europe, if they skulk into some Bay, as if they were beat'.[28] But Conflans was not given the opportunity. He had never imagined that the British would carry such a press of sail under such dangerous conditions, with the light of the winter afternoon dimming in the squalls. *Magnanime* and the *Royal George* had even set their topgallant sails.[29] Despite having spent the summer at sea, in all conditions, even the British were not fully in control of their ships, and their onset was overwhelming: '*les ennemis entraient eux-mèmes dans la baie pèle-mèle avec les derniers de nos vaisseaux, dont plusiers étaient enveloppés*'.[30]

The French retreat was not without its share of professional heroism. While Conflans led his fleet past the Cardinals, the rear commanded by St Andre du Verger had spread into a rough inverted 'V' formation due to faster ships passing those less able to keep up. Although not intentional, this formation had strong defensive capabilities, threatening leading British ships with being engaged on both sides. *Magnifique*, commanded by Bigot de Morogues, was in the extreme end of the line, with *Héros* ahead of him, and St Andre du Verger's flagship *Formidable* on the port beam of *Orient* and *Bizarre* to starboard. Not content with this disposition, St Andre du Verger swung *Formidable* broadside

147

against the British advance, to buy time for the rest of the French fleet to enter the bay.

With the wind at west-south-west it might have been possible for Conflans to have carried out his intention and taken up a defensive line at anchor under Quiberon Point even when closely engaged, but now the wind suddenly veered back to west-north-west and freshened. He was forced to continue to steer north-easterly towards the Vilaine estuary in the extreme north-eastern corner of the bay, beyond Le Croisic harbour north of the mouth of the Loire. In the increasingly confined waters, the movement of the French fleet became congested, and Conflans ordered it to wear in succession, to break out towards the south-west. The result was a chaos of plunging ships and thundering canvas.[31]

'At half-past two', noted Captain Stanhope, the *Magnanime*, *Torbay*, *Dorsetshire*, *Resolution*, *Warspite*, *Swiftsure*, *Revenge*, *Montague* and *Defiance* 'in a close body, but not in any formed line' were almost within gunshot of the French rear.[32] 'Lord Howe, in the *Magnanime*,' wrote Patrick Renny, MD, surgeon of the frigate *Coventry*, 'had led the chase the greatest part of the day,' even though she had carried away her main topgallant yard at 11.00 am and taken an hour to replace it. A very severe rain squall at 3.17 pm from the north brought *Magnanime*, *Montague* and *Warspite*, the three leading British ships, into collision. They managed to clear each other after *Montague* dropped her best bower anchor, and rounded to in twelve fathoms, but *Montague* suffered considerable damage, and the pursuit was delayed. *Dorsetshire* came close to foundering when the squall heeled her over so far water poured into her leeward gun ports. She had to luff up, but quickly regained control. *Magnanime*, Renny continued, 'was now passed by Sir Peter Denis in the *Dorsetshire* and Captain Patrick Baird in the old *Defiance*, who ran along the French line to windward, receiving the fire of every ship that passed without making any return, intending to stop and engage the van of the enemy. Lord Howe followed in the same glorious career, but coming abreast of the Rear Admiral in the *Formidable* was disabled from going further, his foreyard being carried away in the slings. He immediately bore down upon the rear admiral.'[33] In this kind of fighting, the initiative of individual captains and British superiority in firepower and manoeuvre was decisive.

Coventry's surgeon wrote that *Formidable*'s starboard side 'was pierced like a cullender by the number of shot she received in the course of the action'. Du Verger was first wounded and then killed, as were his brother and the ship's second captain. At about 4.00 pm *Torbay* silenced her with two broadsides, and left her to strike her colours to *Resolution*.[34]

In 1747 Captain Keppel had lost his ship near this spot and had briefly been a prisoner of war, but that did not make him shy. 'In the heat of the action,' the *Naval Chronicle* later wrote, 'after having silenced one of the enemy's line of battle ships, he suddenly wore his own ship round, and engaged the *Thesée*, of 74 guns, yard-arm to yard-arm, with such impetuous fury, that he sunk her in half an hour, and the greatest part of her crew perished.'[35] A good part of the fury, however, was from the elements, and *Torbay* should only be credited with an assist. A squall heeled *Thesée* over so suddenly that she foundered from water flooding into her leeward gun ports. *Torbay*, also of seventy-four guns, almost suffered the same fate. Her master wrote in his log that 'at this time We Received so much Water in at our Lee Ports, that we were obliged to fling the Ship up the Wind and She went Round, & soon after the *Defiance*, *Revenge*, *Magnanime*, and *Swiftsure* came up.'[36] Keppel ordered *Torbay*'s boats hoisted out to rescue as many of the French as they could, but in the circumstances it is not surprising that only twenty-two French sailors were pulled from the water. Captain Kersaint was not among the survivors.[37]

Conflans in the *Soleil Royal* tried to lead his fleet out to sea again before it fell dark, and this brought him into action with *Swiftsure* and *Royal George*, which had rounded the Cardinals into the bay at 3.55 pm. 'On the slightest inspection of the chart,' wrote the editor of the *Annual Register*, 'it will appear, that all this sea is sown thick with sands and shoals, and shallows and rocks; our pilots were by no means well acquainted with it; and the wind blew little less than a violent storm, and the waves ran mountain high. In these circumstances they were to attack a very strong squadron of the enemy on their own coast, with which they were perfectly acquainted.'[38] According to this account, the master of the *Royal George* warned Hawke against entering Quiberon Bay, but was answered, 'You have done your duty in

149

this remonstrance; now obey my orders, and lay me alongside the French admiral.' The new moon had been 19 November, so the force of the ebb tide that had started to run at 2.47 pm would have been strong. But the danger was less than it would have been on a flood tide. On the ebb, wind and tide were running together in a south-west or west-south-west direction. Although there would still be a confused sea, the worst conditions form when wind and tide are in different directions. The danger that ships entering the bay would be drawn on to the rocks was less during ebb tide, the breaking water provided some guide to their location, and Hawke counted on using the movements of the enemy to show him the channels.[39]

'At 35 minutes after 4', it was noted in *Royal George*'s captain's log, 'we got up with 4 sail of the enemy ships who all wore and gave us their broadsides; we then began to engage.' Captain Montalais tried to protect the flag by bringing *Superbe* of seventy guns between *Soleil Royal* and *Royal George*.[40] At the second broadside, at 4.41 pm, she was sunk, but Admiral Philip Patton, in his 'Strictures on Naval Discipline and the Conduct of a Ship of War', wrote that *Superbe*, like *Thesée*, was a victim of a squall. They were sunk, he wrote, 'entirely by a want of dexterity in hauling in the guns, and letting down the ports of the lower deck; by which, not only the ships, but about 1500 men, perished in a few minutes. I was myself an eye-witness of this disaster, which has, in many accounts of the action, been erroneously attributed to the fire of the British fleet.'[41] A great many who were drowned were the Breton coastguards, whose normal life consisted of keeping watch from the coastal path and intercepting smugglers. Hawke's chaplain remarked that 'The *Royal George*s gave a cheer, but it was a faint one; the honest sailors were touched at the miserable state of so many hundreds of poor creatures.'[42] Captain Casteloger then interposed *Intrepide* to protect *Soleil Royal*, which in turning to avoid being raked fell away to leeward. Trying to wear around to weather the Four shoal, she collided heavily with *Tonnant* flying de Bauffremont's flag, and another ship following her, and *Soleil Royal* was forced to run to leeward of the shoal into Croisic Road.[43]

At about 5.00 pm *Héros* (74 guns), with four hundred of her crew killed or wounded, struck to *Magnanime*. 'Finding ourselves then very near the shore,' Howe entered into *Magnanime*'s log, 'anchored in 15 fathom water south-west, about three miles distance, from the Isle Dument [sic], causing the prize to do the same ... But a great part of the enemy's van making off from our fleet under favour of the approaching night, by passing near on each side of the prize rendered it unsafe to send a boat on board.' Bad weather later in the evening prevented boat work, and this gave *Héros* the opportunity to rehoist her colours and slip away in the night, although only to strand herself.[44] 'Night was now come and, being on a part of the coast among islands and shoals of which we were totally ignorant, without a pilot, as was the greatest part of the squadron, and blowing hard upon a lee shore,' Hawke reported, 'I made the signal to anchor and came to in fifteen fathom water, the Island of Dumet [in the Vilaine estuary] bearing E by N between two and three miles, the Cardinals W 1/2 S, and the steeples of Croisic SE, as we found next morning.' Captain Digby of *Dunkirk* noted that Hawke hauled down the signal to engage at 5.30 pm, over an hour after sunset and at the middle of the ebb tide.[45] The signal to anchor, two guns, was not understood by all the British ships, and *Dorsetshire*, *Revenge*, *Defiance* and *Swiftsure* did not anchor, but stood out to sea despite the damage they had suffered.

Conflans also hauled down the signal for engaging at 5.30 pm and anchored *Soleil Royal* to avoid running on to the rocks between the Four shoal and the land, not aware that he was alone in the middle of the British fleet that was also anchoring.[46] Nine French ships, including the flagships of de Bauffremont and Budes de Guébriant, were able to weather the Four shoal west of Le Croisic, and escape out to sea. Bauffremont came in for a great deal of criticism for his departure, without signalling the ships under his command that he was doing so. In the dark no one really knew what was happening. Bauffremont said in his report that he had wanted to follow the track taken by *Soleil Royal* before it had been lost to sight, but that his pilot had warned him he would certainly run aground. He said he expected that Conflans would be given the same advice by his pilots, and would be found at Rochefort when he arrived. *Northumberland* arrived in Basque Roads six hours before Bauffremont did in *Tonnant*, and *L'Intrépide* arrived twenty-four hours later having spent the night between Le Croisic and Le Pouliguen north of the Loire. The rest of the ships that eventually met there were from the First Division, de Guébriant's own *Orient*, *Dauphin Royal* and *Solitaire*, and from St André's Third Division, Bigot de Morogues' *Magnifique* and the Prince de Montbazon's *Bizarre*.[47]

Seven of the French fleet were unable to beat out of the bay and were driven into the estuary of the Vilaine. In the *Petite Neptune François*, published in 1761 but based on an earlier work by George Boissaye Du Bocage, was given a description of the difficulties of the approach to the river: 'From the Cardinals to the entrance of the said river the course is about 6 leagues to the north east. But you must steer around the Isle of Dumet lying between them and running into a number of sandy points, which strike into the sea about a quarter of a league, and require tacking about. The ordinary passage is to the West of this Isle, and the Western side of the Entrance of this River is always taken on account of its cleanness. And then you steer a cable's length off the land, or further if you think fit, 'til you have the River open, after which you enter through the middle of the channel, for there are Rocks on the Eastern side of the Entrance of this River: when you got within these Rocks, you may anchor, or else run aground.' At neap tide there would be a minimum depth of nine or ten feet of water in the mouth of the river, but considerably less at spring tide. 'Tho' I give directions for entering those Rivers,' cautioned the author, 'I would not advise any person to enter without the assistance of a pilot.'[48]

'Nothing could be conceived more dreadful than the night which succeeded this action,' wrote the *Annual Register*. 'A violent storm blew all night long. It was a pitchy darkness; a dangerous coast surrounded them on almost all sides. A continual firing of distress guns was heard, without knowing whether they came from friend or enemy; and on account of the badness of the coast and the darkness of the night, our people were equally unable to venture to their assistance.' Hawke's own account was briefer, but to the same point: 'In the night we heard many guns of distress fired; but blowing hard, want of knowledge of the coast, and whether they were fired by a friend or an enemy, prevented all means of relief.'

When dawn broke, Conflans saw the British fleet anchored to windward, and only one other French ship, *Héros*. He ordered

Soleil Royal's cable cut, and took the shortest route to the little port of Croisic: '*le plus près possible du Croisic*'. Conflans has been severely criticized by French authors for losing control, and in the words of Lacour-Guyet, for '*indécision perpétuelle*': having been slow to exit Brest, he chased his enemy, then sought refuge in the Morbihan, and finally tried to escape out to sea.[49] Certainly, this last act was one of despair. Croisic was not a deep-water harbour, and neither was it strongly defended. The description in the *Petite Neptune François* leaves no doubt about the matter: 'The entrance to Croisic is extremely difficult, both on account of the Multitude of rocks that block up the whole Haven, and of the great Currents inward and outward, it is no sooner High Sea than the Ebb forces you back, and one as well as the other carries you directly across the said Rocks; for which reason this harbour is very rarely visited but by small vessels; besides it is dry every tide.'[50] Had Conflans stood out to west of the Four shoal and run for Rochefort he would have been chased, but there was a chance he might have extricated his ship, and saved his reputation. The passage eastward of the Four was fouled with several small shoals, but William Price in his 1796 chart noted that the inside passage was 'the best channel into the River Loire, or Nantes'. Either course would have had some prospect of escape, but as it was, both ships were wrecked, as was the ship Hawke sent in pursuit.[51]

> By daybreak of the 21st [Hawke continued] we discovered one of our ships [the *Resolution* (74 guns)] dismasted ashore on the Four [shoal], the French *Héros* also, and the *Soleil Royal*, which under cover of the night had anchored among us, [now] cut and run ashore to the westward of Croisic. On the latter's moving, I made the *Essex*'s signal to slip and pursue her; but she unfortunately got upon the Four and both she and the *Resolution* are irrecoverably lost, notwithstanding we sent them all the assistance that the weather would permit. About fourscore of the *Resolution*'s company, in spite of the strongest remonstrances of their captain, made rafts and, with some French prisoners belonging to the *Formidable*, put off and I am afraid drove out to sea. All the *Essex*'s are saved with as many of the stores as possible, except one lieutenant and a boat's crew, who were drove on the French shore and have not since been heard of. The remains of both ships are set on fire ...

As soon as it was broad daylight in the morning of the 21st I discovered seven or eight of the enemy's line of battle ships at anchor between Point Penvins and the River Vilaine, on which I made the signal to weigh in order to work up and attack them. But it blowed so hard from the NW that, instead of daring to cast the squadron loose, I was obliged to strike topgallant masts. Most of those ships appeared to be aground at low water. But on the flood, by lightening them and the advantage of the wind under the land, all except two got that night into the River Vilaine.

The weather being moderate on the 22nd, I sent the *Portland*, *Chatham* and *Vengeance* to destroy the *Soleil Royal* and *Héros*. The French on the approach of our ships set the first on fire and soon after the latter met the same fate from our people. In the meantime, I got under way and worked up within Penvins Point, as well for sake of its being a safer road as to destroy, if possible, the two ships of the enemy which still lay without the Vilaine. But before the ships I sent ahead for that purpose could get near them, being quite light and the tide of flood they got in.

All the 23rd, we were employed in reconnoitring the entrance of that river which is very narrow and [has] only twelve foot of water on the bar at low water. We discovered at least seven, if not eight, line of battle ships about half a mile within [and] quite light, and two large frigates moored across to defend the mouth of the river. Only the frigates appear to have guns in. By the evening I had twelve longboats fitted as fireships, ready to attempt burning them under cover of the *Sapphire* and *Coventry*. But the weather being bad and the wind contrary obliged me to defer it till at least the latter should be favourable. If they can by any means be destroyed, it shall be done.

With the help of local pilots, and of the spring tide that increased the depth of water by up to sixteen feet, it had been possible over the course of 21 and 22 November for the French crews to get all the ships in the Vilaine estuary over the bar and into the safety of the river. But to do so, they had to be lightened by removing their guns, which made them vulnerable should the weather permit Hawke to mount his fireship attack. The Duc d'Aiguillon inspected them there on 23 November, and reported to Berryer that all the seven ships of the line and four frigates were undamaged. Because they were disarmed they were unfit for service, and to guard them he established batteries on the headlands at the mouth of the river. Conflans also visited the ships in the Vilaine en route to Versailles, and also took the credit for the establishment of the defensive batteries. He said in his report to Berryer that the British had already laid buoys in the estuary indicating their intention to make an attack, and that it was the intention of the senior captain, Villars de la Brosse, who commanded *Glorieux*, to move the ships further up the river into a place of greater safety. This was not approved by Berryer who wanted the ships to make their way back to Brest, and did not want any expenditure made that could be avoided. But de la Brosse viewed it as impossible to get the ships out of the river except at high water spring, or get them past the waiting British, so he defied his orders, and even established a hospital ashore for sick seamen. When he received more strongly worded orders, he assembled a council of war that collectively stated its professional agreement that an immediate return to Brest was impossible. There they were to remain for two years. On 1 January 1760 the *Inflexible* broke its mooring and was driven ashore, where its hull began to break up. As a result, Louis XV ordered that all the ships in the Vilaine should immediately be decommissioned.[52]

* * *

Tunstall remarked that by 1759 Hawke was no longer a tactical innovator. In signalling for his seven leading ships to draw into a line ahead to engage the enemy's rear, he had merely followed Anson's additional instruction of twelve years before. Nevertheless it had been enough; partly because the French could retreat no further into the bay, so that their whole fleet was involved, and partly because Hawke's captains had developed such a highly aggressive spirit through the long blockade that they did not require special signals to urge them on.[53] The conclusion of Geoffrey Marcus, who in 1960 published the first account of the battle to make detailed use of the journals of the British ships, was that the battle 'was far more a victory over the elements, indeed, than over the French. It was incomparably the finest thing of its sort in our naval history; and it established Hawke for all time in his place amongst the foremost fighting Admirals of his own or any other age.'[54]

155

Hawke's conclusion to his action report has justly become famous:

> In attacking a flying enemy it was impossible, in the space of a short winter's day, that all our ships should be able to get into action or all those of the enemy brought into it. The commanders and companies of such as did come up with the rear of the French on the 20th behaved with the greatest intrepidity and gave the strongest proofs of a true British spirit. In the same manner I am satisfied would those have acquitted themselves whose bad going ships, or the distance they were at in the morning, prevented from getting up ...
>
> When I consider the season of the year, the hard gales on the day of action, a flying enemy, the shortness of the day, and the coast they were on, I can boldly affirm that all that could possibly be done was done. As to the loss we have sustained, let it be placed to the account of the necessity I was under of running all risks to break this strong force of the enemy.[55]

For the French the action off the Cardinals, in Quiberon Bay, was a tragedy made inevitable by Hawke's precipitant onset in a full gale, the ravages of typhus, and capture of crews that had stripped the navy of trained seamen, and finally by the shift of the wind that prevented Conflans leading his fleet to a safe anchorage. Wolters's agent in Paris dispatched on 26 November a long account of the French defeat, which put an end to any immediate threat of invasion: '*Adieu l'Embarquement! En va décharges les Viasseaux du Morbian; le Duc d'Aiguillon s'est rendu au Croissic pour donner du Secours à la Marine.*'[56] With it came a report from Croissic painted in the darkest colours: '*Tout le Resumé de cette Affaire est, qu'il y a eu peu d'Obeissance et beaucoup de Valeur à la Droit; grande Confusion et Ignorance dans le Centre; at mauvaise Manoeuvre dans la Gauche; et ni Habileté ne Tête dans le tout ... Les Ennemis sont restés Sur le Champ de Bataille.*'[57] However, it would be wrong to see all of Conflans' actions in the previous twenty-four hours through the dark glass of the dismal dawn of 21 November. It could be argued that, having no time or opportunity to work up his inexperienced and seasick crews, he was fortunate to have suffered no greater losses. Had the wind not shifted and he had been able to form a defensive

156

line at anchor off the Morbihan, his reputation might have been very different.

No British ships had been lost to the enemy, but two had been lost due to grounding. The conditions had been dangerous in the extreme, and every sailor knew that the dangers of battle were small compared to the dangers of shipwreck, when few could expect to survive. The mandatory court martial on the loss of the *Resolution* clearly brought out the lack of any useful charts to British captains. The French had published a chart atlas, the *Neptune François*, in 1693, with a new edition reworked by Jacques Nicolas Bellin in 1753.[58] British naval officers were expected to provide their own navigational instruments and charts, but the *Neptune* was expensive. Captain Stanhope of *Swiftsure* possessed a copy, but it is quite likely that no one on board the *Resolution* or *Essex* did. Writing to Admiral Anson a few days after the battle, Hawke offered 'to your Lordship's judgement whether it would not be greatly for the benefit of the service to have that book correctly printed on a large scale, and translated, at the King's expense, and given to all the ships that are employed, as well as the best draughts that can be had of the different coasts in any part of the world where our ships may be sent'.[59] Two years later this need was met, to some extent, by the publication in English of Du Bocage's *Petit Flambeau de la Mer* of 1684, with corrections, and given the title of *Le petit Neptune françois: or, the French coasting pilot. Being a particular description of the ... coast of France ...* It was to be another thirty-four years, however, before an Admiralty hydrographic department was formed in August 1795, with Alexander Dalrymple appointed its first head. When John Thomas Serres was commissioned in 1800 to draw the appearance of the French coast, the book of coastal views that he subsequently published was at his own expense and for sale. He called his book *The Little Sea Torch*, to capitalize on the reputation of Du Bocage's work, which was by then more than a century old.[60]

Chapter Seven

Victory

To the professionals in Quiberon Bay, the extent of the British success was not immediately clear. *Formidable* flying the flag of the French rear admiral had been captured; *Thésée* (74 guns) and *Superbe* (70 guns) were sunk; *Soleil Royal* and *Héros* were wrecked and burned; and it was later learned that *Juste* (70 guns) had been wrecked trying to enter the Loire after both of her captains had been killed. Only 150 of her crew got safely ashore.[1] Certainly, there would be no invasion attempt launched that year. But Hawke was not content: 'Had we had but two hours more daylight, the whole had been totally destroyed or taken, for we were almost up with their van when night overtook us.'

Hawke told Anson that he had

> consulted all the young, active men of spirit in the frigates, besides others, about the enemy's ships lying in the Vilaine harbour and have made them reconnoitre them as they lie, over and over again; but am sorry to tell your Lordship that they positively assure me we can do nothing with them, either with fireships or bombs. However they will be rendered entirely useless to the enemy, as I shall keep a watch upon them to prevent anything going to or coming from them – and have reason to believe most, if not all of them, have broke their backs.

In that belief he was wrong, although *Inflexible* (64 guns) was later lost in the Vilaine. The earlier observation that the ships in the Vilaine appeared to be light, however, indicated that they must have thrown their guns into the sea in order to cross the bar into the river. At best, it would be a long task to recover them, and put them back into service.

The wounded on board the *Formidable*, their numbers 'very great & very nauseous', were put ashore to be cared for by French medical professionals, but not without an exchange of angry letters between Hawke and d'Aiguillon. Hawke insisted that the crew of *Héros*, who had surrendered their ship and then fled ashore, should be returned as prisoners of war, but d'Aiguillon correctly maintained that they had a right to try and escape as they had not given any parole. Hawke could do little about that, but he could and did hold up landing half the wounded from *Formidable* until eighty British sailors in French prisons were handed over.[2] The prize was sent into Plymouth. Lieutenant Thompson remarked on the extreme difficulty of getting her there:

> The honours we acquired by beating the French fleet, compensated for all the fatigues of an eight months' cruize, and the dangers of the battle: – but nothing can ever be equivalent to the horrors sustained in our passage home with the *Formidable*: the misfortunes and distress which afflicted the ship and crew, are not to be parallel'd: – she was often sinking from the number of shot holes received in the engagement, – dismasted by the violence of the storm, and for many hours the sport of the wind and waves: – her coppers washed away, – for want of which, her people subsisted four days on the boatswain's tallow. – When the *Dorsetshire* join'd her in this melancholy situation, – she had but ten days half allowance for 500 men, – and found herself under a necessity at that time, of assisting 1200 starved with hunger and fatigue: – but in the midst of these growing misfortunes, a favourable breeze sprung up, and brought us safely to this place.[3]

Consistent with his belief that *Héros* had surrendered and was a lawful prize, Hawke sent Captain Philip Henry Ourry with the *Actaeon* to recover the guns from the wrecks of *Héros* and *Soleil Royal*. He threatened to bombard the town if they were prevented, but the commandant at Croisic, the Marquis de Broc, refused to agree to the working party carrying out its orders, and hurriedly improved the coastal batteries. On 9 December Ourry was back with a bomb ketch, which fired into the town while the sailors recovered some of the guns, and hacked off a gilded statue of Louis XV from where it had stood on the poop of *Soleil Royal*.[4]

Keppel, with Hood commanding *Minerva*, found the rest of the French fleet sheltering in Basque Roads before Rochefort. On 2 December he reported to Hawke:

I proceeded with the squadron under my command to the southward in quest of the enemy's ships and on the 29th anchored off Aix Road. The *Minerva* joined in the evening and her captain informed me that he had stood very near the Isle of Aix and that from his mast head, over the island, he perceived seven large ships of the line, one with a flag at her fore topmast head, besides another ship that was dismasted and in tow of a small vessel. The situation of the enemy's ships, as described by Captain Hood, gave me some reason to imagine they had got up very near the mouth of the Charente.

At daybreak the following morning, I weighed with the squadron and proceeded to the Isle of Aix and, as I passed the Point, I discovered the enemy's ships as follows: three frigates and four line of battle ships close in between Fort la Pointe and Isle Madame, and three line of battle ships within Fort la Pointe. This appearance agreed exactly with Captain Hood's description excepting the dismasted ship, which I did not see. There appear four more very large and rigged [ships] as high up the Charente as the Vergeron. The situation and distance of the nearest of the enemy's ships was such as rendered it impracticable to offer an attempt upon them, they being farther up by miles than any ship can go without warping through the mud and being dismantled.[5]

Hawke suggested to the Admiralty that he be directed to leave about twelve sail of the line with three fifty-gun ships and four or five frigates as a guard on the coast from Port Louis to Rochefort, under the command of an admiral. And now that he had resources available, he sent *Sapphire*, *Aeolus* and *Coventry* to capture Île d'Yeu to interrupt French coastwise traffic. Unfortunately it was found that the wells on the island were inadequate for watering the squadron.[6]

In January Hawke informed the Admiralty that 'every plan of operation' he had formed against the ships sheltering in the Vilaine

River and at Rochefort had been defeated either by bad weather or by lack of provisions. All that was possible was the continued blockade of the coast. Difficult as it had been to provision the fleet off Brest in the summer, it was a real challenge to do so in Quiberon Bay during the winter. The bitter sailors invented a now-famous stanza to express their feelings:

> Ere Hawke did bang Monsieur Conflans
> They gave us bread and beer,
> Now Monsieur's beat we've naught to eat
> Since they have naught to fear!

Their sufferings, however, sufficed to prevent the French getting the squadron out of Rochefort until the end of the war. A convoy did escape from Bordeaux on 10 April 1760, three of which reached the Gulf of St Lawrence in a little over a month, but they were too late. The British garrison in Quebec had been brought to battle at St Foy by French and Canadian forces on 26 April and driven with heavy losses back behind the city gates. Starving and scurvious, they could not have held out had the reinforcements reached the French before the Royal Navy seventy-gun ship of the line *Vanguard* arrived on 9 May. As it was, the French ships were defeated by five British ships dispatched from Louisbourg, and once the Quebec garrison had recovered and been resupplied it was able to go on the offensive. In September Montreal surrendered.[7]

While there remained any danger of the French getting their transports out of the Morbihan, under light escort, there was thought still to be some danger of an invasion. Without a battle fleet to escort it, the most likely destination was believed to be Ireland. Accordingly the Duke of Bedford, who had been made Lord Lieutenant of Ireland in 1756 by the Devonshire–Pitt administration, warned the houses of the Irish parliament in Dublin. This created consternation and a run on the banks that was only stopped by the Duke buying up local currency. But there was no indication that a French invasion would be welcomed even by the Catholic population. Smollett wrote that

> On the contrary, the wealthy individuals of the Romish persuasion
> offered to accommodate the government with large sums of money,

in case of necessity, to support the present establishment against all its enemies; and the Roman Catholicks of the city of Cork, in a body, presented an address to the Lord-Lieutenant, expressing their loyalty in the warmest terms of assurance ... Finally, they expressed the most earnest wish that his Majesty's arms might be crowned with such a continuance of success, as should enable him to defeat the devices of his enemies.[8]

Horace Walpole thought this excitement made the wretched state of the garrison at Carrickfergus, when Captain Thurot arrived a few months later, reflect all the more poorly on Bedford's administration. 'It was no joke to the Duke of Bedford.'[9]

But it was not to Ireland that Choiseul was looking in the aftermath of disaster. Wolters's Paris agent had reported on 7 December that the transports in the Morbihan had been discharged from government service.[10] Choiseul had devised a new plan for a landing in England, of which he informed the Spanish government on 14 April 1760.[11] This time he ordered that the invasion army, 50,000 men, should be concentrated well inland, between the Meuse and the Lower Rhine, where a cover story could be sustained that it was intended as a reserve for the army in Westphalia. The cover would be extended by limiting the number of transports to be accumulated, in Dunkirk and Calais. They would have to make repeated crossings of the Channel over a period 'of at least five weeks' to ferry the soldiers when the time was right. As before, the sea crossing was to be made possible by diverting the attention of the British navy – but this time the diversion was only possible if Choiseul could obtain the support of Spain, which he wanted to dispose its forces to suggest an attack on Gibraltar, while actually invading Portugal. While the British were busy saving Gibraltar and Lisbon from the Spaniards, control of the English Channel would be seized and held with a Franco-Spanish fleet of twenty-two ships of the line that was to be concentrated at Ferrol at the northwestern tip of Spain. The most realistic aspect of the plan was that Choiseul recognized the impossibility of bringing the Toulon fleet and the Spanish squadron at Cartagena past Gibraltar where Admiral Saunders was in command of superior forces, and the impossibility of getting the squadron at Rochefort to sea past the English blockade.

163

Both Britain and France had financed their war on credit, but first the loss of Quebec and then the defeat at Quiberon Bay had undermined the ability of France to obtain credit at reasonable rates. So hollow were French finances that the French controller general who was appointed in March 1759, Etienne de Silhouette, had his name popularly attached to a style of portraiture that observed the forms but lacked any substance. In 1759 the army budget was 152 million livres, which was overspent by another 17 million. The navy budget was 57 million, which was also overspent. Thirty million had been spent in the attempt to invade Britain, and bills of exchange were issued for nearly twenty-seven million livres just to build the landing craft. So desperate were French naval finances that dockyard workers at Toulon were laid off. Silhouette tried to impose new taxes without the approval of Parliament, creating political hostility, and bills totalling fifty-three million livres issued by Intendent François Bigot to support the defence of Canada were defaulted.[12]

The Spanish treasury was applied to, and could provide no immediate assistance, but Choiseul's calculation that he could persuade Spain to throw in its lot with France was to prove sound. The leader of the peace party in the French government, Marshall the Duc de Belle Île, died on 25 February 1761, and Choiseul was appointed war minister in his place, with his cousin César Gabriel de Choiseul, Duc de Praslin, nominally succeeding him at the Foreign Ministry. The invasion army was not considered adequate to subjugate Britain, but if safely got ashore it would suffice to devastate British credit, and bring an end to the war on terms not unfavourable to France.

* * *

Hawke had sent his flag captain, Campbell, to carry his personal report to Admiral Anson, in which the only requests he made were that Lieutenant Stuart, who had been appointed acting Captain of *Fortune* sloop and had been killed in action, should be confirmed in his rank so that his wife and children would be better looked after, and the other was for the promotion of Lieutenant Chaloner Ogle of the *Ramillies* to captain's rank. In the circumstances Hawke's recommendation should have been good enough, but this was the eighteenth century, and it was also important to drop the names of Lady Kingston, who was Ogle's first cousin, and of Lord Scarborough and Sir George Saville, as having 'a great regard for him'. Anson would have known that Ogle was a kinsman of Hawke's old patron, and he was indeed promoted master and commander in December. Campbell was given the traditional £500 sword for carrying the dispatch to the king, but allegedly was not interested in the knighthood that was also traditional.

Hawke asked nothing for himself, but the government was determined to reward him handsomely, and Anson replied that the Duke of Newcastle, First Lord of the Treasury, had agreed to grant him a pension of £1,500 per annum for thirty-two years, 'the longest term the King can grant'. When in March 1760 the pension was formally granted it was in fact to be for £2,000 per annum for his own life and for those of his two older sons in succession. Of more immediate concern to Hawke on board *Royal George* in Quiberon Bay was that he had 'now been thirty-one weeks on board without setting my foot on shore, and cannot expect my health will hold out much longer'.[13] But he was pleased by the royal approbation: 'I long for an opportunity to throw myself at his feet with the most loyal assurance of the dutiful sense I do, and ever shall, entertain of his goodness.'

He was finally relieved of his command and sailed from Quiberon Bay in *Torbay* on 11 January 1760, and struck his flag at Plymouth on 18 January. On 21 January he was received by the king, 'graciously', but his majesty did not offer a peerage to one of the most successful and loyal admirals in British history, who had just relieved the country from the fear of invasion. A week later he was in his seat in the House of Commons as member for Portsmouth when the Speaker informed him that the House had unanimously resolved to express its appreciation:

> Your expedition was of the nearest and most affecting concern to us – the immediate defence of his Majesty's kingdom against a disappointed and enraged enemy, meditating in their revenge, our destruction at once. Your trust, therefore, Sir, was of the highest nature; but to which your characters of courage, fidelity, vigilance, and abilities, were known to be equal. You soon freed us from fears, and have answered all our hopes, that bravery and conduct could give, or turbulent seas and seasons would admit of; even the last did not disturb or diminish your spirit and vigour. You had

overawed the enemy in their ports, in their chief naval force, till shame, perhaps, or desperation, brought them forth at last.

Hawke's reply was the dignified response of a simple man: 'In doing my utmost I only did the duty I owed my King and Country, which ever has been, and shall be, my greatest ambition to perform faithfully and honestly to the best of my ability.'[14] In February he again begged Anson to support his obligation to the widows of old sailors – this time of the warrant officers and captain of *Ramillies* which was wrecked on Bolt Head in a gale, with the loss of almost everyone on board.[15] Later he was elected one of the Elder Brethren of Trinity House, and honoured with the freedom of the city of Dublin.

The public mingled its rejoicing with mockery of their frustrated enemy. Special prayers had been ordered for the second Sunday in December, and Charles Wesley was to publish another collection of hymns, *Hymns to be Used on the Thanksgiving Day, Nov. 29, 1759, and After it*.[16] For his production of *The Harlequin's Invasion* David Garrick, the director of Drury Lane theatre, wrote his famous song 'Heart of Oak', which was set to music by Dr William Boyce. His original words were:

> Come cheer up my lads, 'tis to glory we steer,
> To add something more to this wonderful year;
> To honour we call you, as freemen not slaves,
> For who are so free as the sons of the waves?
>
> Refrain:
> Heart of oak are our ships,
> Heart of oak are our men
> We always are ready; Steady, boys, steady!
> We'll fight and we'll conquer again and again
>
> Our worthy forefathers, let's give them a cheer,
> To climates unknown, did courageously steer.
> Through oceans to deserts, for freedom they came,
> And dying, bequeathed us, their freedom and fame.
>
> Refrain:

But even in the short term the triumph was incomplete.

* * *

In order to keep up the pressure on France, Pitt came up with the idea that Belle Île, the largest island in Quiberon Bay, should be occupied with a military force that by its presence would oblige the French to maintain a large garrison along the coast of the mainland. This plan was part of a general strategy of negotiating peace from a position of strength. Frederick had encouraged London to reach a settlement with Paris, and there was growing weariness with the war among the public. As Sir Julian Corbett put it, 'Pitt ... saw the country committed to negotiations for peace; but for him that was only a reason for pressing the war to its utmost.' Amherst was alerted to a plan to divert some of his professionals against Dominica, St Lucia and Martinique from his assault on Montreal, and a plan that had been developed to strike against Île de France (Mauritius) was redirected to Belle Île because its impact would be known about in time to affect any formal peace negotiations, and because the continued threat of invasion was taken seriously enough not to want to send any considerable detachment of the fleet into the Indian Ocean. It was known through interception of diplomatic correspondence that the Spanish government was working to establish a common strategy with France.[17]

After six months' leave, Hawke returned to command the blockading force in Quiberon Bay, and was tasked with locating the best landing beaches. To Pitt's intense annoyance, he dismissed the option of taking Belle Île as he had dismissed General Mordaunt's idea in 1757 of capturing Île d'Oléron following the failure to take Rochefort. Hawke preferred a landing on the mainland that could directly destroy the naval resources of the enemy. Suppose Belle Île taken, he wrote, 'will the possession of a place detached by water from the Continent draw troops from any part of that Continent to retake it, while we are masters of the sea?' Hawke proposed simultaneous landings at the Vilaine and Morbihan to destroy the French ships, with a third landing at St Jacques on the peninsula between them to provide a defensible redoubt. How long it could have been held, however, and how large a French army would have been needed to contain it, can only be conjectured. At any rate, Anson hurried Hawke's reply into the king's closet before showing it to Pitt, and George II declared Hawke's plan 'infinitely more practicable'. Newcastle was delighted at Pitt's discomfiture, and Pitt said he washed his hands of the project.[18]

Hawke's plan might well have been carried forward but for the sudden death of the king on the following day, October 25. From the time of the Battle of Minorca, George II had been Hawke's patron, and now he was gone. Newcastle believed that Hawke's letter, and the king's death, eclipsed his career.

In the new circumstance, with George II out of the way, Pitt brought forward the Belle Île scheme again. The idea that garrisoning the island would oblige the French to keep back soldiers intended for Germany proved to be exaggerated, but Belle Île in British hands would support cruiser operations against French trade, and most important, it was French home territory that could be exchanged at a peace treaty for Minorca. Hawke loyally undertook the detailed planning, but on 27 December the operation was put on hold. On 18 February 1761 he was permitted to return home, arriving at Spithead on 11 March, and eighteen days later Keppel sailed from Spithead flying a commodore's broad pendant to command the naval aspects of the delayed assault on Belle Île. Forewarned, the French had reinforced their positions.

On 8 April Keppel put the troops commanded by General Studholme Hodgson ashore at Locmaria Bay at the eastern end of Belle Île. This, the *Naval Chronicle* noted, 'the natural strength of the place, and the superior force of the enemy rendered ineffectual, and the assailants were repulsed with some loss. This check, together with a severe gale of wind which immediately succeeded it, threw the fleet into disorder, and for a while disconcerted the enterprise.' A second attempt was made, as Keppel reported, 'where, from the impracticable appearance it had to them, the enemy were no otherways prepared, than by a corps of troops posted to annoy the boats'. 'This success', continued the *Naval Chronicle*,

paved the way to the reduction of the island. The whole of the forces was now landed, and the cannon with great difficulty were dragged up the rocks, and for two leagues along a rugged and broken road. The siege was then commenced with the utmost vigour; and though the garrison, commanded by the Chevalier de St. Croix, at first threatened an obstinate resistance, yet the lines that covered the town being carried by a furious attack, the enemy abandoned the town, and retired to the citadel, which they maintained for a considerable time.

The garrison capitulated on 7 June 1761, and marched out with the honours of war.[19]

The laurels on the badge of the Royal Marines are believed to honour the gallantry they displayed during that action. A medal was struck with the head of Britannia and the legend 'Belle Isle Taken'.[20] But the strategic consequences were fewer than had been hoped for. French garrisons along the coast were increased, but not at the expense of the army in Germany.[21] And while attention was concentrated on its capture, some of the ships sheltering in the Vilaine were able to escape. Their captains having let Berryer down, he was willing to look further down the ranks, and agreed to the Duc d'Aiguillon's suggestion to choose as senior officer a lieutenant, the Chevalier de Ternay. The plan was to lull the British into thinking nothing was to be attempted, and then quickly to bring forward a part of the squadron for sea. On 7 January 1761 de Ternay managed to get two ships and two frigates out of the Vilaine during a dense fog, evade the blockade, and safely get all but one of the frigates into Brest.[22] In January and April 1762 he was to repeat his feat, taking advantage of a storm to bring out the four remaining serviceable ships in the Vilaine. He was then put in command of two of the ships and two of the frigates to mount a successful raid on Newfoundland as part of Choiseul's deception plan. The Admiralty obtained intelligence that an expedition was being planned at Brest, and Hawke, who was now formally commissioned as Commander in Chief but was still being sent detailed ship deployments, was ordered to guard against it. But despite the watch on the harbour mouth, de Ternay escaped from Brest before he could be stopped, and succeeded in capturing St Johns, Newfoundland, and destroying 500 fishing boats, before returning safely to Brest.[23]

Chapter Eight

An Armed Peace
and an Empire Lost

'After thanking God first, & Lord Anson secondly, & the brave Admirals & Captains in the third,' Sir Joseph Yorke wrote to his sister Elizabeth, Anson's wife, on hearing news of Hawke's victory in Quiberon Bay, 'let me wish you joy from the bottom of my heart, for the most glorious tidings that have ever come to our Lot since we can remember, & in all probability for the most decisive Coup de Grace we ever gave the French nation ... They are, as well may be, in a terrible Consternation, & I hope will think no more of disturbing us in our Beds.'[1] But as the British envoy to The Hague, Yorke was to observe during the next decades the terrible price that Britain was to pay for the scale of its humiliation of France. War is a dangerous game, and its reverberations can blight more than one generation.

At the end of 1759, the editor of the *Gentleman's Magazine* had noted the arguments that were being heard about whether Canada should be returned to France as part of a peace treaty, and offered his own solution – 'let us never take it. The French still hold out in Montreal and Trois Rivieres, in hopes of succour from France. Let us but be a little too late with our ships in the River St. Lawrence, so that the enemy may get their supplies up next spring, as they did the last, with reinforcements sufficient to enable them to recover Quebec, and there is an end to the question.'[2] But that sort of wisdom rarely appeals to the public.

171

While arranging prisoner exchange following the victory in Quiberon Bay, Lord Howe had been told by d'Aiguillon that he had authority to negotiate a separate peace with Britain, and Hawke had sent Howe home to report to Anson and Pitt. Immediately following the succession of the Bourbon Charles III to the Spanish throne in August 1759 Pitt had been approached with the idea of a Spanish mediated peace. Charles had a reputation for being pro-French, and Pitt deflected the proposal by agreeing to participate in a Congress of the Powers. Choiseul liked the idea, because a Congress was more likely to drive a wedge between Britain and Prussia than it was to reach a peace settlement. The congress was located at The Hague, and Yorke found himself Britain's chief negotiator in pointless procedural wrangling that lasted until the attempt collapsed in May 1760.[3]

The Duke of Bedford, who had been made Master of the Horse following his retirement from Ireland, had been an early and consistent advocate for making a generous peace with France. He was not a minister, but George III insisted that he be sent copies of official dispatches, and he was to be made the chief emissary when peace was finally negotiated in 1762. He recognized that Britain's victories were a poisoned legacy. Writing to the Duke of Newcastle in May 1761, he warned against any thought of retaining all the territories that had fallen to British arms. The French planter population of Guadaloupe would be impossible to govern, and Senegal and Goree, while 'of infinite use to our Commerce ... if possessed by a military force, will be the Grave of our People'. The retention of Canada and the French part of the Newfoundland fishery posed both particular and general dangers: 'I don't know whether the neighbourhood of the French to our Northern American Colonies, was not the greatest security of their dependence on their Mother Country, who I fear will be slighted by them when their apprehensions of the French are removed.' Nor was the possible disloyalty of the American colonies the greatest danger. The collapse of New France endangered the balance of power in Europe, and ensured there would be no real peace: 'should England attempt to seclude France entirely from the North American fishery,' Bedford noted, 'it would not only be inadmissible by them, but would give umbrage to Spain and all other maritime Powers, as it would be a great step towards gaining the monopoly of a trade, which is the great source of all maritime power, and might be as dangerous for us to grasp at, as it was for Lewis the 14th when he aspired to be the Arbiter of Europe, and might be as likely to produce a grand Alliance against us, as his ambitious views did against him.' The concern that Spain, and possibly the Netherlands, would be driven to throw their lot in with France was soon to be justified.[4]

Even before Charles III succeeded to the throne of Spain, when he had been king of the Two Sicilies, he had appreciated that the Spanish empire would be at risk were Britain to weaken significantly the ability of France to maintain her own imperial position, and on his succession he recalled from exile the Anglophobe Zenón de Somodevilla y Bengoechea, Marquis of the Ensenada. French defeat in Quiberon Bay only increased his concern about the growing naval power of Britain. In January 1761 one of Ensenada's followers, the Marquis de Grimaldi, was given the diplomatic post in Paris. Following George III's accession he made his former tutor, John Stuart, Third Earl of Bute, a privy councillor, and on 24 March with Newcastle's support he was sworn in as Secretary of State for the Northern Department. Bute was convinced of the need to seek a treaty with France, and a diplomatic agent, Hans Stanley, was dispatched from London to Paris on 24 May 1761 to explore the prospects for a peace settlement. But his instructions included the warning 'to give watchful attention to the conduct and motions of the Spanish ambassador' in Paris.[5]

Pitt's unwillingness to make concessions to France about the Newfoundland fishery reflected his conviction that there was little prospect of concluding peace at a time when Spain was making ready to join the war, and Choiseul's failure to address British concerns about the future of the Channel ports of Dunkirk, Ostend and Nieuport suggested that he was not serious in his negotiations. Bedford agreed on making no concession on that question: 'I have never myself been much in apprehension of invasion of England,' he wrote to Bute on 9 July, but 'for the satisfaction of the nation, too great security cannot be taken to guard against any future alarms'.[6]

Choiseul was to write in 1765 for Louis XV a *Memoire Justificatif presente au Roi* in which he described his duplicitous peace negotiations which were intended to draw Spain into the war, and divert British energies to the pillage of the Spanish empire.[7] He was successful in these aims, and even succeeded in bringing a change in British leadership. On 15 August 1761 the Family Compact between France and Spain was signed along with a Special Convention by which they agreed to an offensive and defensive alliance, and Spain hurried forward its preparations for war. Pitt regarded war with Spain as preferable to Spain's hostile neutrality, but the aging Anson threw his weight on the side of the peace party. Unable to obtain ministerial support to take pre-emptive action against the Spanish flota of treasure ships, to ensure Spain could not meet the financial cost of war, Pitt resigned in October.[8] But by then Choiseul's machinations had gone too far for Bute and Newcastle to bring forward the peace process.[9] Undeterred by the succession of British victories following the Battle of Quiberon Bay, at Montreal, in Dominica and at Belle Île, to which were added victories at Pondicherry and in Westphalia, Charles III declared war on Britain in January 1762.

In Corbett's words, 'in his vision of England as sole mistress of the sea', Pitt 'fell into an error as enticing and as fatal as that which brought the Grand Monarque and Napoleon to their ruin. Magnificent as was his strategy, it broke the golden rule.'[10] Writing in 1907 those were prescient words; Corbett could not gloss over the part played by Pitt's strategy in stoking the conflict that was to keep Britain at war for most of the next fifty-two years, and a century and a half later was to drive a wedge between Britain and the United States that weakened their responses to the threat of German militarism.

In immediate terms, the Spanish declaration of war was little threat. The British Admiralty knew its job well enough that it did not let concern about Spanish assaults on Gibraltar and Portugal cause it to lose sight of the need to prevent an invasion of England. The French plan to embark an invasion force from Dunkirk in stages was discovered by British agents.[11] In February 1762 Hardwicke forwarded to Newcastle intelligence from France, with the comment that 'however desperate the attempt of an Invasion may seem without its being Supported by a Fleet, I have been informed that I might certainly depend upon its being most un-doubtedly a part of the present plan of France. They are far from thinking themselves capable of making a Conquest; but throwing England into Confusion, destroying its Credit & the Confidence of the Public & of foreigners they think Sufficient to answer all their Views.'[12] The Belle Île garrison was hurried to Lisbon in time to stiffen Portuguese resistance to the Spanish invasion, and Hawke chose a rendezvous for the covering force ten leagues off Ferrol, where it served to prevent the combined fleet sheltering there getting into the Channel to support the small Dunkirk flotilla, which never put to sea. The extension of war opened opportunities for British soldiers and sailors to obtain laurels and wealth in attacks on the Spanish empire. Among the prizes taken by the Saunders squadron at Gibraltar was the *Hermione* from Lima, worth half a million pounds in prize money. A major amphibious operation was mounted, successfully, against Havana, with Commodore Keppel acting as second in naval command. Colonel Robert Draper, who had been involved in planning the Belle Île expedition, obtained permission to lead an expedition to seize Manila in the Philippines from its Spanish government, using naval and military forces already in India.[13]

But in the longer term, revival of the dynastic partnership of the Bourbon Kings of France and Spain was to have a decisive impact on Britain's future. France retained something from the wreck of her empire when the peace negotiations were concluded at Paris on 10 February 1763, due to the determination with which Louis XV fought the war to a standstill in Germany in the years following Quiberon Bay, and due to the perception of the dangers by Bute, and by Bedford who arrived in Paris as plenipotentiary for the negotiation of peace on 12 September. George III had made Bute his prime minister on 27 May 1762 following the resignation of the Duke of Newcastle over the sums to be voted to support the war in Germany.[14] Guadaloupe, Martinique and St Lucia had in the end all fallen to British arms, but all were returned to France. Canada was retained by Britain largely because the French had found it such a financial burden that they were prepared to sacrifice it, and because British public opinion led by Pitt would not have tolerated its surrender. France, however, was ceded control of the islands of St Pierre and Miquelon close to the south coast of Newfoundland to make possible the continuation of

French fishery despite the loss of Île Royale, which became part of British Nova Scotia.

Peace diplomacy had been fraught. Not only was the surrender of conquered territory deeply resented by the public, but Bute's determination to obtain a peace settlement was not matched by his skill as a diplomat, and Frederick complained of treachery. Peace could not have been concluded had not the news of the fall of Havana arrived in time to force Choiseul's hand; in order to secure a treaty a deal was offered to Spain to accept from France the cession of Louisiana in compensation for the cession to Britain of Florida, itself in compensation for the British evacuation of Cuba. No compensation was required for the return of Manila, because its capture was not known about in Europe at the time of the conclusion of the treaty. Bute appointed Henry Fox as parliamentary leader to obtain the assent of Parliament to the treaty, using all the techniques of bribery and bullying.

* * *

Like the 1919 Peace of Paris that failed to create the circumstances for enduring peace, that of 1763 neither prevented the recovery of French sea power nor abated the hostility between Britain and France. The opposition in Britain to its conclusion was symptomatic of the mercantilist concept of the world as a zero-sum game in which there can be only winners and losers. Scholars are beginning to ask why the political leaders in those countries did not recognize that their interests lay in partnership, but the fact is that few did. The treaty did strike a bargain between the belligerents, but it was no more than a grudging contract, and the years following the Seven Years War were anything but peaceful.

In post-war London it was accepted that France was bound to seek revenge for her defeat at the hands of Britain. 'It is not easy to imagine', noted the instructions given to the Duke of Richmond when he was dispatched as ambassador to France in 1765, 'that, after so great Disgraces both by Sea and Land, and after the Cession of so vast a Territory to Our Crown in Consequence of their late unsuccessful War, the Court of France, as well as That of Spain, should not have Thoughts of putting Themselves in a Condition to recover in Time their lost Possessions, and retrieve

176

the Reputation of their Arms.' Indeed, as early as 7 April 1763 Louis XV sent instructions to the Duc de Broglie, his ambassador in London, to devise yet another plan for the invasion of England, and his aid-de-camp La Rosière, who had a reputation as a cartographer, spent a year in England for the purpose.[15] The Spanish navy survived the war relatively intact, and the Spanish government was convinced of the necessity of planning for a renewal of the conflict with Britain. The attitude of Charles III and his countrymen was well summed up by an 'old Spaniard', de Munian, who told the British charge d'affaires in Madrid in 1766, Lewis de Visme, that the British 'as Masters of the Sea, [were] too powerful not to be oppressive, and [that he] is firmly of opinion that no Peace with them can be secure'.[16] In 1767 the Comte d'Ossun, French ambassador in Madrid, warned Choiseul that Spain wanted war with Britain as soon as possible, perhaps in twelve years. Choiseul's own position was little different, although there never was complete harmony between French and Spanish ends, nor complete co-operation in preparing for them.[17]

In September 1764 it was estimated that it would cost the Navy Board £2,003,785 to put in condition a fleet of the best 121 ships that had survived the war. In 1768 Charles Jenkinson, later First Earl of Liverpool but at the time a commissioner of the Treasury, epitomized the dominant concern of British post-war naval planning when preparing 'Heads of Defence of the Extra Estimates of the Navy'. He remarked that 'We shall begin the next war with two Enemies at a time.'[18] 'The two great ends of security & oeconomy may seem at first view to combat each other but it is our duty to reconcile them,' Jenkinson cautioned. 'Security must have the first place,' he concluded, but unless the debt incurred by the Navy Board during the war was paid down it would be evident to all that Britain could not afford to risk another war. It is ironic that one of the means experimented with to pay for defending the empire was the Stamp tax, which proved to be a catalyst for colonial revolt.

During the years following the Peace of Paris, the balance between expenditure on ship repair, and paying down the debt, and the conduct of Britain's foreign policy depended upon the reliability of intelligence gathered on the French and Spanish navies. Hawke was eventually to be made First Lord of the

Admiralty 11 December 1766. When he wanted information about the French dockyards in the winter of 1768–1769 it was to Robert Wolters that he applied. Wolters's answer reflects the difficulties: 'Sending a person on purpose to a French Port I have long since been obliged to give up, as I have not been able to find one that would have courage to see clearly and to make a true report.'[19] Often Wolters's agents supplied the only information available, and their reliability was born out by Hawke's own opinion when he visited France himself in 1770.[20]

As early as January 1763 Wolters's agent in Versailles reported that Choiseul was inclined 'to reduce the Army to Nothing, in order to increase the Fleet, to introduce the same Oeconomy into every Office, and to pursue it, so far as to enable Him to discharge the Debt contracted this War ... to put the Finances in about Twelve Years ... on a better Footing, than they were on in 1755.'[21] Wolters forwarded reports from Paris and Geneva confirming that Choiseul's plan was to prepare for a naval war of revanche.[22] In 1761 he took the post of Minister of the Marine in order to oversee the reconstruction of the navy, instituted a series of reforms designed to improve naval morale, and embarked on a programme of ship construction.[23] The Versailles agent, however, also reported that there was doubt about what success he would have. In his 1765 'Memoire Justificatif presente au Roi' Choiseul claimed that he had built up the fleet to sixty-three ships and thirty-one frigates *tous en etat d'aller a la mer et en etat de tous points*.[24] But there was a degree of wishful thinking in this. In reality, new construction and repair was not adequate even to hold in check the decay in the French fleet. On 30 May 1765 an unknown Admiralty intelligence source drew up an 'Abstract of the French Navy' that reported no more than a total of thirty-six capital ships fit for service.[25] It was known in London that none of the ships under construction were being built at the expense of the crown. They were all ships laid down late in the war as patriotic gifts from various cities. In 1767 the Versailles correspondent expressed his opinion that the French court 'sincerely wish to avoid war' because 'the Finances are so ruined'. Three months later he added that 'the Duc de Choiseul & every other Minister must avoid War for, at least, Ten years'.[26] Abstracts of the French fleet dated 10 September and 26 November 1766 list only

178

thirty-nine and forty-two ships of the line respectively that were thought to be in good condition.[27] On 1 January 1768 Wolters provided a 'Liste de la Marine de France' that showed a maximum of only forty-one capital ships that could be in good condition, out of a total of fifty-nine. There was good evidence of sound condition for only twenty-three.[28] Discouraged by his lack of success, Choiseul returned to the Foreign Ministry. His cousin, the Duc de Praslin, who had been acting as Foreign Minister, took over the Marine. It was not until 1 January 1770 that Wolters drew up a list of the French fleet that included thirty-three ships of the line for which there was evidence that they were in good repair, out of a total of fifty-eight, of which six were definitely not fit for service.[29]

* * *

In dealing with the dangerous peace, naval leadership was provided by a succession of First Lords, the Earl of Halifax, the Earl of Sandwich, Hawke, and Sandwich again, following Hawke's retirement in 1771. Hawke's appointment was made by Pitt, who evidently had come to value his honest professionalism. Elevated to the Lords as the Earl of Chatham and brought into the Duke of Grafton's administration in July 1766, Pitt needed to replace Sir Charles Saunders, who had been knighted for his service at Quebec but was closely associated with the Rockingham group. Anson had wanted Hawke as a member of the Board in 1757, but his lack of political connections had then been a disadvantage. And that lack was to make him vulnerable during his period in office. In appointing him, Pitt passed up the opportunity to strengthen his political position in order to have the best man for the job. As a naval officer, Hawke was in a stronger position to resist political encroachment on naval patronage, but it could be dangerous to refuse to serve the families of the aristocracy. He was to sustain a rate of shipbuilding which compares well with that of the Earl of Sandwich, who held that office in the summer of 1763 and was to succeed Hawke in 1771. On 15 January 1768 Hawke was promoted to the highest rank in the navy, to be the sole Admiral of the Fleet, and on 20 May 1776 he was belatedly elevated to the peerage as Baron Hawke of Towton in Yorkshire. The inscription on the monument that was to be eventually raised to him following his death in 1781 concludes: 'a prince, unsolicited, conferred on him dignities he disdained to ask'.[30]

Several of the naval officers who had played important parts in the Quiberon Bay operations under Hawke's command had roles in the post-war navy. Keppel had prospered from the Havana expedition to the sum of nearly £25,000, and on 21 October 1762 he was promoted at the age of thirty-seven to rear admiral of the blue. From the beginning of the peace, his career was to be marked by his political attachment to the Marquis of Rockingham, along with his cousin the Duke of Richmond and his friend Sir Charles Saunders. He was Member of Parliament for Windsor from 1761 to 1780, and in Rockingham's first administration (July 1765 to July 1766) Saunders and Keppel were both members of the Admiralty Board. When Grafton succeeded Rockingham at the Treasury Saunders became first lord, but his and Keppel's loyalties were strongly to their clan, and both resigned for political reasons when another of Hawke's captains, George Edgcumbe, now Rear Admiral Lord Edgcumbe, a fellow Rockingham whig, was dismissed as groom of the bedchamber. It was this circumstance that brought Hawke to the Admiralty as First Lord.

Keppel was the obvious man to appoint as Channel Fleet commander during the 1770 Falkland Islands crisis. The dispute with France and Spain was settled before he could hoist his flag, but in 1778 he was to command the fleet in the Battle of Ushant during the American Revolutionary war. Unfortunately his, and the Rockingham group's, affected support for the American revolutionaries was highly divisive, and was a major factor in the defeats Britain suffered at that time.

Another name from the blockade of Brest to be important in the subsequent years of peace was that of Captain Hervey, both as a naval commander and as a politician. Before he had joined Hawke's command outside Brest he had fought and won election to Parliament from the rotten and very expensive borough of Bury St Edmunds by eleven votes to ten; taking his seat in January 1759. Having missed the Battle of Quiberon Bay, he returned there for the operations leading to the capture of Belle Île in 1761. Following the conclusion of peace, he attached himself politically to George Grenville, who forced himself upon George III as prime minister in 1763. As a result, Hervey was returned to parliament from the Admiralty borough of Saltash.

Lord Howe had also acquired a seat in parliament during the war, being returned unopposed on 23 May 1757 for the government as MP for Dartmouth. He was to hold this seat for twenty-five years. He had also married an heiress, Mary Hartopp, giving him the resources following the end of the war to live the political life. He was to vote regularly with Pitt, the Earl of Chatham, and with the Earl of Grafton, but he was appointed to the Board of Admiralty by Grenville between April 1763 and the end of July 1765 when the Earl of Sandwich was first lord, and on the fall of the Grenville administration the Marquis of Rockingham made Howe treasurer of the navy, a post he held with a three-month break in 1766 until Chatham went into opposition in January 1770.

* * *

To confront the anticipated danger from France and Spain, British foreign policy in the years following the conclusion of the Peace of Paris was based on a structure of deterrence, employing the potential that existed in the battle fleet. In the belief that only clear indication of British determination would keep the Bourbon monarchs honest, squadrons were dispatched to demonstrate, and if necessary to take direct action. In 1764 the British government of George Grenville responded to French and Spanish encroachments in the West Indies, at Turks Island and Honduras, in Newfoundland waters at St Pierre, and in the River Gambia.[31] Less successful efforts were made by Grenville's successors to resolve without the use of force problems with Spain over the unpaid portion of the ransom agreed to at the capture of Manila by the defeated governor, Archbishop Rojo, with France over the demilitarization of the port of Dunkirk as had been stipulated in the peace treaty, and in 1768 over the French annexation of Corsica. Frederick Lord North came to head the British government in January 1770. Recognizing the dangerous consequence of the lost prestige when Britain did not prevent the French annexation of Corsica, he, with the Secretary of State for the Northern Department, the Earl of Rochford, reacted strongly when France appeared to be working to establish a defence relationship with the Ottoman Porte that could establish French control of the eastern Mediterranean, and when Spain seized a British post in the Falkland Islands. Timing his reaction for the autumn when British trade was returning home with full crews who could be pressed into the navy, North ordered an emergency mobilization. In three separate steps, fifty-five ships of the line were brought forward for service.

It was naval advice that the government used to justify its inactivity when Corsica was invaded. On 17 November 1768 there was a call for papers in the Commons concerning Corsica.[32] Hervey initiated the defence for the government. He declared that Corsica was not an important source of naval reserves of men, or of timber, which he described as brittle. Howe supported Hervey's principal conviction, although he disagreed in detail: 'I can't agree with the Honourable Gentleman in thinking that Corsica in the hands of the French is of no importance, but as to going to war, that is nothing to the point. You suffer'd in your trade in Queen Ann's time. In a future war with regard to Corsica, it would not lay you under great danger, if Corsica were in possession of the French, for they [i.e. the merchant ships?] must have convoys ...' Hawke told the Commons that he was of the same opinion. Saunders declared: 'I think it would be better to have gone to war with France, than let them have Corsica,' but Hawke replied: 'Upon no other ground do I speak than from what I know from experience, & from that experience I differ in opinion from the Hon[oura]ble Gentleman who spoke last.'

The navy, under Hawke's leadership, met the challenge of effective deterrence in the Falklands crisis. By 4 January 1771 the guardships at Plymouth, Portsmouth and Chatham could be fully manned should their recruiting parties be called in. The remainder of the fifty-five ships ordered brought forward for service were still 7,000 men short of complement, but the muster-books show that at the beginning of 1771 the first forty ships ordered were sixty-one-and-a-half per cent manned, so that it would have been possible to man fully twenty-four ships.[33] This number is consistent with the experience of the Seven Years War, during the first year of which it had only been possible to raise 25,824 men, enough to man 39 ships of the line. 'The Utmost Efforts being exerted during the last War to raise men', after seven years of war the navy had been able to muster 84,770.[34] The evident capacity of the Royal Navy to go to war in 1771 ensured that it would not have to.

Hawke resisted the idea of sending a fleet to the Mediterranean, disagreeing with weakening the battle fleet by sending into distant waters a squadron which would not be strong enough to defend itself. He later told the Commons that 'he did not understand sending ships abroad when, for aught he knew, they might be wanted to defend our own coast'.[35] However, he promoted Howe rear admiral on 18 October 1770, crediting George III with the decision to promote him over the heads of other captains waiting their turn, and as one of his last acts as First Lord of the Admiralty Hawke appointed Howe on 26 November Commander in Chief Mediterranean despite his lack of seniority.

After his resignation in February 1770 from the Treasury, the Duke of Grafton had put out feelers to Lord North to take Hawke's place at the Admiralty. As First Lord of the Treasury he should have been able to ensure that the navy was not short; nevertheless his secretary Thomas Bradshaw reported: 'I have talked seriously to him [i.e. North] upon the wretched & dangerous state of the navy.' Urging that a good man be appointed to replace George Cockburne as Comptroller when the latter died, Bradshaw 'apprised Lord North of the importance of filling up this office properly, especially at this time, when, from the weakness of the Admiralty it was doubly necessary that the Comptroller of the Navy should be a man of ability & diligence'.[36] According to Bradshaw and Grafton, North agreed that the navy needed greater attention and agreed that a vote to reduce the debt would serve to meet current expenditure while it would not raise alarms.[37] The 1770 vote to reduce the debt was only £100,000 however, and every rival's efforts to unseat Hawke failed. Even Sandwich was put off with the assurance that North was 'firmly desirous of seeing that department under your management' but that no vacancy was foreseen.[38]

The poor condition some of the guardships were found to be in during the Falklands mobilization gave edge to the complaints about Hawke's leadership at the Admiralty. The damage sustained by ships supposedly just fitted, not to mention the need to dock a guardship that was supposed to be ready for sea, alarmed the Earl of Rochford, and George III was concerned that the ships had not been cleaned: 'if the remainder which are now supposed to be ready should turn out to be in the same condition, the most dreadful consequence may be apprehended from it.' Rochford, however, was able to tell the king on 9 December that Hawke had said that the twenty-two ships ordered out of Ordinary had been both docked and sheathed, although the guardships had only had their annual cleaning and would have to be docked again in the spring. With this the king expressed himself satisfied. The reaction of the Admiralty and the Navy Board was to treat the accidents as trivial. On 12 December Hawke reassured the Commons: 'I do take upon me to say th[at] we are forwarder now than we were then [in 1755].' When Keppel replied: 'I don't say every ship is bad, but those you h[ave] tried are bad,' Hawke was only able to say that Guardships 'are not intended to be sent abroad, they are a deal forwarder than the ships in ordinary to be sent out to cruise upon the enemy'.[39] MacKay has suggested that the fault lay with the failure of the Navy Board to keep Hawke informed about the difficulty maintaining in condition for service the ships that had been constructed during the war out of green wood, in such a hurry that they could not be properly seasoned.[40] But was the problem only a political one? The bottom line is that more ships were available for sea duty during the Falklands mobilization than the press gangs could man.[41]

Hawke was as assiduous in his attendance at the Board of Admiralty as he had been when keeping watch on Brest eleven years before. The Board met six days a week, Monday to Saturday, and Hawke presided at every meeting from 11 September 1770 to mid-November, when his health began to break down.[42] At the end of the first week of January he was forced by increasingly bad health to announce his resignation to the cabinet, but his resignation did not indicate a failure in his department and it did not lead to a change of policy. Sandwich quietly accepted the office which North had promised, and when he inspected the dockyards in the spring he reported eighty ships of the line fit for service, and forty-three others reparable.[43]

In the years following Hawke's 1759 watch on Brest the operational lessons learned since the beginning of the French wars were increasingly applied. Plymouth and Portsmouth dockyards were extensively rebuilt, to accommodate more stores. The job took thirty years. Plymouth was given the largest rope walk in the Royal Dockyards. Between 1778 and 1783 the labour force at Plymouth expanded to equal that at Portsmouth. The success of this work was demonstrated in 1778 when Keppel brought the Channel Fleet into Plymouth to refit following the Battle of Ushant. Keppel refused to take the fleet all the way into the Hamoaze River because he wanted to be able to return to sea should the French appear. Damage to yards, rigging and sails was repaired in the sound, and where possible by the ships' crews. The least damaged ships stayed outside the sound, in Cawsand Bay. The wounded were brought ashore to Stonehouse Hospital. Having arrived on 31 July, Keppel was able to sail again on 23 August with all but one of his ships. That was three days longer than it took Lieutenant Général de la Marine Louis Guillouet, Compte d'Orvilliers, to complete in Brest, the French main dockyard, the repairs his fleet needed. The introduction of copper sheathing of ship bottoms, beginning in 1760, ensured that ships deployed for extended periods would be able to maintain their cruising speed.

*　*　*

The outcome of the Falklands crisis led to Choiseul being exiled to his estates by Louis XV, but it is never wise to humiliate your enemies, and deterrence is never comfortable. In 1772 the states-man and author Edmund Burke described the situation as 'an armed peace. We have peace and no peace, war and no war. We are in a state to which the ingenuity of our ministry has yet found no apt name.'[44] In 1773 it was again necessary to order a naval mobilization to forestall a French naval deployment to the Baltic to control Swedish politics. The outcome for Britain was not entirely satisfactory because the hope of forming an alliance with Russia had to be sacrificed. London did not feel any great concern for British security because of the evident capacity of the navy. But it would have been wiser to have tried harder to improve relations with France. Britain was to pay the price for the victories of 1759 and those of the 1760s, not so much because the French were able to bear the cost of war, as because the opportunity presented itself.

It was the American 'rebellion', which was really a civil war, and the weakness of Britain's leadership that brought the house of cards tumbling to the ground. The Boston Tea Party on 16 December 1773 focused London's attention on the revolt in America, but the style of British foreign policy was not at once affected.[45] The receipt of news in London of the Battle of Bunker Hill, when on 17 June 1775 British soldiers ordered to suppress an armed insurrection were repelled by American farmers, however, produced a profound change in the security policy of the British government. In part because of the technical demands of the military campaign on the far side of the Atlantic, but primarily because the confidence of the North administration was undermined. Attention was focused on events in America, distracting attention from the all-important task of isolating the colonial revolt from European intervention. Having embarked on a policy of deterrence in 1763, it could not be abandoned easily without paying a price.

The hope in London, that the line could be held in Europe by sustaining the image of deterrence without its underlying muscle, while settling the rebels, was too transparent in Paris. Superior strategic direction by the Admiralty and by the Secretary of State for the Colonies, Lord Germain, might have managed the complexities of American tactical operations and European deterrence, but there was no one in the administration in London who proved to have outstanding ability. Sandwich had been an unusually effective peacetime administrator, but he had no genius for strategy, and unfortunately he attracted bitter political opposition. Hervey had been on the Admiralty Board from 1771 until April 1775, but he had succeeded his brother as Earl of Bristol in March and his new responsibilities claimed his attention. Sandwich was held to have betrayed his old friends when he reached high office, and they were out to discredit him at all costs. Their sympathy with the American cause had some reality to it, but more policy. Their parliamentary attacks spread to the fleet, and were to prove highly destructive to discipline and morale. Were Hawke still First Lord he might have been able to shrug off the political dissent, and avoid Sandwich's strategic mistakes. As it was, the Royal Navy that fought the Americans, French, Spaniards, and ultimately the Dutch, was a fleet divided against itself.

French strategic objectives for the European theatre in 1778 were to contain British resources in home waters, so that a detachment could be deployed to take decisive action overseas. The French Marine was able to use the Brest fleet, safely positioned behind its massive defences, to prevent a major dispersal of the British Channel Fleet, while the fleet at Toulon was used overseas. Sandwich had intended to send to the Mediterranean a fleet to watch Toulon, and follow the Toulon fleet should it break out, but his concern for safety in the Channel had prevented him. Admiral Keppel, Channel Fleet Commander, insisted that he needed more than twenty ships ready for service, even though the intelligence from Brest indicated that the French were far from ready. In July 1778 Louis XVI called the British bluff and declared war only weeks before the French Brest Fleet, commanded by the Comte d'Orvilliers, sought action off Ushant, in a battle that was most remarkable for the reappearance of the sort of service conflict in the British fleet that had been seen at the Battle of Toulon in 1744. Both Keppel and his subordinate flag officer, Vice Admiral Sir Hugh Palliser, were to be tried by court martial. When Spain entered the war in June 1779, Britain found herself in a more difficult situation than she had had to face in her previous conflicts.

Charles Gravier, Chevalier de Vergennes, who had replaced Choiseul as French Foreign Minister in 1774 on the succession of Louis XVI, had no interest in invading England. The plan that had been devised by La Rosière had been approved by the French Council during the Falklands crisis, but it was never to be used. Vergennes' reasoning strongly reflected the experiences of both France and Britain in the Seven Years War, and resonated with Bedford's warning against frightening Europe by humiliating France: 'Even if I could destroy England, I would abstain from doing so, as from the wildest folly.'[46] France had learnt that threatening any major disruption in the strategic balance of European affairs would lead to a general coalition against her. It was Britain that now suffered that fate. Her victory in the Seven Years War had been so decisive that it eliminated the incentive for her old allies to confront Bourbon aggression.

It was recognized as a central requirement of British strategic planning that an alliance with a continental military power or powers was needed in order to give Britain greater influence in European affairs, and in particular to ensure that the French could not concentrate their efforts upon building naval forces. The Duke of Newcastle had warned in 1749 that 'France will outdo us at sea, when they have nothing to fear by land.'[47] However, the Swedish crisis in 1773, when Britain had threatened naval action if France became involved in the affairs of the Baltic, had put an end to Britain's hope of a Russian alliance; Frederick had not forgiven Britain for what he considered to have been its betrayal in 1762 when the Anglo-Bourbon peace was negotiated before Prussian ambitions were satisfied; and with the succession to the French throne of Louis XVI an Austrian Archduchess, Marie Antoinette, was Queen of France.

Nevertheless, the threat of invasion was always latent in the power of the French army, and Vergennes' caution was to be overcome, to a limited extent, by Spain. Spain was unwilling to support directly the American colonists, but agreed to make war to recover Gibraltar and Spanish interests in Honduras, and to support French efforts to seize more of the Newfoundland fishery, recover Senegal and Dominica, and to restore her position in India. In April 1779 France and Spain signed an offensive alliance against England, the Convention of Aranjuez. Spain could not afford to support a protracted war, and pressed the French to undertake joint operations in the Channel. Vergennes still refused to countenance a full-scale invasion of England, but a plan was developed for the occupation of the Isle of Wight, from whence the dockyard at Portsmouth could be destroyed, or even occupied. Other port cities could also be subjected to attack, with the intended result that Britain's credit would be destroyed. Without credit, it would be necessary for her to seek peace.

Sandwich lamented to George III that this was the first time that Britain had been forced to engage 'in a war with the House of Bourbon thoroughly united, their naval forces unbroken, and having no other war or object to draw off their attention and resources'.[48] Thirty French ships of the line under the command of d'Orvilliers were to be joined by thirty-six Spanish ships to bring overwhelming force against the Channel Fleet. This had been brought up to a strength of forty ships of the line, and command had been given to the elderly Sir Charles Hardy, who had been promoted a full admiral in 1771 because he was the only one who was outside the political quarrel between ministerial and opposition admirals. To compensate for the fact that he had last been at sea twenty years before, he was given a flag captain of superior talent, Richard Kempenfelt. The latter was to remark that 'There is a fund of good nature in the man, but not one grain of the Commander-in-Chief ... My God, what have you great people done by such an appointment.'[49] Charles Wesley trotted out his *Hymns on the Expected Invasion* again, with the new date attached, and the Franco-Spanish combined force dominated the English Channel for several weeks until disease defeated the invasion attempt.

The always-futile attempt to assert control over the American colonies by force, while insecure in home waters, put the British navy in a situation similar to that endured by the French during the Seven Years War. Finally, tactical mistakes when Rear Admiral Sir Thomas Graves encountered a French fleet commanded by Rear Admiral the Comte de Grasse in the mouth of Chesapeake Bay on 5 September 1781 led to the surrender of British forces at Yorktown, and the independence of the United States.

Thus it is was that the triumphs of 1759, and especially the Battle of Quiberon Bay, that ensured that New France would cease to exist and that Canada would become part of the British Empire, also ensured that London's authority in the thirteen American colonies that later became the United States would be challenged, and that the independence of the United States would be made possible by the combined forces of Bourbon France and Spain. But history did not stop there. The decisive French intervention into American affairs did more than make possible American independence. It also bankrupted France, which led to the French Revolution, and ultimately to the French declaration of war against Britain and most of the rest of Europe in 1793.

Appendix 1

From the Captain's Log of *Swiftsure*

Captain Sir Thomas Stanhope, 20 November 1759.

The first part of this 24 Hours We had little Wind & fair Weather. At 10 PM Fresh Gales & Clear, the Fleet steering to the SE: till 3 AM when they brought too with the Starboard Tack and the Main Topsail to the Mast, & continued in that Position till Seven & then made Sail. At ½ past 8 One of the Frigates ahead made the Signal for seeing a Fleet, soon after which the Adm:l Sir Edw:d Hawke made a Signal for the Fleet under his Command to draw into a Line of Battle a Breast at the Distance of two Cables Lengths assunder. At ½ past nine the *Magnanime* made the Signal for discovering the aforementioned Fleet to be that of the Enemy. In a short time after Sir Edw:d chang'd the Signal for the Line to one for a General Chace, the Enemys Ships (who were now within Sight of Our whole Fleet) not being form'd into any regular Order, & by their Motions seemingly confused. The whole English Fleet gave Chace accordingly and at Noon Nine of Our best sailing ships were in the Pursuit advanc'd abreast of Belle Isle, the West End of that Island bearing N: distant 3 Leagues.

Fresh Gales with frequent heavy Squalls. The Chace continu'd, Our Ships gaining fast on the Enemy. We now could plainly discover the Enemy's Fleet to consist of Twenty One Ships of the Line, three Frigates, & Six Small Barks, steering for that Part of Quiberon Bay which lies between the Rock call'd the Cardinals & the Island of Dumet. At ½ past two P.M. His Majesty's Ships, *Magnanime, Torbay, Dorsetshire, Resolution, Warspite, Swiftshure, Revenge, Montague* & *Defiance* in a close Body, but not in any form'd Line were almost within gun shot of the Enemy's Rear; the rest of the English Ships being about 2 Leagues astern: three of Our advanced Ships abovemention'd were all engaged

191

sometimes very close, at other Times further off, as the Necessity of keeping clear of each other occassion'd. The *Montagu, Magnanime* & *Warspite* by some Accident fell on board each other, & remain'd so for some time, by which the Enemy strech'd ahead & to Windward of them. After they were clear'd of each other, the *Magnanime* renew'd the Action with One of the Enemy's Ships that had been driven to Leeward, which Ship soon after struck to her: The French Commander in Chief observing his Rear to be hard press'd, tack'd with two other Ships in order to put Our most advanc'd Ships between two Fires. The *Swiftsure* receiv'd some Damage from each of them, & by the last Fire from the French Admiral's Ship had her Tiller Rope shot & her Foretopsail Yard carried away in the Slings, which occasion'd her broaching too, & She for some time lay muzzled; by which accident She was left out of further Action, & being at the same time near the Island of Dumet She wore & lay too under a Mizen, the only Sail She then had to set. About 4 o'Clock the French Rear Admiral's Ship surrender'd & a short time after One of the Enemy's ships that had doubled, Sunk. Before 5 o'Clock Sir Edw:d Hawke with the rest of the Ships drawing very near the Enemy, they made what Sail they could to avoid him, but several of them were nevertheless very warmly engag'd by the *Royal George*, and some others of His majesty's Ships; till the Evening clos'd, by this time the *Swiftsure* had set her Foresail and having a Windward Tide and endeavour'd to stand out to Sea, making more Sail as the Damages She had received could be repair'd. In standing out of the Bay close haul'd on the Starboard Tack, with the Wind at NNW & NW by W. We had Soundings from 9 to 10, 11, 14, 17, 20 & 24 Fathoms, from which last Depth of Water & from the Distance the Ship had run, We judg'd her to be out of all Danger from the Shoals, & by the *Neptune François* to have weathered the Four about a Mile, the Remainder of the Night was emply'd in repairing Our Damages. At Day light (in wearing to rejoin the Fleet) the Ship roll'd away the Main Topmast, which carried with it all the Starboard Side of the Main Top, split the Mainsail, & did other Damage. The rolling Sea We then had made it necessary to bring the Ship to her former Tack, by which We sav'd the Topsail & most of the Topmast Rigging; the clearing & saving of which employ'd Us till Noon. In the Action the *Swiftsure* had only three Men kill'd & Eighteen wounded.[1]

Appendix 2

Neptune's Resignation

The wat'ry God, great Neptune, lay,
In dalliance soft, and amorous play,
On Amphitrite's breast;
When Uproar rear'd its horrid head,
The Tritons shrunk, the Neriads fled,
And all their fear confess'd.

Loud thunder shook the vast domain,
The liquid world was wrapt in flame,
The god amazed spoke:
'Ye winds, go forth, and make it known,
Who dares to shake my coral throne,
And fill my realms with smoke!'

The Winds, obsequious at his word,
Sprung strongly up, t' obey their lord,
And saw two fleets a-weigh;
The one, victorious Hawke, was thine;
The other, Conflans' wretched line,
In terror and dismay.

Appal'd, they view Britannia's sons,
Deal death and slaughter from their guns,
And strike the deadly blow!
Which caus'd ill-fated Gallic slaves
To find a tomb in briny waves,
And sink to shades below.

With speed they fly, and tell their chief,
That France was ruin'd past relief,
And Hawke triumphant rode:
'Hawke! (cry'd the fair) pray who is he
That dare usurp this pow'r at sea.
And thus insult a god?'

The Winds reply, 'In distant lands,
There reigns a King, who Hawke commands;
He scorns all foreign force;
And, when his floating castles roll
From sea to sea, from pole to pole,
Great Hawke directs their course:

'Or, when his winged bullets fly,
To punish fraud and perfidy,
Or scourge a guilty land,
Then gallant Hawke, serenely great,
Tho' death and horror round him wait,
Performs his dread command.'

Neptune with wonder heard the story
Of George's sway, and Britain's glory,
Which time shall ne'er subdue;
Boscawen's deeds, and Saunders' fame,
Join'd with brave Wolfe's immortal name,
Then cry'd, 'Can this be true?

'A King! he sure must be a god!
Who has such heroes at his nod,
To govern earth and sea!
I yield my trident and my crown,
A tribute due to such renown!
Great George shall rule for me!'

From a broadside, Anon, *Neptune's resignation. Written on the naval victory obtained by Sir Edw[ard] Hawke, Nov. 20, 1759, over the French, off Belleisle.* [1785?]

194

References

Abbreviated references to Archives

BL   British Library
MOD   Ministry of Defence
NMM   National Maritime Museum
PRO   Public Record Office, National Archives

Chapter 1

1. Jonathan R Dull, *The French Navy in the Seven Years War.* Lincoln, University of Nebraska Press, 2005, pp. 20–34, 37, 79–80, 86–88, 105–108, 142–144.
2. Andrew Lambert, *Admirals: The Naval Commanders Who Made Britain Great.* London, Faber and Faber, 2008, pp. 121–156.
3. Ruddock F Mackay, *Admiral Hawke.* Oxford, Clarendon Press, 1965, p. 304.
4. BL, Add. MS 32,996, ff. 87–88, Newcastle Memoranda, 21 and 22 April 1755.
5. Horace Walpole (1717–1797), *Memoirs of King George II*, 3 vols. New Haven, Yale University Press, 1985, vol. 2, pp. 69–71.
6. Jean-François Brière, 'Pêche et Politique à Terre-Neuve au XVIIIe siècle: La France veritable gagnante du traité d'Utrecht?' *Canadian Historical Review* 64 (1983), pp. 168–187.
7. *Annual Register for the Year 1759*, London periodical, vol. 2, December 1759, p. 5.
8. James S Pritchard, *Louis XV's Navy, 1748–1762: A Study of Organization and Administration.* Kingston, McGill-Queen's University Press, 1987, pp. 7–14; Dull, *The French Navy*, pp. 77, 117–119; Guy Le Moing, *La Bataille Navale des 'Cardinaux' 20 November 1759*. Paris, Economica, 2003, pp. 116–117.

9. Dull, *The French Navy*, pp. 94–100, 120–125.
10. Ibid., pp. 129–131.
11. Pritchard, *Louis XV's Navy*, p. 14.
12. BL, Add. MS 32,889, ff. 94, 199, 254, 328, 329, 439, 444; 32,890, f. 52, Yorke–Newcastle correspondence, 16, 23, 27 March, 3, 10, 13 April 1759.
13. *Annual Register 1759*, p. 94.
14. BL, Add. MS 32,998, f. 249, Newcastle: Considerations for my Lord Mansfield, 6 February 1759.
15. Add. MS 32,889, ff. 199, 329, 339, Yorke–Newcastle correspondence, 23, 27 March, 3 April 1759.
16. Dull, *The French Navy*, pp. 112–114, 118.
17. Mackay, *Admiral Hawke*, p. 88.
18. Dull, *The French Navy*, pp. 133–135.
19. Le Moing, *La Bataille Navale des 'Cardinaux'*, pp. 7–8.
20. Georges Lacour-Gayet, *La Marine Militaire de La France sous Le Règne de Louis XV*. Paris, Honoré Champion, 1902, p. 321.
21. Carl von Clausewitz, Anatol Rapoport ed., *On War*. Harmondsworth, Penguin Classics, 1982, p. 164.
22. Sir Julian Corbett, *England in the Seven Years War*, 2 vols. London, Longmans, Green & Co, 1907 [1918], pp. 19–20.
23. 'The ministers have not allowed me any part in planning the project ... my only responsibility is to follow the King's orders.' Le Moing, *La Bataille Navale des 'Cardinaux'*, pp. 15–16.
24. BL, Add. MS 32,892, ff. 55–56, Newcastle–Devonshire, 14 June 1759.
25. BL, Add. MS 32,892, ff. 247, 260 and 262, 'Memorable Passages out of Pieces Secrettes' and Hardwicke–Newcastle, 27 June 1759.
26. Corbett, *England in the Seven Years War*, vol. 2, pp. 10–15; Lacour-Gayet, *La Marine Militaire*, pp. 302–303.
27. BL, Add. MS 32,889, f. 339, Newcastle–Yorke, 3 April 1759; 32,891, f. 467, Newcastle, *Memorandum for the King*, 7 June 1759; 32,892, f. 57, 14 and 27 June 1759; PRO, ADM 2/83, f. 110, Lord's Letters, 21 June 1759; Geoffrey Marcus, *Quiberon Bay*. London, Hollis and Carter, 1960, pp. 70–71.
28. PRO, ADM 1/3945, pp. 245–246, [Wolters's agent] Paris, 4 June 1759.
29. 'He has received from the land and sea forces the honours due to his rank, and in the evening the whole town was illuminated.'
30. PRO, ADM 1/3945, p. 309, [Wolters's agent] Brest, 4 July 1759.
31. 'The intent of that expedition cannot be discovered.'
32. PRO, ADM 1/3945, pp. 350, 369, [Wolters's agent] Paris, 27 July and 6 August 1759.

33. Corbett, *England in the Seven Years War*, vol. 2, p. 31; Dull, *The French Navy*, pp. 151–152.
34. Dull, *The French Navy*, pp. 9–12, 272-4.
35. BL, Add. MS 32,890, f. 122, *Considerations on the Present State of Affairs*, 18 April; 146v–147v, *State of Foreign Affairs*, 17 April 1759; Reed Browning, *The Duke of Newcastle*. New Haven and London, Yale University Press, 1972, p. 268.
36. BL, Add. MS 32,891, f. 39, *Memorandum for the King*, 8 May 1759.

Chapter 2

1. Nicholas Tracy, *The Collective Naval Defence of the Empire: 1900 to 1940*. Aldershot, Navy Records Society, vol. 136, 1997, #6, 'Papers relating to a Conference between the Secretary of State for the Colonies and the Prime Ministers of Self-Governing Colonies, June 30–Aug 11 1902,' Appendix iv, 'Memorandum on Sea-Power and the Principles Involved.'
2. Sir Julian Corbett, *Some Principles of Maritime Strategy*. London, Longmans, Green & Co, 1911, p. 20.
3. Eli F Heckscher, M Shapiro trans., *Mercantilism*, 2 vols. London, Allen & Unwin, 1931, vol. 2, p 29. See Robert Livingston Schuyler, *The Fall of the Old Colonial System*. London, Oxford University Press, 1945.
4. William Cobbett etc., *The Parliamentary history of England England from the earliest period to the year 1803*, 36 vols. London, T C Hansard, 1812, 9 April 1745, vol. 13, p. 1272.
5. Dull, *The French Navy*, p. 50.
6. Ibid., p. 98.
7. David Aldridge, 'Swedish Privateering, 1710–1718 and the Reactions of Great Britain and the United Provinces,' in *Commission Internationale d'Histoire Maritime. Course et Piraterie*. Paris, Institut de Recherche et d'Histoire de Textes Editions du Centre National de la Recherche Scientifique, 1975, pp. 416–440.
8. Benjamin Hoadly, *An Enquiry into the Reasons of the Conduct of Great Britain with Regard to the Present State of Affairs in Europe*. Dublin, 1727 (quoted in Sir Herbert Richmond, *The Navy as an Instrument of Policy*. Cambridge, Cambridge University Press, 1953, p. 397).
9. Alice Clare Carter, *Neutrality or Commitment: The Evaluation of Dutch Foreign Policy, 1667–1795*. London, Edward Arnold, 1975, pp. 53–58. See also Norbert Laude, *La Compagnie d'Ostende et son activite coloniale au Bengale 1725–30*. Bruxelles, 1944.

10. Quoted in Richard Pares, *Colonial Blockade and Neutral Rights, 1739–1763*. Oxford, Clarendon Press, 1938, p. 172.
11. See Nicholas Tracy, *Attack on Maritime Trade*. London, Macmillan, 1991, pp. 54–68.
12. See R B Merriman, *The Rise of the Spanish Empire*, 4 vols. New York, Macmillan, 1918–1934, vol. 4, pp. 207, 436; J A Williamson, *Hawkins of Plymouth*. London, Adam and Charles Black, 1969, p. 159; Sir Walter Raleigh, 'Of a war with Spain, and our Protecting the Netherlands,' in *Three Discourses of Sir Walter Raleigh*. London, Benjamin Barker, 1702; and M Oppenheim ed., *The Naval Tracts of Sir William Monson*, 5 vols. London, 1892, vol. 1, p. 46.
13. Quoted in Richmond, *The Navy as an Instrument of Policy*, p. 291.
14. Henry Kamen, 'The Destruction of the Spanish Silver Fleet at Vigo in 1702,' *Bulletin of The Institute of Historical Research* XXXIX (1966), pp. 165–173.
15. Jonathan Swift, Herbert Davis ed., *Political Tracts 1711–1713*, 'The Conduct of the Allies' (November 1711). Oxford, Blackwell, 1951–1953, p. 22.
16. David J Starkey, 'British Privateering, 1702–1783, with particular reference to London,' PhD, University of Exeter, 1985, p. 366, Table 87, *passim*. See also Pares, *Colonial Blockade and Neutral Rights*, p. 18.
17. Swift, *Political Tracts*, p. 22.
18. Kenneth Raymond Andrews, *Elizabethan Privateers*. Cambridge, Cambridge University Press, 1964, pp. 3–21, s.v. 'Privateering and the Sea War' and pp. 222–240, 'The Consequences of Privateering.'
19. Francis R Stark, *The Abolition of Privateering and the Declaration of Paris*. New York, Ams Press, 1967 (reprint of 1897 edition), pp. 49–57.
20. N A M Rodger, 'The New Atlantic Naval Warfare in the Sixteenth Century,' in N A M Rodger, *Essays in Naval History, from Medieval to Modern*. Farnham, Ashgate, 2009.
21. *Zamora*: 'The power of an order in council does not extend to prescribing or altering the law to be administered by the court ... If the court is to decide, judicially, in accordance with what it conceives to be the law of nations, it cannot, even in doubtful cases, take its direction from the crown, which is party to the proceedings.' See A C Bell, *A History of the Blockade of Germany, 1914–18*. London, 1937 (confidential to 1961), p. 463 and James Wilford Garner, *Prize Law During the World War*. New York, Macmillan, 1927, section 126.
22. Corbett, *England in the Seven Years War*, vol. 2, p. 5.

23. See C H Firth and R S Rait, *Acts and Ordinances of the Interregnum 1642–1660*. London, 1911, vol. 2, p. 66; Peter Kemp, *Prize Money*. Aldershot, Gale & Polden, 1946 and *The Oxford Companion to Ships and the Sea*. Oxford, Oxford University Press, 1976, s.v. 'Prize Money'; and Carl E Swanson, 'Predators and Prizes: Privateering in the British Colonies During the War of 1739–1748,' PhD, University of Western Ontario, 1979, pp. 31–56. Note, the text of William and Mary 4–5, 1692, does not agree with the information given in Kemp.

24. 32 George II, c. 25; Corbett, *England in the Seven Years War*, vol. 2, pp. 7–8. Newcastle remarked that 'Mr. Pitt's behaviour on the Prize Bill was manly & Honorable,' although he did try and make political capital by arguing for a reduction of the size limit to ships of ten guns. BL, Add. MS 32,891, f. 5v, Newcastle–Hardwicke, 6 May 1759.

25. James C Riley, *The Seven Years War and the Old Regime in France: The Economic and Financial Toll*. Princeton, Princeton University Press, 1986, pp. 319–320.

26. Richard Pares, *War and Trade in the West Indies 1739–1963*. London, Frank Cass, 1963, p. 390.

27. Corbett, *England in the Seven Years War*, vol. 1, p. 5.

28. Riley, *The Seven Years War*, pp. 104–107, 111, 114–117, 128–129.

29. Corbyn Morris, *An essay towards deciding the question, whether Britain be permitted by right policy to insure the ships of her enemies? Addressed to the Right ... The second edition, with amendments*. London, 1758; and see Patrick Crowhurst, *The Defence of British Trade 1689–1815*. Folkstone, England, Dawson, 1977, s.v. 'Marine Insurance'; and A H John, 'The London Assurance Company and the Marine Insurance Market of the Eighteenth Century,' *Economica* XXV (1958), pp. 126–141.

30. See also John H Pryor, *Geography, Technology and War: Studies in the Maritime History of the Mediterranean, 649–1571*. Cambridge, Cambridge University Press, 1988, p. 162.

31. Richard D Bourland Jr, 'Maurepas and his Administration of the French Navy on the Eve of the War of the Austrian Succession 1737–1742,' PhD Dissertation, Notre Dame, Indiana, 1978, pp. 146, 434–435. See Chanoine Victor Verlaque, *Histoire du Cardinal de Fleury et de son Administration*. Paris, 1878, p. 132.

32. C P Crowhurst, 'The Admiralty and the Convoy System in the Seven Years War,' *The Mariner's Mirror* 57 (1971), pp. 163–173.

33. D J Llewelyn Davies, 'Enemy Property and Ultimate Destination During the Anglo-Dutch Wars 1664–7 and 1672–4,' *British Yearbook of International Law*, 1931, p. 21.

34. Anon, *Channel Pilot*. London, Hydrographer of the Navy, 1965, vol. 2, p. 27. See also: N A M Rodger, 'Weather, Geography and the Age of Sail,' in Rodger, *Essays*.

35. Michael Duffy, 'The Establishment of the Western Squadron as the Linchpin of British Naval Strategy,' in Michael Duffy ed., *Parameters of British Naval Power, 1650–1850*. Exeter, University of Exeter Press, 1992, pp. 60–82.

36. Sir Herbert Richmond, *Papers relating to the Loss of Minorca, 1756*. London, Navy Records Society, vol. 42, 1913, p. 96.

37. H W Richmond ed., *The Private Papers of George, Second Earl Spencer*. London, Navy Records Society, vol. 58, 1924, vol. 3, p. 296, n. 1.

38. B McL Ranft ed., *The Vernon Papers*. London, Navy Records Society, vol. 99, 1958, p. 459. See also pp. 445–446, 451, 532–533.

39. Ruddock F Mackay, *The Hawke Papers: A Selection: 1743–1771*. Aldershot, Navy Records Society, vol. 129, 1990, #186, Instructions 18 May 1759; R Middleton, 'British Naval Strategy, 1755–1762: The Western Squadron,' *Mariner's Mirror* 75 (1989), p. 357.

40. N A M Rodger, 'The Victualing of the British Navy during the Seven Years War,' *Bulletin du Centre d'Histoire des Espaces Atlantiques* II (Bordeaux, 1985), p. 44, and reprinted in Rodger, *Essays*.

41. Geoffrey J Marcus, 'Hawke's Blockade of Brest,' *Journal of the Royal United Services Institute* (1959), pp. 475–488; Stephen F Gradish, *The Manning of the British Navy during the Seven Years War*. London, Royal Historical Society, 1980, pp. 140–171; Brian Tunstall ed., *The Byng papers, selected from the letters and papers of Admiral Sir George Byng, first viscount Torrinton and of his son Admiral the Hon. John Byng*. Navy Records Society, 1930–, vol. 1, pp. 84–85; PRO, ADM 110/2, 11 July 1705; Christopher Lloyd ed., *The Health of Seamen*. London, Navy Records Society, vol. 107, 1965, p. 121.

42. James Lind, *A Treatise of the Scurvy. In three parts. Containing an inquiry into the nature, causes, and cure, of that disease, etc.* Edinburgh, 1753.

43. PRO, ADM 1/87, Anson to Admiralty, 2 May 1747.

44. Mackay, *The Hawke Papers*, #230, Hawke–Clevland, 23 July 1759; Mackay, *Admiral Hawke*, p. 223; J Marsh, 'The Local Community and the Operation of Plymouth Dockyard, 1689–1763,' in Michael Duffy et al, *The New Maritime History of Devon*. Conway Maritime Press, 1992, 1994.

45. Memorandum c. 8 July 1805 and Admiralty to Cornwallis, 9 July 1805, both published in Sir John Knox Laughton, *The Letters and*

Papers of Charles Lord Barham, Admiral of the Red Squadron, 1758–1813. London, Navy Records Society, vol. 3, 1911, pp. 255–259.

Chapter 3

1. Edward Hawke Locker, *The naval gallery of Greenwich Hospital: comprising a series of portraits and memoirs of celebrated naval commanders*. London, Harding and Lepard, 1832.
2. Mackay, *The Hawke Papers*, pp. xiii–xv.
3. Mackay, *Admiral Hawke*, pp. 25–34.
4. Mackay, *The Hawke Papers*, #16, pp. 15–17; Brian Tunstall and Nicholas Tracy, *Naval Warfare in the Age of Sail*. London, Conway, 1990, pp. 83–91.
5. Edward Pelham Brenton, *Life and correspondence of John, earl of St. Vincent*. London, Henry Colburn, 1838, vol. 2, p. 289.
6. Tunstall and Tracy, *Naval Warfare*, p. 97; NMM, CLE/2/19, Sailing and fighting instructions: notebook on signals c. 1747.
7. Père Paul Hoste, *L'Art des Armées Navales ou Traité des Evolutions Navales, qui contient des regles utiles aux officiers généraux, et particuliers d'une Armées Navales; avec des examples itez de ce qui c'est passé de considérablesur la mer depuis cinquante ans*. Lyon, 1697.
8. Tunstall and Tracy, *Naval Warfare*, p. 100; MOD, NM/29, Signals for the use of the fleet (1756), with memoranda on the use of signals, twice signed by Edward Hawke.
9. D Bonner-Smith ed., *The Barrington Papers: Selected from the Letters and Papers of Admiral the Hon. Samuel Barrington*. London, Navy Records Society, vols 77 and 81, 1937–, pp. 231–232 (30 August 1758), pp. 259–260.
10. Mackay, *Admiral Hawke*, p. 81.
11. Mackay, *The Hawke Papers*, #39; see also #49, Court Martial of Captain Thomas Fox, pp. 61–85.
12. The Court Martial condemned Captain Thomas Fox to be dismissed from his ship.
13. PRO, ADM 49/162 (bound volume), 'An account of the Annual Charge of each of the Guardships in the last Peace at a Medium of Three Years.'
14. PRO, ADM 7/651, Guardships 1764–1770. Twenty guardships were kept on the books from July 1765, but anything up to four of the guardships were often away performing various services, generally on foreign stations. Furthermore, from July 1766 until 1771 there

were never fewer than two of them paid off and repairing. This was not a matter of routine maintenance because during most of the period the same two ships were paid off.

Chapter 4

1. Gradish, *The Manning of the British Navy*, p. 30–31; BL, Add. MS 32,996, Newcastle Memorandum, 1755–1756, ff. 50–97, 18 March 1759; PRO, ADM 1/991, Hawke, 8 March 1755; ADM 3/63, 10, 13 March 1755.
2. BL, Add. MS 32,996, ff. 149 and 160–162, Newcastle Memorandum, St James, 29 June 1755 and 1 July 1755.
3. Mackay, *The Hawke Papers*, #99, Secret Instructions from the Lords Justices.
4. Ibid., #101, note.
5. Dull, *The French Navy*, p. 38.
6. Mackay, *The Hawke Papers*, #102, #104, Hawke to Clevland, 1 and 9 October 1755.
7. Ibid., #109, Secret Instructions to Hawke, 22 April 1756.
8. BL, Add. MS 35,359, ff. 383–384, 6 December 1755.
9. Gradish, *The Manning of the British Navy*, pp. 30–37.
10. Dudley Pope, *At Twelve Mr. Byng Was Shot*. Philadelphia: J B Lippincott, 1962, *passim*; Gradish, *The Manning of the British Navy*, pp. 35–40; Dull, *The French Navy*, pp. 51–52.
11. Tunstall and Tracy, *Naval Warfare*, pp. 107–111, 235–240.
12. BL, Add. MS 32,865, f. 159, Anson to [Newcastle] 31 May 1759; and ff. 167–169, Versailles, 1 June 1756.
13. Mackay, *Admiral Hawke*, p. 146.
14. Mackay, *The Hawke Papers*, #112, Admiralty to Hawke, 8 June 1756.
15. David Erskine ed. (Augustus John Hervey, Earl of Bristol, 1724–1779), *Augustus Herve's Journal, being the intimate account of the life of a captain in the Royal Navy ashore and afloat, 1746–1759*. London, W Kimber, 1953, pp. 217, 220; Mackay, *Admiral Hawke*, pp. 52, 147.
16. Mackay, *The Hawke Papers*, #116, Hawke to Clevland, 12 September 1756.
17. Dull, *The French Navy*, pp. 53–54, 60–61.
18. Mackay, *The Hawke Papers*, #122, Secret Instructions from the King to Hawke, 5 August 1757.
19. Ibid., #130, Hawke to Mordaunt, 8 August 1757.
20. Ibid., #142 [September 1757]; Mackay, *Admiral Hawke*, pp. 264–268.

21. Mackay, *The Hawke Papers*, #151, Memorandum, 20 September 1757.
22. Ibid., #161, Hawke to Pitt, 21 October 1757.
23. [Clerk], *The Secret Expedition impartially disclos'd: or, an Authentick faithful narrative of all occurrences that happened to the fleet and army commanded by Sir E- H- [i.e. Edward Hawke] and Sir J- M- [i.e. John Mordaunt], from its first sailing to its return to England ... By a commissioned officer on board the fleet, etc.* London, J Staples etc. [1757].
24. Mackay, *Admiral Hawke*, p. 176; Hawke Papers, Out-Letters, 29 and 30 September 1757.
25. P C York III, *The Life and Correspondence of Philip Yorke, Earl of Hardwicke*, 3 vols. Cambridge, Cambridge University Press, 1913, vol. 3, p. 186, Anson–Hardwicke, 6 October 1757.
26. Mackay, *Admiral Hawke*, p. 177.
27. Ibid., p. 181.
28. Mackay, *The Hawke Papers*, #164, Lords of Admiralty to Hawke, 5 March 1758; Mackay, *Admiral Hawke*, pp. 188, 199.
29. Mackay, *The Hawke Papers*, #174, Hawke to Clevland, 11 April 1758.
30. Ibid., #176, Hawke to Clevland, 30 April 1758.
31. Anon, *The state farce: or, they are all come home. In which is introduced, a scene representing Britannia weeping in the Centre of the Stage attended by the ghosts of the Duke of Marlborough and Admiral Hosier, being more applicable to the present times than anything yet published, Multum in Parvo.* London, printed for J Scott and sold by the booksellers of London and Westminster, 1758.
32. Le Moing, *La Bataille Navale des 'Cardinaux'*, pp. 7–8, 15.
33. Mackay, *The Hawke Papers*, #177, 178a and b, Hawke to Clevland, 10 May 1758, Clevland's Draft Minute on Hawke's Submission to the Board, and Formal Admiralty Minute on Hawke's Submission to the Board, 12 May 1758; Mackay, *Admiral Hawke*, pp. 196–199.

Chapter 5

1. BL, Add. MS 32,891, f. 39, Newcastle, *Memorandum for the King*, 8 May 1759; *Journal of the House of Commons*, vol. 28 (1757–1761), pp. 600–601.
2. *Annual Register 1759*, p. 7.
3. Marcus, *Quiberon Bay*, p. 74; BL, Add. MS 32,892, f. 247, 'Memorandum of Remarkable Passages out of the Pieces Secrettes,' 27 June 1759.

4. Charles Wesley, *Hymns on the Expected Invasion, 1759*. London, Strahan, 1759, #6.
5. Dull, *The French Navy*, p. 64.
6. Browning, *The Duke of Newcastle*, pp. 264–265.
7. *Annual Register 1759*, p. 100.
8. BL, Add. MS 32,890, f. 114, Newcastle to Hardwicke, 17 April, 1759; 32,891, f. 39, Newcastle Papers, *Memorandum for the King*, 8 May 1759.
9. BL, Add. MS 32,891, f. 39, Memorandum for the King, 8 May 1759.
10. Boys' early life experience had included surviving a fire at sea that destroyed an East India Company slave galley, leaving him and twenty-two others in a sixteen-foot open boat without food or water to make a thirteen-day passage to Newfoundland. Six of them survived by eating the bodies of those who died.
11. A Flat-Bottomed Boat, as it appeared (at Havre de Grace Road) in going from Havre to Honfleur, *The London Magazine, or Gentleman's Monthly Intelligencer*, London periodical, 1759, p. 384.
12. Tobias Smollett MD (1721–1771), *The History of England, from the Revolution to the death of George the Second. (Designed as a continuation of Mr. Hume's History.)* 5 vols. Printed for T Cadell and R Baldwin [by H Baldwin and son], 1800, vol. 4, p. 492; David Syrett ed., *The Rodney Papers: Selections from the Correspondence of Admiral Lord Rodney*. Ashgate, Navy Records Society, vols 148, 151, 2005, #569 (PRO, ADM 1/93) Rodney to Clevland, 6 July 1759. BL, Add. MS 32,892, ff. 406 and 474–477, copy of Rodney's reports of 4 and 6 July 1759, and Clevland to Newcastle, 8 July 1759.
13. Corbett, *England in the Seven Years War*, vol. 2, p. 25.
14. 'The horrors of war, it is impossible to depict for you the consternation: women, children and the elderly driven out; the roads filled with people in flight with their possessions.' PRO, ADM 1/3945 p. 311 [Wolters's agent] Havre, 5 July 1759.
15. Rodney, #600–605 (PRO, ADM 1/93), Rodney to Clevland, 7, 11, 14 and 16 September 1759; Corbett, *England in the Seven Years War*, vol. 2, p. 47.
16. Erskine, *Augustus Hervey's Journal*, p. 301.
17. Mackay, *The Hawke Papers*, #179, #180, #181, Admiralty to Hawke, 9 May, and to Victualling Board, 11 May 1759.
18. Ibid., #186, Admiralty to Hawke, 18 May 1759.
19. Dull, *The French Navy*, pp. 121, 161; Mackay, *The Hawke Papers*, #176, c. 18 May 1759.

20. 'Everything is more and more ready for immanent departure of the fleet.' PRO, ADM 1/3945, p. 317 [Wolters's agent] Brest, 6 July 1759.
21. Mackay, *The Hawke Papers*, #188, #190, #191, Hawke to Anson, 19 or 20 May, to Clevland, 20 May, and Line of Battle, 20 May 1759.
22. Ibid., #197, Admiralty to Hawke, 5 June 1759.
23. Ibid., #186 and #193, Admiralty to Hawke, 18 May, and Hawke to Clevland, 27 May 1759.
24. Ibid., #194, Admiralty to Hawke, 1 June 1759.
25. Ibid., #193, Hawke to Clevland, 27 May 1759; Erskin, *Hervey's Journal*, pp. 237, 302.
26. Mackay, *The Hawke Papers*, #196, Hawke to Clevland, 4 June 1759.
27. Ibid., #198, Hawke to Clevland, 6 June 1759.
28. Ibid., #199–201, Hawke to Cross, Rogers and Clevland, 6 and 8 June 1759.
29. Lloyd, *The Health of Seamen*, p. 121.
30. Mackay, *The Hawke Papers*, #204–208, #211, Hawke to Clevland 12, 13, 15, 17 and 22 June 1759.
31. Erskine, *Augustus Hervey's Journal*, p. 303.
32. Mackay, *The Hawke Papers*, #206–207, #211, #225, Hawke to Clevland 15, 17 and 22 June, Edgcumbe to Hawke 20 July 1759.
33. *Annual Register 1759*, p. 100.
34. Florence Maris Turner ed., *Diary of Thomas Turner*. London, John Lane, The Bodley Head, 1925, p. 52.
35. Mackay, *The Hawke Papers*, #209–210a, #212–212a, Hawke to Clevland, 18–21 June, 3 July 1759.
36. Ibid., #214–218, Hawke/Hervey, 3–7 July 1759.
37. *London Evening Post*, London periodical, 4 August 1759.
38. Mackay, *The Hawke Papers*, #222–223b, Instructions from Hawke to Clements, Hervey to Hawke, 15 July, and Hawke to Clevland, 16 July 1759.
39. Richmond, *Papers relating to the loss of Minorca*, p. 96.
40. Mackay, *The Hawke Papers*, #224, #226–226a, Admiralty to Victualling Board, 19 July, Hervey to Hawke 20 July 1759.
41. Ibid., #227, #229, Hervey to Hawke, 21–22 July 1759.
42. Erskin, *Augustus Hervey's Journal*, p. 305.
43. Mackay, *The Hawke Papers*, #230–231, Hawke to Clevland and to Hervey, 23 July 1759.
44. Ibid., #230, #235, #244, Hawke to Clevland, 23, 24 July and 4 August 1759.

45. Quoted in Marcus, *Quiberon Bay*, p. 63.

46. Edward Thompson 1738?–1786, *Sailor's letters. Written to his select friends in England, during his voyages and travels in Europe, Asia, Africa, and America*, 2 vols. London, T Becket and P A de Hondt; W Flexney and C Moran, 1767, p. 111, Letter 39 to H.M. Esq., off the port of Brest 23 July 1759; Thomas Campbell, *Specimens of the British Poets: With Biographical and Critical Notices, and an Essay on English Poetry*. Philadelphia, Henry Carey Baird 1853, p. 638.

47. Mackay, *The Hawke Papers*, #233–234, #241, #243, #245, #249, #251, #253, #256, #263, Hawke–Ommanney 23–24, 27 July, Minutes on Hawke to Cleveland 2 and 12 August, Hawke to Young, 2 August, Victualling Board to Hawke 6 August, Admiralty to Victualling Board 13 August, Hawke–Pett 14, 21 August, Hawke to Hanway, 8 September 1759. Also see: N A M Rodger, 'The Victualling of the British Navy in the Seven Years War,' in Rodger, *Essays*.

48. Ibid., #230 and #241, Hawke to Clevland, 23 July and 2 August 1759; PRO, ADM 1/92 , Hawke to Pitt, 1 August 1759; Birr Castle, Hawke Papers, Hawke's Journal, 1 August 1759; Thompson, *Sailor's Letters*, p. 111, Letter 39 to H.M. Esq., off the port of Brest 23 July 1759, postscript 2 August.

49. Mackay, *The Hawke Papers*, #238–239, #244, Hawke to Clevland, 29, 30 July, 4 August 1759.

50. *Annual Register 1759*, p. 118, 5 October 1759; Marcus, *Quiberon Bay*, pp. 100–103.

51. Mackay, *The Hawke Papers*, #247, Duff to Hawke 6 August 1759.

52. Ibid., #255, #257, Clevland to Hawke, 18, 22 August 1759.

53. Mackay, *Admiral Hawke*, p. 220.

54. Mackay, *The Hawke Papers*, #259, Hawke to Clevland, 28 August 1759; Marcus, *Quiberon Bay*, pp. 86–87; see also ADM 52/853 (3), Log of George Harrison, Master – *Firm*, 14 April 1759–13 April 1760.

55. Mackay, *The Hawke Papers*, #261–262a, #264, Hawke to Clevland 4 and 7 September with insert from Lord Bristol 24 August 1759.

56. PRO, ADM 1/3945, p. 441, [Wolters's agent] Vannes, 12 September 1759.

57. Le Moing, *La Bataille Navale des 'Cardinaux'*, pp. 20–22.

58. Corbett, *England in the Seven Years War*, vol. 2, p. 35.

59. Tunstall and Tracy, *Naval Warfare*, pp. 111–112.

60. *Annual Register 1759*, p. 23.

61. Robert Beatson, *Naval and Military Memoirs of Great Britain, from the Year 1727, to the Present Time*, 3 vols. London, J Strachan; Edinburgh, P Hill, 1790 [reprint of 1804 edition, Boston, Gregg Pres, 1972], vol. 2, p. 318.

62. PRO, ADM 1/384 (4), Boscawen to Clevland, 20 August 1759; Tunstall and Tracy, *Naval Warfare*, pp. 111–115; Dull, *The French Navy*, p. 137; Léon Guérin, *Histoire maritime de France, depuis la fondation de Marseille jusqu'à la prix de Nimègue*. Paris, 1863 [1843], vol. 4, pp. 369–372.

63. Mackay, *The Hawke Papers*, #264, #266, Instructions, 10 September, Hawke to Clevland 12 September 1759.

64. Ibid., #267, Milnes to Hawke, 14 September 1759.

65. Ibid., #282b, Reynolds to Hawke, 19 September 1759.

66. Ibid., #265a–b, Reynolds to Hawke and Minute, 7 September 1759.

67. Ibid., #266a, Hawke to Reynolds, 11 September 1759.

68. Ibid., #268, #270, #278, #279, Instructions, 14 September, Hawke to Clevland 18 September 1759.

69. Mackay, *Admiral Hawke*, p. 227.

70. Mackay, *The Hawke Papers*, #278, #279, Hawke to Clevland, 23 September, Extract from Minutes of Hood's Court Martial 24 September, Swinton to Hawke 24 September, Clevland to Hawke 3 October 1759.

71. Ibid., #282, #282a–d, #283, #288, Reynolds to Hawke and Minute of Consultation, 19 September, Hawke to Clevland 28 September and 3 October, Hawke to Duff, 4 October 1759.

72. Ibid., #287, #290, #291, Clevland to Hawke, 3 October, Hawke to Clevland 7 October, and to Duff 8 October 1759.

73. Marcus, *Quiberon Bay*, pp. 98–99, 108; PRO, ADM 1/92 f. 89, Harvey [to Hawke] copy, 4 August 1759.

74. Mackay, *The Hawke Papers*, #284, Hawke to Anson, 29 September, to Clevland 1 October, Duff to Hawke, 30 September 1759.

75. Ibid., #289, #293, Clevland to Hawke, 5 October, Hervey to Hawke 9 October 1759.

76. Ibid., #288, #289, #302, Hawke to Duff, 4 October, and Clevland to Hawke, 5 and 19 October 1759.

77. Ibid., #294, #294a, #295, #295a, Hawke to Duff and to Clevland, 10 October, Duff to Hawke 7 October 1759.

78. Mackay, *Admiral Hawke*, p. 230.

79. Marcus, *Quiberon Bay*, p. 112.

80. Mackay, *The Hawke Papers*, #297–298, Hawke to Clevland, 13 October 1759.

81. Ibid., #310b, Porter to Hawke, n.d.

82. PRO, ADM 1/802, Thomas Hanway to Clevland, 14 October 1759; ADM 1/802, In-Letters from Commander in Chief, Plymouth, 14 October 1759.

83. Marcus, *Quiberon Bay*, p. 128; NMM Hawke Papers, In-Letter Book, 4 and 5 November 1759.

84. Mackay, *The Hawke Papers*, #301, Hawke to Clevland, 17 October 1759.

85. Ibid., #310a, Duff to Hawke, 18 October 1759.

86. Ibid., #303, #306, Hervey to Hawke 20 October and Hawke to Clevland 21 October 1759.

87. Ibid., #309, #317, #317a, Hawke to Hervey, 23 October, to Clevland 5 November, insert from Hervey 2 November 1759.

88. Ibid., #310, Hawke to Clevland, 24 October 1759.

89. PRO, ADM 1/3945 pp. 485, 505, [Wolters's agent] Paris, 19 October, and Brest, 22 October 1759.

90. Mackay, *The Hawke Papers*, #314–316, Clevland to Hawke 29–30 October, Hawke to Clevland 30 October 1759.

91. Ibid., #317, Hawke to Clevland, 5 November 1759.

92. Ibid., #319, Hawke to Clevland, 10 November 1759.

93. NMM, Hawke In-Letter Book, 5 November 1759.

94. Mackay, *The Hawke Papers*, #327a, List of the French Squadron which came out of Brest, 14 November 1759.

95. PRO, ADM 1/3945 pp. 537, 545, [Wolters's agent] 13 and 16 November 1759.

96. Marcus, *Quiberon Bay*, p. 134; Louis Dutens, *Mémoires d'un voyageur qui se repose: contenant des anecdotes historiques, politiques et littéraires, relatives à plusieurs des principaux personnages du siècle.* London, Cox, Fils and Baylis (Bossange, Masson et Besson), 1807, pp. 142–143.

97. PRO, ADM 1/92 (2), f. 47a, Captain Ourry's Intelligence of the French Fleet, 14 November 1759; ADM 52/754, Master's Log, *Actaeon*.

98. Mackay, *The Hawke Papers*, #322, #323, Hawke to Geary, and to Clevland, 17 November 1759.

99. Marcus, *Quiberon Bay*, pp. 141–142; PRO, 30/8/55, Saunders to Pitt, 19 November 1759.

Chapter 6

1. Le Moing, *La Bataille Navale des 'Cardinaux'*, pp. 20–22; Corbett, *England in the Seven Years War*, vol. 2, pp. 87–88.

2. 'I proscribe only that you do not lose sight of he main purpose of our present operations, which is to protect the fleet in the Morbihan.'

3. Le Moing, *La Bataille Navale des 'Cardinaux'*, pp. 16–25; Guérin, *Histoire maritime de France*, vol. 4, pp. 367–368; Lacour-Gayet, *La Marine Militaire de la France*, pp. 323–327; Corbett, *England in the Seven Years War*, vol. 2, p. 45, *et seq.*; Marcus, *Quiberon Bay*, pp. 84–85.

4. Walpole, *Memoirs of King George II*, vol. 3, pp. 99–100.

5. Le Moing, *La Bataille Navale des 'Cardinaux'*, pp. 103–105; William Harrison, *Mona Miscellany*. Douglas, Isle of Man, printed for the Manx Society, 1873.

6. Pritchard, *Louis XV's Navy*, p. 80–88.

7. Dull, *The French Navy*, p. 161.

8. Mackay, *Admiral Hawke*, p. 234.

9. Le Moing, *La Bataille Navale des 'Cardinaux'*, pp. 18–20.

10. Thompson, *Sailor's Letters*, vol. 2, p. 123, letter 41 to G.T. Esq., Quiberon, 20 November 1759.

11. Corbett, *England in the Seven Years War*, vol. 2, p. 234.

12. Le Moing, *La Bataille Navale des 'Cardinaux'*, pp. 19–20.

13. Corbett, *England in the Seven Years War*, vol 2, pp. 57–58.

14. Marcus, *Quiberon Bay*, p. 140; PRO, ADM 52/1094 (3) and 1005, Master's Logs of *Vengeance* and *Rochester*.

15. Maréchal de Conflans, 24 Novembre 1759, Guérin, *Histoire maritime de France*, vol. 4, pp. 509–511.

16. 'That was my plan, and you may judge it yourself, Sir, by applying it to a chart.' Tunstall and Tracy, *Naval Warfare*, p. 116; O Troude, *Batailles navales de la France*, 4 vols. Paris, Challamel, 1867–1868, vol. 1, p. 385; Corbett, *England in the Seven Years War*, vol. 2, pp. 56–57.

17. NMM, HOL/16: Brest, Chez à Malassis, Imprimeur du Roi et de la Marine, 1759; Tunstall and Tracy, *Naval Warfare*, p. 115.

18. Tunstall and Tracy, *Naval Warfare*, pp. 119–122.

19. Mackay, *The Hawke Papers*, #327, Hawke to Clevland, 24 November 1759; Marcus, *Quiberon Bay*, p. 144; Le Moing, *La Bataille Navale des 'Cardinaux'*, p. vii.

20. John Charnock, *Biographia Navalis*, 6 vols. London, R Faulder, 1794–1798, v. 187; Mackay, *Admiral Hawke*, p. 351.

21. Thompson, *Sailor's Letters*, vol. 2, p. 123, letter 41 to G.T. Esq., Quiberon, 20 November 1759.

22. Marcus, *Quiberon Bay*, p. 145; PRO, ADM 51/965, Captain's Log, *Swiftsure*.

23. Mackay, *Admiral Hawke*, p. 214.

24. *Universal Magazine*, May 1758, 'Capture of l'Orphée and Le Foudroyant, by a naval officer,' Gibraltar Bay, 2 April 1758.

25. Mackay, *The Hawke Papers*, #327b, Line of Battle, 20 November 1759.
26. Maréchal de Conflans, 24 Novembre 1759, Guérin, *Histoire maritime de France*, vol. 4, pp. 509–511; Troude, *Batailles navales de la France*, vol. 1, pp. 387–388; Lacour-Gayet, *La Marine Militaire de la France*, p. 333; Marcus, *Quiberon Bay*, p. 147.
27. Corbett, *England in the Seven Years War*, vol. 2, p. 61.
28. BL, Add. MS 35,389, f. 186 [Yorke to his sister], 16 November 1759.
29. PRO, ADM 52/862 and 935, Master's Logs, *Royal George* and *Magnanime*.
30. 'The enemies came into the bay pell-mell with the last of our vessels, several of which were enveloped.'
31. Guérin, *Histoire maritime de France*, vol. 4, pp. 373–375; Corbett, *England in the Seven Years War*, vol. 2, p. 66; Dull, *The French Navy*, p. 162.
32. PRO, ADM 51/965, Captain's Log, *Swiftsure*.
33. Tunstall and Tracy, *Naval Warfare*, p. 116, from the transcription of General Henry Renny. An incomplete and inaccurate version of Renny's memoirs was printed in W H Long's *Naval yarns: letters and anecdotes, comprising accounts of sea fights and wrecks, actions with pirates and privateers etc from 1616 to 1831*. London, Gibbings, 1899.
34. Marcus, *Quiberon Bay*, pp. 151–152; PRO, ADM 52/1070, Master's Log of *Torbay*, 51/4308, Captain's Log of *Resolution*.
35. *Naval Chronicle*, vol. 7, London periodical (1802), p. 285.
36. PRO ADM 52/1070, Master's Log, *Torbay*, 20 November 1759.
37. Marcus, *Quiberon Bay*, p. 153; Le Moing, *La Bataille Navale des 'Cardinaux'*, pp. 55–56.
38. *Annual Register 1759*, p. 52.
39. William Price, *A Chart of Quiberon Bay*, London, 20 August 1796; Le Moing, *La Bataille Navale des 'Cardinaux'*, p. viii.
40. Marcus, *Quiberon Bay*, p. 155; PRO, ADM 51/811 (6), Captain's Log of *Royal George*.
41. Philip Patton, *Strictures on Naval Discipline, and the Conduct of a Ship of War: Intended to Produce an Uniformity of Opinion Among Sea-officers*. 1810; Charles Ekins, *Naval Battles, from 1744 to the Peace in 1814, Critically Reviewed and Illustrated*. London, Baldwin, Cradock and Joy, 1824, p. 46.
42. *Gentleman's Magazine*, London periodical, December 1759, pp. 557–558.
43. Le Moing, *La Bataille Navale des 'Cardinaux'*, pp. 57–60; Mackay, *Admiral Hawke*, p. 249.

44. PRO, ADM 51/3895, Captain's Log *Magnanime*; Lacour-Gayet, *La Marine Militaire de la France*, p. 333; Le Moing, *La Bataille Navale des 'Cardinaux'*, pp. 57–58.
45. Marcus, *Quiberon Bay*, p. 156.
46. Le Moing, *La Bataille Navale des 'Cardinaux'*, pp. vii–viii.
47. Ibid., p. 69; Guérin, *Histoire maritime de France*, p. 374.
48. Georges Boissaye Du Bocage, *Le petit Neptune François*. T Jefferys, 1761, p. 63.
49. Guérin, *Histoire maritime de France*, vol. 4, pp. 375, 515–517; Lacour-Gayet, *La Marine Militaire de la France*, pp. 335–340.
50. Du Bocage, *Le petit Neptune François*, p. 64.
51. Price, *A Chart of Quiberon Bay*; Le Moing, *La Bataille Navale des 'Cardinaux'*, pp. 71–73.
52. Le Moing, *La Bataille Navale des 'Cardinaux'*, pp. 89–96.
53. Tunstall and Tracy, *Naval Warfare*, p. 117.
54. Marcus, *Quiberon Bay*, p. 162.
55. Mackay, *The Hawke Papers*, #327, Hawke to Clevland, 24 November 1759; Le Moing, *La Bataille Navale des 'Cardinaux'*, pp. 77–78.
56. 'So much for the invasion! The ships in the Morbihan are to be discharged; the Duc d'Aiguillon has taken himself to Croissic to provide relief for the sailors.'
57. 'This business can be summed up as: there were little obedience and much valor to the Right; great confusion and ignorance in the Center; and bad operation in the Left; without a competent leader in the whole … the enemies remained on the battle field.' PRO, ADM 1/3945, pp. 553–556, 565–566, [Wolters's agent] Paris 26 November, Croissic 24 November 1759.
58. J N Bellin, *Le Neptune François, ou Atlas nouveau des cartes marines*. Paris, Imprimerie Royale, 1693 [Paris, Dépôt des Cartes et Plans de la Marine, 1753].
59. Mackay, *The Hawke Papers*, #328, Hawke to Anson (draft) [late November 1759].
60. Serres, John Thomas. *The Little Sea Torch: or True Guide for Coasting Pilots*. London, J Debrett, 1801. See Nicholas Tracy, *Britannia's Palette: The Arts of Naval Victory*. Montreal, McGill-Queen's University Press, February 2007, pp. 230–235.

Chapter 7

1. Le Moing, *La Bataille Navale des 'Cardinaux'*, pp. 74–77. In 1968 the wreck of the *Juste* was located.
2. Mackay, *Admiral Hawke*, p. 259; Le Moing, *La Bataille Navale des 'Cardinaux'*, pp. 79–82.

3. PRO, ADM 1/92 (2), f. 63, Hawke to Clevland, 2 December 1759, and f. 61, 'List of Officers'; Thompson, *Sailor's Letters*, vol. 2, p. 133, letter 42 to G. T., Plymouth, 23 December 1759.

4. Marcus, *Quiberon Bay*, p. 166; Le Moing, *La Bataille Navale des 'Cardinaux'*, pp. 83–84.

5. Mackay, *The Hawke Papers*, #331a, Keppel to Hawke, 2 December 1759.

6. Mackay, *Admiral Hawke*, p. 262; Mackay, *The Hawke Papers*, #334, Hawke to Clevland, 9 December 1759; NMM, Hawke Out-Letter book, 9, 26 December 1759.

7. Le Moing, *La Bataille Navale des 'Cardinaux'*, pp. 105–107.

8. Smollett, *History of England*, vol. 4, pp. 507–508.

9. Walpole, *King George II*, vol. 3, p. 100.

10. PRO, ADM 1/3945, p. 573, [Wolters's agent] Paris, 7 December 1759.

11. Cesáreo Fernandez Duro, *Armada Espanola*, Museo Naval, Madrid, 1973 (facsimile of 1895–1903 edition), vol. 7, p. 53, Appendix; and see Corbett, *England in the Seven Years War*, vol. 2, pp. 302–307; Mackay, *Admiral Hawke*, p. 283.

12. Dull, *The French Navy*, pp. 158–160.

13. Mackay, *The Hawke Papers*, #336, Hawke to Clevland, 26 December 1759.

14. *Naval Chronicle*, London periodical, vol. 7 (1802), pp. 468–469.

15. Mackay, *The Hawke Papers*, #332, 338, 340, Anson to Hawke, 1 December 1759, and n., p. 357, Hawke to Clevland 7 January, and to Anson [late February] 1760.

16. Charles Wesley, *Hymns to be Used on the Thanksgiving Day, Nov. 29, 1759, and After it*. London, Strahan, 1759.

17. Corbett, *England in the Seven Years War*, vol. 2, pp. 147–170.

18. Mackay, *The Hawke Papers*, #343, #344, Hawke to Anson, 17 October, and Hawke to Pitt, 15 December 1760; BL, Add. MS 32,913, ff. 326–331, Newcastle to Hardwicke, 25 October 1769; Mackay, *Admiral Hawke*, pp. 268–274.

19. *Naval Chronicle*, vol. 7, pp. 286–287.

20. Belle Isle Taken, 1761. Head of Britannia to left: Cap of Liberty in front; trident behind. Figure of Victory advancing to right carrying a full cornucopia and a French standard in triumph. Edge engraved: WILLIAM PITT ADMINISTRING. By John Kirk.

21. Corbett, *England in the Seven Years War*, vol. 2, pp. 176–177.

22. Mackay, *The Hawke Papers*, #347, Hawke to Clevland, 13 January 1761.

23. Pritchard, *Louis XV's Navy*, p. 69.

Chapter 8

1. BL, Add. MS 35,389, f. 188 [Hardwicke to his sister], 30 November 1759.
2. *The Gentleman's Magazine*, 1759, p. 621.
3. Corbett, *England in the Seven Years War*, vol. 2, pp. 72–77.
4. BL, Add. MS 32,922, f. 451 Bedford to Newcastle, 9 May 1761; published in Theodore Calvin Pease, *Anglo-French Boundary Disputes in the West, 1749–1763*. The Trustees of the Illinois State Historical Library, 1936, p. 295. See also Bedford to the Earl of Bute, 9 July 1761, Lord John Russell ed., *Correspondence of John, fourth Duke of Bedford*, 3 vols. London, 1842–1846, vol. 3, pp. 22–29.
5. Francis Thackeray, *A History of the Right Hon. William Pitt, Earl of Chatham*, 2 vols. London, 1827, vol. 1, p. 509; Corbett, *England in the Seven Years War*, vol. 2, p. 154.
6. Bedford to Bute, 9 July, and Bute's answer, 12 July, Russell, *Correspondence*, vol. 3, p. 23 *et seq.*
7. Duc de E F Choiseul, *Memoire Justificatif presente au Roi*, cited in *Memoires du duc de Choiseul, 1719–1785*. Paris, 1904, pp. 405–406
8. BL, Add MS 32,924, Newcastle to Devonshire, 28 June 1761; Pitt to Stanley, 26 June, Thackeray, *A History of the Right Honorable William Pitt*, vol. 1, p. 549.
9. Browning, *The Duke of Newcastle*, pp. 280–282.
10. Corbett, *England in the Seven Years War*, vol. 2, pp. 206–207.
11. PRO, ADM 2/1332, f. 16, Secret Orders, 3 February 1762; BL, Add. MS 32,934, ff. 355–357; Corbett, *England in the Seven Years War*, vol. 2, p. 315.
12. BL, Add. MS 32,934, ff. 355–357, Hardwicke to Newcastle [15 February 1762], with intelligence from a m. L'Anglais dictated by one Cramond in the confidence of Silhouette.
13. Nicholas Tracy, *Manila Ransomed: The British Expedition to the Philippines in the Seven Years War*. Exeter, Exeter University Press, 1995.
14. Browning, *The Duke of Newcastle*, pp. 287–290.
15. P Coquelle, 'Le projets de descent en Angleterre de après les archives de aiffaires étrangères,' *Revue d'Histoire Diplomaticque*, vol. 15 (1901), pp. 619–624.
16. PRO, SP 94/175, 22 September. See V L Brown, 'Studies in the History of Spain in the Second Half of the Eighteenth Century,' *Smith College Studies in History*, vol. 15, October 1929.

17. See P Coquelle, 'Le Comte de Guerchy, ambassadeur de France a Londres, 1763-1767,' *Revue des Etudes Historiques*, vol. 64 (1908), p. 467.
18. BL, Add. MS 38,366, ff. 359–366, undated but subsequent to the economies of 1767 and can therefore only refer to the 1768 estimates. Punctuation supplied.
19. PRO, ADM 1/3972, Wolters to Stephens, 28 February 1769.
20. Mackay, *Admiral Hawke*, p. 323.
21. PRO, SP 81/142, in Cressener to Secretary of State, 24 January.
22. PRO, SP 84/503, Paris 3 January 1763, and Geneva 23 February 1763.
23. See A Temple Patterson, *The Other Armada*. Manchester, Manchester University Press, 1960, p. 30 and H M Scott, 'The Importance of Bourbon Naval Reconstruction to the Strategy of Choiseul after the Seven Years War,' *International History Review* (January 1979), pp. 17–35.
24. '... all complete and ready for sea in all respects'. Choiseul, *Memoire Justificatif presente au Roi*, cited in *Memoires du duc de Choiseul*, pp. 405–406.
25. PRO, ADM 1/4352, Abstract of the French Navy, 30 May 1765

GUNS	116	90	80	74	70	64	60	TOTAL
Fit for Service	1	1	1	11	1	21		36
Repairing				2	2			4
Bad condition	11			5		2		18
Building		1		2	2			5

See also PRO, SP 84/513, Wolters, 30 November 1765. It was reported that one ship of 90 guns (*Ville de Paris*), one 74 and two 56s had been launched in 1764, and in 1765 one 64 (*Artesian*) and two more 56s had joined them. One 90 (*Bretagne*, which had been intended to have 110 guns), two 80s (*St. Esprit* which was nearly finished, and *Languedoc*) and three 74s (*Lyonnais*, *Marseillais* and *Bourgogne*) were being built. One 80 (*Orient*), three 74s and one 64 were being rebuilt.

26. PRO, SP 81/147, Versailles 12 April, and Paris 5 July, in Cressener to Conway, nos 23 and 39, 20 April and 14 July 1767.
27. PRO, 30/8/85, f. 351, and Add. MS 38,339, f. 254.
28. PRO, SP 84/520. A copy of this list is in ADM 1/3972, and in the Hardwicke papers Add. MS 35,878.

29. PRO, SP 84/536. 7 × 80 to 90 guns (including *Couronne* a built-up 74 and *Tonnant*, but not *Orient* reduced to a 74); 27 × 70 (only the *Dauphine Royal* [70] known to be in bad condition, 2 under repair, 6 new since the war, and 11 rebuilt); 23 × 64 guns (2 in bad condition, one of which [*Rencontre*] had been condemned, 3 new ships, and 6 rebuilt); 8 × 50–56 guns; and a total of 44 small ships.

30. *Naval Chronicle*, vol. 7 (1802), p. 471.

31. Nicholas Tracy, *Navies, Deterrence and American Independence.* Vancouver, University of British Colombia Press, 1986, pp. 42–68.

32. BL, Egerton MS 215, pp. 161–195, Debate on Seymour's motion.

33. PRO, SP 42/47 (Admiralty to Rochford, 25 December, and Rochford to Admiralty, 21 and 26 December, and to Secretary at War, 26 December), WO1/680; and SP 42/48 ('State of the Guardships etc. 31 December' in Stephens to Sutton, 4 January 1771).

34. PRO, 30/8/79, f. 279.

35. *Parliamentary History* vol. 16, col. 1331; BL, Egerton MS 223, f. 194, Hawke 12 December, see Mackay, *Admiral Hawke*, p. 103.

36. West Suffolk Record Office 423/615, Bradshaw to Grafton, 24 July 1770.

37. Sir William R Anson ed., *Autobiography and Political Correspondence of Augustus Henry, Third Duke of Grafton K.G.: From Hitherto Unpublished Documents in the Possession of his Family.* London, John Murray, 1898, p. 257; and West Suffolk Record Office 423/311, pt. 2.

38. Quoted in George Martelli, *Jemmy Twitcher: A Life of the Fourth Earl of Sandwich, 1718–1792.* London, Jonathan Cape, 1962, pp. 292.

39. The Hon. Sir J Fortescue ed., *The Correspondence of King George the Third*, 6 vols. London, Macmillan, 1927, #843, #846 and #851, Rochford–George III correspondence 6–9 December; BL, Egerton MS 223, f. 181; and see Admiralty to Navy Board, 1 December, ADM 2/544 p. 461, and reply, 10 December, ADM/B/184.

40. Mackay, *The Hawke Papers*, #379, Admiralty to Navy Board, 23 June 1767.

41. Ibid., #490, Fragment of a letter, Hawke to Martin Bladen Hawke [1771?]; Edward Hawke, *A seaman's remarks on the British ships of the line from the 1st of January 1756 to the 1st of January 1782, with some occasional observations on the fleet of the House of Bourbon.* London, 1782.

42. Mackay, *The Hawke Papers*, p. 448.

43. Longleat House, Thynne MSS 'Admiralty Affairs', 'From Lord Sandwich 1776', 'Remarks on the State of His Maj.s Fleet 20 June

1776', 'Precis of Advices & Intelligence 20 June 1776' and cabinet minutes 20 June 1776; G R Barns and J H Owen eds, *The Private Papers of John, Earl of Sandwich, First Lord of Admiralty, 1771– 1782*, 4 vols. London, Navy Record Society, 1932–1938, vol. 1, p. 212, cabinet minutes 20 June 1776; and Fortescue, *George III*, nos 1894–1896.

44. 2 December 1772. Edmund Burke, *The Speeches of the Rt. Hon. Edmund Burke*. London, 1816, vol. 1, p. 138.
45. See Tracy, *Navies, Deterrence and American Independence*, pp. 118–158.
46. Temple Patterson, *The Other Armada*, pp. 37–39.
47. BL, Add. MS 35,410, ff. 153–154, to Hardwicke, 10 September 1749.
48. Fortescue, *The Correspondence of King George the Third*, #2776.
49. Laughton ed., *The Letters and Papers of Charles Lord Barham*, vol. 1, pp. 293, 323.

Appendix 1

1. ADM 51/965.

Bibliography

Primary Sources

British Library

Additional MSS 32,865; 32,889; 32,890; 32,891; 32,892; 32,897; 32,913; 32,922; 32,924; 32,934; 32,996; 32,998. Official correspondence of Thomas Pelham-Holles, Duke of Newcastle, 1697–1768.

Additional MSS 35,359; 35,389; 35,410, 35,878. Hardwicke Papers, correspondence and collections of the first four Earls of Hardwicke and other members of the Yorke family.

Additional MSS 38,339; 38,366. The Liverpool Papers, correspondence and papers, official and private, of the first three Earls of Liverpool, with a few earlier papers of the family.

Egerton MSS 215; 223. Reports of the debates of the House of Commons, 1768 and 1770.

Egerton MS 3,444. Leeds papers, vol. CXXI (ff. 274), correspondence and papers of Lord Holdernesse relating to naval and military affairs, 1748–1762 (mostly of the years 1755–1760). Included are papers relating to the seizure and detention of neutral vessels by British men of war.

Longleat House

Thynne MS 'Admiralty Affairs', 'From Lord Sandwich 1776', 'Remarks on the State of His Maj.s Fleet 20 June 1776', 'Precis of Advices & Intelligence 20 June 1776' and cabinet minutes 20 June 1776.

Ministry of Defence

NM/29 Signals for the use of the fleet (1756), with memoranda on the use of signals, twice signed by Edward Hawke.

Public Record Office: National Archives

ADM 1 In-Letters to Admiral

1/87 Letters from Flag Officers, Channel Fleet: including Admiral Anson, 1743–1747

1/92 Letters from Flag Officers, Channel Fleet: including Admiral Hawke, 1759–1762

1/93 Letters from Flag Officers, Channel Fleet: including Admirals Hardy, Geary and Rodney, 1759–1763

1/384 Letters from Commanders in Chief, Mediterranean, 8 August 1759

1/802 Letters from Commander in Chief, Plymouth

1/919 Letters from Commanders in Chief, Portsmouth, January–May 1755.

1/3945 Intelligence papers: secret correspondence from Robert and Marguerite Walters of Rotterdam, covering dates 1759

1/3972 Intelligence papers: 2nd series, 1761–1778

1/4352 Secret Letters: miscellaneous papers, 1756–1800

ADM 2 Out-Letters, Admiralty

2/83 Lords' Letters: Orders and Instructions

2/544 Secretary's Letters: Public Officers and Flag Officers

2/1332 Secret Orders

ADM 3 Admiralty: Minutes

3/63 Board's Minutes: 25 January 1753–1 July 1755

ADM 7/651 Guardships 1764–1770

ADM 49/162 (bound volume), 'An account of the Annual Charge of each of the Guardships in the last Peace at a Medium of Three Years.'

ADM 51 Admiralty: Captains' Logs

51/811 Captain's Log: *Royal George*

51/965 Captain's Log: *Swiftsure*

51/3834 Captain's Log: *Firm*

51/3895 Captain's Log: *Magnanime*

51/4308 Captain's Log: *Resolution*

ADM 52 Admiralty: Masters' Logs

52/754 Master's Log: *Actaeon*

52/853 Master's Log: *Firm*, 24 February 1759–21 May 1763

52/862   Master's Log: *Royal George*
52/935   Master's Log, *Magnanime*
52/1005   Master's Log: *Rochester*
52/1070   Master's Log: *Torbay*
52/1094   Master's Log: *Vengeance*

ADM 110 Navy Board: Victualling Office, Out-Letters
110/2   Letter Book, 1702–1705

PRO 30/8 William Pitt, First Earl of Chatham
30/8/55   Correspondence of William Pitt and Lady Hester (Grenville) his wife
30/8/70   Note books and letter book
30/8/78–79 Admiralty papers, 1759–1767
30/8/85   Papers, 1st Series, Continental Europe, papers relating to France, 1748–1761

SP 42 State Papers Domestic, Naval
42/43–52 Lords of the Admiralty, 1762–1778
42/64–65 Supplementary, 1760–1775
42/136   Miscellaneous, sick and wounded

SP 81/142 State Papers, Foreign, Archbishopric of Cologne, Bishopric of Liège, etc, George Cressener (Maastricht), 1763 Jan–Dec.

SP 81/147 State Papers, Foreign, George Cressener (Maastricht), 1767.

SP 84/501–545 State Papers, Foreign, Holland, 22 vols, Intelligence from Wolters in Rotterdam.

SP 92/70–82 State Papers, Foreign, Savoy and Sardinia.

SP 94/175 State Papers, Foreign, Spain, Lewis de Visme.

WO1/680 War Office In-Letters, 1770–1775.

National Maritime Museum

ADM/B/184 Navy Board letters to Admiralty, 1770.

CLE/2/19 Sailing and fighting instructions: notebook on signals c.1747. Hawke Papers Journal, In-Letter Book, and Out-Letter Book, 1759.

HOL/16 Brest, Chez à Malassis, Imprimeur du Roi et de la Marine, 1759.

West Suffolk Record Office
423/615 Correspondence of the Earl of Grafton.

Secondary Sources

Records

Firth, C H and Rait, R S, *Acts and Ordinances of the Interregnum 1642–1660.* London, 1911.
Journal of the House of Commons, vol. 28 (1757–1761).
Parliamentary History, vol. 16.

Journals

Annual Register for the Year 1759, London periodical, vol. 2.
Gentleman's Magazine, 1759, London periodical.
London Evening Post, 1759, London periodical.
The London Magazine, or Gentleman's Monthly Intelligencer, 1759, London periodical.
Naval Chronicle, vol. 7, 1802, London periodical.
Read's Weekly Journal, 1759, London periodical.
The *Universal Magazine*, 1759, London periodical.

Theses

Bourland, Richard D Jr, 'Maurepas and his Administration of the French Navy on the Eve of the War of the Austrian Succession (1737–1742),' PhD Dissertation, Notre Dame, Indiana, 1978.
Starkey, David J, 'British Privateering, 1702–1783, with particular reference to London,' PhD, University of Exeter, 1985.
Swanson, Carl E, 'Predators and Prizes: Privateering in the British Colonies During the War of 1739–1748,' PhD, University of Western Ontario, 1979.

Published Books and Articles

Aldridge, David, 'Swedish Privateering, 1710–1718 and the Reactions of Great Britain and the United Provinces,' in *Commission Internationale d'Histoire Maritime: Course et Piraterie*. Paris, Institut de Recherche et d'Histoire de Textes Editions du Centre National de la Recherche Scientifique, 1975.
Anderson, F, *Crucible of War*. London, Faber and Faber, 2001.
Andrews, Kenneth Raymond, *Elizabethan Privateers*. Cambridge, Cambridge University Press, 1964.
Anon, *Channel Pilot*. London, Hydrographer of the Navy, 1965.

Anon, *A complete channel pilot: comprehending the English and French coasts, from the Thames mouth to the Bay of Biscay*. London, printed for Robert Sayer and John Bennett [1781?].

Anon [Master in the Royal Navy], *The new and complete channel pilot; or sailing directions for navigating the British Channel on the English and French coasts, ... adapted to Sayer's charts of that channel, ... The whole carefully revised by a master in the Royal Navy*. London, sold by J Heskett [1760?].

Anon, *The state farce: or, they are all come home. In which is introduced, a scene representing Britannia weeping in the Centre of the Stage attended by the ghosts of the Duke of Marlborough and Admiral Hosier, being more applicable to the present times than anything yet published, Multum in Parvo*. London, printed for J Scott and sold by the booksellers of London and Westminster, 1758.

Anson, Sir William R ed., *Autobiography and Political Correspondence of Augustus Henry, Third Duke of Grafton K.G.: From Hitherto Unpublished Documents in the Possession of his Family*. London, John Murray, 1898.

Barns, G R and Owen, J H eds, *The Private Papers of John, Earl of Sandwich, First Lord of Admiralty, 1771–1782*, 4 vols. London, Navy Records Society, 1932–1938.

Beatson, Robert, *Naval and Military Memoirs of Great Britain, from the Year 1727, to the Present Time*, 3 vols. London, J Strachan; Edinburgh, P Hill, 1790, reprint of 1804 edition, Boston, Gregg Press, 1972.

Bell, A C, *A History of the Blockade of Germany, 1914–18*. London, 1937 (confidential to 1961).

Bellin, J N, *Le Neptune François, ou Atlas nouveau des cartes marines*. Paris, Imprimerie Royale, 1693 [Paris, Dépôt des Cartes et Plans de la Marine, 1753].

Boissaye Du Bocage, Georges (1626–1696), *Le petit Neptune françois: or, the French coasting pilot. Being a particular description of the ... coast of France ... Translated from the Petit flambeau de la mer of Du Bocage. With large improvements from the great Neptune françois, Bellin, Belidor, &c ...* Engraved by Thomas Jefferys, printed for T Jefferys, 1761.

Bonner-Smith, D ed., *The Barrington Papers: Selected from the Letters and Papers of Admiral the Hon. Samuel Barrington*. London, Navy Records Society, 1937.

Brenton, Edward Pelham, *Life and correspondence of John, earl of St. Vincent*. London, Henry Colburn, 1838.

221

Brière, Jean-François, 'Pêche et Politique à Terre-Neuve au XVIIIe siècle: La France veritable gagnante du traité d'Utrecht?' *Canadian Historical Review* 64 (1983), pp. 168–187.

Brown, V L, 'Studies in the History of Spain in the Second Half of the Eighteenth Century,' *Smith College Studies in History*, vol. 15, October 1929.

Browning, Reed, *The Duke of Newcastle*. New Haven and London, Yale University Press, 1972.

Burke, Edmund, *The Speeches of the Rt. Hon. Edmund Burke*. London, 1816.

Campbell, Thomas, *Specimens of the British Poets: With Biographical and Critical Notices, and an Essay on English Poetry*. Philadelphia, Henry Carey Baird, 1853.

Carter, Alice Clare, *Neutrality or Commitment: The Evaluation of Dutch Foreign Policy, 1667–1795*. London, Edward Arnold, 1975.

Charnock, John, *Biographia Navalis; or, Impartial memoirs of the lives and characters of officers of the navy of Great Britain, from the year 1660 to the present time ... With portraits and other engravings, by Bartolozzi, &c.*, 6 vols. London, R Faulder, 1794–1798.

Choiseul, Duc de E F, *Memoires du duc de Choiseul, 1719–1785*. Paris, 1904.

Clausewitz, Carl von, Rapoport, Anatol ed., *On War*. Harmondsworth, Penguin Classics, 1982.

[Clerk], *The Secret Expedition impartially disclos'd: or, an Authentick faithful narrative of all occurrences that happened to the fleet and army commanded by Sir E- H- [i.e. Edward Hawke] and Sir J- M- [i.e. John Mordaunt], from its first sailing to its return to England ... By a commissioned officer on board the fleet, etc.* London, J Staples, etc. [1757].

Cobbett William, *The Parliamentary history of England from the earliest period to the year 1803*, 36 vols. London, T C Hansard, 1812.

Coquelle, P, 'Le projets de descent en Angleterre de après les archives de aiffaires étrangères,' *Revue d'Histoire Diplomaticque* 15 (1901), pp. 591–624.

——, 'Le Comte de Guerchy, ambassadeur de France a Londres, 1763–1767,' *Revue des Etudes Historiques* 64 (1908).

Corbett, Sir Julian, *England in the Seven Years War*, 2 vols. London, Longmans, Green & Co, 1907 [1918].

——, *Some Principles of Maritime Strategy*. London, Longmans, Green & Co, 1911.

Crowhurst, C Patrick, 'The Admiralty and the Convoy System in the Seven Years War,' *The Mariner's Mirror 57* (1971), pp. 163–173.

——, *The Defence of British Trade 1689–1815*. Folkstone, England, Dawson, 1977.

Davies, D J Llewelyn, 'Enemy Property and Ultimate Destination During the Anglo-Dutch Wars 1664–7 and 1672–4,' *British Yearbook of International Law* (1931), p. 21.

Dodington, George Bubb (1691–1762), *The Diary of the late George Bubb Dodington, Baron of Melcombe Regis: from March 8, 1748–9, to February 6, 1761 ... now first published by Henry Penruddocke Wyndham*. Dublin, 1784.

Duffy, Michael, 'The Establishment of the Western Squadron as the Linchpin of British Naval Strategy,' in Michael Duffy ed., *Parameters of British Naval Power, 1650–1850*. Exeter, University of Exeter Press, 1992, pp. 60–82.

Dull, Jonathan R, *The French Navy and the Seven Years War*. Lincoln, University of Nebraska Press, 2005.

Duro, Cesáreo Fernandez, *Armada Espanola*. Museo Naval, Madrid, 1973 (facsimile of 1895–1903 edition).

Dutens, Louis, *Mémoires d'un voyageur qui se repose: contenant des anecdotes historiques, politiques et littéraires, relatives à plusieurs des principaux personnages du siècle*. London, Cox, Fils and Baylis (Bossange, Masson et Besson), 1807, pp. 142–143.

Ekins, Charles, *Naval Battles*. London, Baldwin, Craddock and Joy, 1824.

Erskine, David ed. (Augustus John Hervey, Earl of Bristol, 1724–1779), *Augustus Hervey's journal, being the intimate account of the life of a captain in the Royal Navy ashore and afloat, 1746–1759*. London, W Kimber, 1953.

Fortescue, The Hon. Sir J ed., *The Correspondence of King George the Third*, 6 vols. London, Macmillan, 1927.

Garner, James Wilford, *Prize Law During the World War*. New York, Macmillan, 1927.

Gradish, Stephen F, *The Manning of the British Navy during the Seven Years War*. London, Royal Historical Society, 1980.

Guérin, Léon, *Histoire maritime de France, depuis la fondation de Marseille jusqu'à la prix de Nimègue*. Paris, 1863 [1843].

Harrison, William, *Mona Miscellany*. Douglas, Isle of Man, printed for the Manx Society, 1873.

Hawke, Edward, *A seaman's remarks on the British ships of the line from the 1st of January 1756 to the 1st of January 1782, with some occasional observations on the fleet of the House of Bourbon.* London, 1782.

Heckscher, Eli F, Shapiro, M, trans, *Mercantilism,* 2 vols. London, Allen & Unwin, 1931.

Hoadly, Benjamin, *An Enquiry into the Reasons of the Conduct of Great Britain with Regard to the Present State of Affairs in Europe.* Dublin, 1727.

Hoste, Père Paul, *L'Art des Armées Navales ou Traité des Evolutions Navales, qui contient des regles utiles aux officiers généraux, et particuliers d'une Armées Navales; avec des examples itez de ce qui c'est passé de considérablesur la mer depuis cinquante ans.* Lyon, 1697.

John, A H, 'The London Assurance Company and the Marine Insurance Market of the Eighteenth Century,' *Economica* XXV (1958), pp. 126–141.

Johnston, A J B, *Endgame 1758: The Promise, the Glory, and the Despair of Louisbourg's Last Decade.* Lincoln and London, University of Nebraska Press, 2007.

Kamen, Henry, 'The Destruction of the Spanish Silver Fleet at Vigo in 1702,' *Bulletin of The Institute of Historical Research* XXXIX (1966), pp. 165–173.

Kemp, Peter, *The Oxford Companion to Ships and the Sea.* Oxford, Oxford University Press. 1976.

——, *Prize Money.* Aldershot, Gale & Polden, 1946.

Lacour-Gayet, Georges, *La Marine Militaire de la France sous Le Règne de Louis XV.* Paris, Honoré Champion, 1902.

Lambert, Andrew, *Admirals: The Naval Commanders Who Made Britain Great.* London, Faber and Faber, 2008.

Laude, Norbert, *La Compagnie d'Ostende et son activite coloniale au Bengale 1725–30.* Bruxelles, 1944.

Laughton, Sir John Knox, *The Letters and Papers of Charles Lord Barham, Admiral of the Red Squadron, 1758–1813.* London, Navy Records Society, 1911.

Le Moing, Guy, *La Bataille Navale des 'Cardinaux' 20 November 1759.* Paris, Economica, 2003.

Lind, James, *A Treatise of the Scurvy. In three parts. Containing an inquiry into the nature, causes, and cure, of that disease, etc.* Edinburgh, 1753.

Lloyd, Christopher ed., *The Health of Seamen.* London, Navy Records Society, vol. 107, 1965.

——, *Naval Miscellany IV.* Navy Records Society, London, 1902–present.

Locker, Edward Hawke, *The naval gallery of Greenwich Hospital: comprising a series of portraits and memoirs of celebrated naval commanders*. London, Harding and Lepard, 1832.

Long, W H, *Naval yarns: letters and anecdotes, comprising accounts of sea fights and wrecks, actions with pirates and privateers etc from 1616 to 1831*, London, Gibbings, 1899.

Mackay, Ruddock F, *Admiral Hawke*. Oxford: Clarendon Press, 1965.

—— ed., *The Hawke Papers: A Selection: 1743–1771*. Aldershot, Navy Records Society, vol. 129, 1990.

Marcus, Geoffrey J, 'Hawke's Blockade of Brest,' *Journal of the Royal United Services Institute* (1959), pp. 475–488.

——, *Quiberon Bay, The Campaign in Home Waters, 1759*. London, Hollis and Carter, 1960.

Marsh, J, 'The Local Community and the Operation of Plymouth Dockyard, 1689–1763,' in Michael Duffy et al, *The New Maritime History of Devon*, 2 vols. London, Conway Maritime Press, 1992, 1994.

Martelli, George, *Jemmy Twitcher: A Life of the Fourth Earl of Sandwich, 1718–1792*. London, Jonathan Cape, 1962.

Merriman, R B, *The Rise of the Spanish Empire*, 4 vols. New York, Macmillan, 1918–1934.

Middleton, R, 'British Naval Strategy, 1755–1762: The Western Squadron,' *Mariner's Mirror* 75 (1989), p. 357.

Morris, Corbyn. *An essay towards deciding the question, whether Britain be permitted by right policy to insure the ships of her enemies? Addressed to the Right ... The second edition, with amendments.* London, 1758.

Oppenheim, M ed., *The Naval Tracts of Sir William Monson*, 5 vols. London, 1892.

Pares, Richard, *Colonial Blockade and Neutral Rights, 1739–1763*. Oxford, Clarendon Press, 1938.

——, *War and Trade in the West Indies 1739–1963*. London, Frank Cass, 1963.

Patton, Philip, *Strictures on Naval Discipline, and the Conduct of a Ship of War: Intended to Produce an Uniformity of Opinion among Sea-officers*. 1810.

Pease, Theodore Calvin, *Anglo-French Boundary Disputes in the West, 1749–1763*. The Trustees of the Illinois State Historical Library, 1936.

Pope, Dudley, *At Twelve Mr. Byng Was Shot*. Philadelphia: J B Lippincott, 1962.

225

Price, William (Master of the *Theseus*), *A Chart of Quiberon Bay*. London, 20 August 1796.

Pritchard, James S, *Louis XV's Navy, 1748–1762: A Study of Organization and Administration*. Kingston, McGill-Queen's University Press, 1987.

Pryor, John H, *Geography, Technology and War: Studies in the Maritime History of the Mediterranean, 649–1571*. Cambridge, Cambridge University Press, 1988.

Raleigh, Sir Walter, 'Of a war with Spain, and our Protecting the Netherlands,' in *Three Discourses of Sir Walter Raleigh*. London, Benjamin Barker, 1702.

Ranft, B McL ed., *The Vernon Papers*. London, Navy Records Society, vol. 99, 1958.

Rashed, Zenab Esmat, *The Peace of Paris, 1763*. Liverpool, Liverpool University Press, 1951.

Richmond, Sir Herbert, *The Navy as an Instrument of Policy*. Cambridge, Cambridge University Press, 1953.

——, *Papers relating to the Loss of Minorca, 1756*. London, Navy Records Society, vol. 42, 1913.

—— ed., *The Private Papers of George, Second Earl Spencer*. London, Navy Records Society, vol. 58, 1924.

Riley, James C, *The Seven Years War and the Old Regime in France: The Economic and Financial Toll*. Princeton, Princeton University Press, 1986.

Rodger, N A M, *Essays in Naval History, from Medieval to Modern*. Farnham, Ashgate, 2009..

Russell, Lord John ed., *Correspondence of John, fourth Duke of Bedford*, 3 vols. London, 1842–1846.

Schuyler, Robert Livingston, *The Fall of the Old Colonial System*. London, Oxford University Press, 1945.

Scott, H M, 'The Importance of Bourbon Naval Reconstruction to the Strategy of Choiseul after the Seven Years War,' *International History Review* (January 1979), pp. 17–35.

Serres, John Thomas, *The Little Sea Torch: Or True Guide for Coasting Pilots*. London, J Debrett, 1801.

Smollett, Tobias MD (1721–1771), *The History of England, from the Revolution to the death of George the Second. (Designed as a continuation of Mr. Hume's History.)* 5 vols. Printed for T Cadell and R Baldwin [by H Baldwin and son], 1800.

Stark, Francis R, *The Abolition of Privateering and the Declaration of Paris*. New York, Ams Press, 1967 (reprint of 1897 edition).

Swift, Jonathan, Davis, Herbert ed., *Political Tracts 1711–1713*, 'The Conduct of the Allies' (November 1711). Oxford, Blackwell, 1951–1953, vol. 6, pp. 1–66 (p. 22).

Syrett, David ed., *The Rodney Papers: Selections from the Correspondence of Admiral Lord Rodney*. Ashgate, Navy Records Society, vols 148, 151, 2005.

Temple Patterson, A, *The Other Armada*. Manchester, Manchester University Press, 1960.

Thackeray, Francis, *A history of the Right Honorable William Pitt, earl of Chatham: containing his speeches in Parliament; a considerable portion of his correspondence, when secretary of state, upon French, Spanish, and American affairs, never before published* ... 2 vols. London, 1827.

Thompson, Edward, 1738?–1786, *Sailor's letters: Written to his select friends in England, during his voyages and travels in Europe, Asia, Africa, and America*, 2 vols. London, T Becket and P A de Hondt; W Flexney and C Moran, 1767.

Tracy, Nicholas, *Attack on Maritime Trade*. London, Macmillan, 1991.

——, *Britannia's Palette: The Arts of Naval Victory*. Montreal, McGill-Queen's University Press, 2007.

——, *The Collective Naval Defence of the Empire: 1900 to 1940*. Aldershot, Navy Records Society, vol. 136, 1997.

——, *Manila Ransomed: The British Expedition to the Philippines in the Seven Years War*. Exeter, Exeter University Press, 1995.

——, *Navies, Deterrence and American Independence*. Vancouver, University of British Colombia Press, 1988.

Troude, O, *Batailles navales de la France*, 4 vols. Paris, Challamel, 1867–1868.

Tunstall, Brian ed., *The Byng papers, selected from the letters and papers of Admiral Sir George Byng, first viscount Torrinton and of his son Admiral the Hon. John Byng*. London, Navy Records Society, 1930–.

—— and Tracy, Nicholas, *Naval Warfare in the Age of Sail*. London, Conway, 1990.

Turner, Florence Maris (Mrs Charles Lamb) ed., *Diary of Thomas Turner*. London, John Lane, The Bodley Head, 1925.

Verlaque, Chanoine Victor, *Histoire du Cardinal de Fleury et de son Administration*. Paris, 1878.

Walpole, Horace (1717–1797), *Memoirs of King George II*, 3 vols. New Haven, Yale University Press, 1985.

Wesley, Charles, *Hymns on the Expected Invasion, 1759*. London, Strahan, 1759.

——, *Hymns to be Used on the Thanksgiving Day, Nov. 29, 1759, and After it.* London, Strahan, 1759.

Williamson, J A, *Hawkins of Plymouth.* London, Adam and Charles Black, 1969.

Yorke, P C III, *The Life and Correspondence of Philip Yorke, Earl of Hardwicke,* 3 vols. Cambridge, Cambridge University Press, 1913.

Index

231

238